C000258392

UFO SCOTLAND

RON HALLIDAY has been investigating paranormal phenomena for over twenty years. He is currently chairman of Scottish Earth Mysteries Research, and appears regularly on television and radio to discuss all aspects of the paranormal. He is a frequent contributor to newspapers and magazines, and is the author of *UFOs: The Scottish Dimension* (1997) and the editor of *McX* (1997). Educated at the Universities of Edinburgh and Stirling, Ron is Assistant Registrar at the University of Stirling.

UFO
SCOTLAND

RON HALLIDAY

First published 1998
by B&W Publishing Ltd
Edinburgh

ISBN 1 873631 83 9

British Library Cataloguing in Publication Data:
A catalogue record for this book is available
from the British Library.

PICTURE CREDITS:

Thanks are due to the following
for their invaluable assistance
with the photographs in this book:

Alec Bell, Brian Curran, James MacLean,
Andrew McMichael, Ian Macpherson, Margaret Ross;
The Fortean Picture Library for the George Adamski and
Cedric Allingham pictures, the Solway Spaceman photo,
the Bob Taylor photo and artwork;
The Dunfermline Press Group for the Ian Macpherson photo;
The *Scotsman* Photo Library;
Tony Stone Images.

All pictures are copyright.

Cover Design: Winfortune & Co

Printed by WSOY

UFO
SCOTLAND

CONTENTS

CONTENTS

INTRODUCTION

I have to admit that I wasn't naturally attracted to the subject of ufology. The supernatural on the other hand fascinated me even as a child. Hardly surprising as my grandmother was 'psychic' and saw spirits, although I was not consciously aware of this at the time. But when I thought of the mysterious world beyond, the images that came to my mind were of ghosts or strange entities that might be found wandering through the woods. I frightened myself to sleeplessness by reading at bedtime *The Haunting of Borley Rectory* and *Psychical Research Today*—both, I might say, still worth looking at.

My father was a scientist, and open-minded enough to consider psychical research a subject that should be investigated. It didn't have to be believed, but it should be examined. Nevertheless, the notion of silver discs hurtling through space, and beings from other planets, just didn't enter into my mind. On the one hand I suppose it's rather strange that it didn't, but on the other hand it does suggest that media stories don't necessarily influence people as easily as might be thought. I was fed on a regular diet of the *Eagle* comic with Dan Dare, Professor Peabody and the evil genius, the 'Mekon', who must have been an early 'grey'—a skinny, large-headed, grey-coloured, evil extraterrestrial who rode about on an open chair-sized disc with no obvious power source. I took it all as fiction, and media frenzy over places like Warminster, and indeed the whole UFO phenomenon, passed me by so completely that I never noticed it. I avidly read newspapers and I honestly cannot recall a single UFO story from either the 1960s or most of the 1970s. When I thought of the 'paranormal' I did not rate UFOs as subject matter worth considering.

Which, when I look back, is rather odd. It wasn't that I didn't believe that UFO incidents were taking place, it was just that I didn't find them anything like as interesting as the fact that a person might have seen a ghost and the implications that had for our lives on Earth.

However, I did notice reports of the 1979 Bob Taylor incident on Dechmont Law. It didn't attract me to the subject, but it did make me think about the possibility that UFO sightings and other strange incidents—ghosts, hauntings—might be linked in the sense that they occurred in the same area or close to each other. At the time I was working on a book on witchcraft cases and looking for a clue as to why there were areas where accusations of witchcraft formed a cluster (a witch 'hot-spot'). A new avenue of thought had begun to open up for me regarding the UFO phenomenon, as it seems to have done for many people at around the same time.

When I first became involved in Scottish ufology there were

very few Scottish investigators, and in fact only Malcolm Robinson and Steuart Campbell seemed to be active. Steuart Campbell had done impressive work on the Bob Taylor incident (and other cases), but although a member of BUFORA (The British UFU Research Association) he was, in fact, sceptical of UFOs as a phenomenon that could not be explained rationally. He eventually produced *The UFO Mystery Solved*, a broad account of UFO incidents with each one explained in rational terms, mainly as mirages of stars or planets (I paraphrase here—for a detailed explanation, read the book).

Steuart Campbell has been heavily criticised for his attempt to create a unified theory of UFOs, that they're all cases of mistaken identity. But he has pinpointed a real problem. Do individual UFO cases stand up to scrutiny? I think this is a key issue because it is pointless referring to the sheer volume of reports as overwhelming evidence of the reality of UFOs. We have to accept that many sightings do have a rational explanation, so shouldn't we be willing to take on board the fact that *all* UFO incidents may have a straightforward answer?

If that is your opinion I hope that the events described in the following pages will convince you otherwise, or at least encourage you to consider the possibility that some UFOs are just that—unidentified flying objects. I certainly didn't start out with the view that UFO reports were a genuine inexplicable phenomenon. It was the encounters I had with UFO witnesses over the years which convinced me that something strange was taking place in the skies over Scotland.

Yes, I have met people who have clearly seen what they believe to be a 'mysterious object', but is not. One individual rang me up to report a strange red object she and her husband had watched for some time hovering in the skies above their house. She was amazed when I told her it could well be the planet Mars as it was prominent at that time of year and could readily be seen with the naked eye. UFO investigator Ken Higgins wrote a fascinating account of the bright lights flashing over the skies of West Lothian reported to him by a family convinced they were seeing UFOs. Although it was the early hours of the morning, Ken with typical determination went out to look. After driving round for some time he located the UFO source. A jeep club were racing each other round open countryside. The bobbing of the car lights was producing the UFO lights in the sky. But what if Ken hadn't bothered to get out of bed to take a look? Another UFO sighting logged.

So far I accept that sceptics have a point. But where I take a radically different road is in response to close up reports. Or cases where individuals claim to have encountered alien entities or strange beings. This is not simply 'mistaken identity'. We have events here which challenge fundamentally the accepted way in which we view the world.

If we take Pat Macleod's encounter in a built-up area of Edinburgh, we can hardly dismiss it as a misidentification of an everyday object. The strange orb she saw hovering over the road has no clear natural explanation. Pat has no axe to grind on the matter so, if you want to dismiss the incident, you can either argue that she invented it (which I utterly reject as an explanation) or that she hallucinated it. I take the latter solution more seriously, but I also reject it because it is far too simplistic an answer to close up encounters like this. ('Oh, saw a space-ship did she? It was obviously a hallucination.') In my view the depth and extent of close encounters precludes hallucination as a solution. People may wish to refer to UFOs as modern day 'fairy stories', with the implication that anyone interested in them dislikes the 'real world'. In response I would say that those who reject the UFO phenomenon do so because they cannot accept the fact that the 'real' world may be less certain than they imagine. There are people who find such uncertainty very disturbing, and who will reject all threats to their fixed outlook in an attempt to retain their world view.

So on its own, even without claims of government cover-ups and ET contact, the UFO phenomenon does threaten stability, which is why according to some ufologists there is a world-wide conspiracy to clamp down on the UFO phenomenon and also to discredit it. Certainly, the USA is vast enough to hide secret bases where extraterrestrial technology (the famous crashed discs) could be stored, copied and tested. In Scotland the MoD owns huge areas of land where any activity could be carried out. I often wonder why the MoD needs to hold on to such enormous acreage as most of it rarely seems to be used—though it may be that I've been too short-sighted and some of these sites have been put to mysterious use. There are parts of Scotland where people just never visit because access is so difficult. ET flying discs could be stored here as geographically we're in a good situation for communication with London, the USA and Western Europe.

I would also add that I don't accept the view that national secrets will always find a way into the public domain. John Kennedy, US President, was killed in public yet those involved in his murder have never been brought to justice. What we've seen instead (for various reasons) is an extensive and lengthy cover-up. Scapegoating, as in the 'lone gunman' explanation, has proved to be an effective way to divert attention and satisfy short-term public concern. The same 'answer' solved the Martin Luther King assassination and Robert Kennedy's death. Major events can undoubtedly be covered up, and the public will not necessarily find out the truth even when certain people may have access to information which could provide an explanation.

So returning to the UFO phenomenon, the fact that governments deny that UFOs are an inexplicable phenomenon should not really weigh too heavily. I agree that it does not mean that governments are in contact with alien intelligences. I have no direct evidence that they are. Yes, I've heard many claims, even been told of Scottish incidents which show this, but I've yet to see the documentary evidence to back this up. Maybe it is true. Maybe one day someone from a military base in Scotland will speak up. It simply hasn't happened yet. The military in Scotland don't seem to have caught up with the public relations exercise mounted by London officials. In spite of the involvement of military aircraft in a number of UFO incidents, they remain incapable of admitting their interest. A little more openness to the public—who after all are paying the bills—wouldn't, I suggest, be a bad thing.

For the moment then it's all down to the public both to report and investigate UFO reports. And what an incredible scene it is. Strange lights in the sky. Solid objects of unearthly design hurtling by overhead. Tall and small alien beings of a variety of colours. Contact with and abduction by creatures who may want our bodies to experiment on. It's hard to believe that anyone would not be interested in this mysterious world!

Many of the witnesses are themselves bemused by what has happened to them. In some cases, like Allistair McNeil's, the experience is uplifting. In others, like those of Gary Wood or Karen, it becomes perplexing, even frightening. The closer witnesses get to whatever is behind the UFO phenomenon the more puzzling or disconcerting it becomes. One of the biggest divides at present is between those who believe aliens are a threat to us and those who view their intentions as peaceful. If aliens do exist with advanced technology it is surprising that if they wanted to 'zap' us they haven't done so already. But that, of course, will only be a relevant comment if aliens really are visiting the earth.

Can we rely on individual accounts of encountering aliens, especially when details only come out through hypnosis? Regression hypnosis has been heavily criticised by professional psychiatrists as a tool for recovering repressed memories. Can we really forget completely all memories of an event, and even if we can does hypnosis actually allow us to reopen that memory? Or does it create new 'memories', recollections of incidents that never really took place? If we had to rely on regression hypnosis alone then all those involved in ufology would surely have to agree that we are treading on thin ice. Fortunately, we do have conscious recall, incidents of alien contact which witnesses can clearly remember and describe. I'm not saying that this evidence is beyond dispute (when is it ever!), but it does mean that we don't have to rely on controversial hypnosis techniques to bring alien contact incidents into the open. Regression therapy can remain a separate topic for discussion. I will say, however, that Gary Wood of the A70 case, whose alien abduction account depends solely on hypnosis, is convinced that the regression sessions he went through helped him come to terms with his experience rather than harmed him.

It goes without saying that I don't have the one hundred per cent convincing evidence that will prove beyond doubt UFOs come from other planets. But strange things happen almost every day of the week in the air above us, and often on the ground too. I don't agree that UFOs are a 'phantom'. There is a 'UFO reality', although exactly what we are dealing with remains to be decided.

ACKNOWLEDGEMENTS

First and foremost I would like to thank the witnesses, all of whose experiences of the UFO phenomenon throw a different slant on the accepted view of the world. They have shown considerable courage in coming forward and letting the public know of the events in which they have been involved. They deserve to be taken seriously.

I would like to thank my father, Dr R. Halliday, for first stimulating my interest in the paranormal. Probably not in the direction he imagined! My wife Evelyn has my heartfelt thanks for tolerating without complaint my sudden disappearances to all parts of Scotland and the many hours spent at the typewriter. Thanks too to my children Tanya, Gareth and Euan for making sure that I have never missed a phone call from a witness with an experience to report.

I would also thank my colleagues in Scottish Earth Mysteries Research, especially Brian Wilson and Viv Alexander, for their support in investigating the Scottish UFO phenomenon. Finally I would thank my publishers, B&W, for their willingness to publish a book on Scottish ufology, and Simon Cave for his constructive suggestions on the text and contents of this book.

Ron Halliday

UFO
SCOTLAND
1

WAY UP OVER THE LOTHIANS
EDINBURGH AND THE WEST LOTHIAN AREA

Unidentified Flying Objects have been reported from every
country in the world, but strangely UFO sightings are not
evenly spread. Scotland has had more than its share of
unexplained incidents. And even within Scotland there are
notorious 'hot-spots', areas where the frequency of UFO
sightings is out of all proportion to what you would expect on
a strict population basis.

Take the Lothians. Edinburgh and its surrounding districts
of East, Mid and West Lothian have played an important role
through many centuries of Scotland's history, and Edinburgh
will soon be home to Scotland's first parliament for 300 years.
Hardly the place to find wide-eyed citizens ready to accept

any odd light in the sky as a UFO. Yet in the 1990s this area of Scotland emerged as one of the key spots for documented UFO reports. It was also the site of one of the world's most famous UFO encounters.

LIVINGSTON INCIDENT

9 November 1979 dawned cold and clear. The 3 a.m. edition of *The Scotsman* newspaper led on the furore over an alleged IRA stunt. Jim Callaghan, Prime Minister at the time, had condemned the BBC for allegedly filming an IRA propaganda exercise in Northern Ireland. On an inside page, Albert Morris's light-hearted column was entitled: 'Reflections of an Alien Kind'. In the article he discussed the attitude of extraterrestrials to an encounter with Earthlings and wrote: 'It is not space monsters we have to fear . . . but mankind itself'. It was almost as if he had foreseen the astonishing event that was to take place that very morning.

Robert David Taylor was well respected as an honest, dedicated forestry worker. A few years off retirement age at 61, Bob was employed by Livingston Development Corporation in their Forestry Commission, working in the woodland areas in the vicinity of the new town. At around 10.30 a.m. on 9 November 1979 Bob, in the company of his dog Lara, a seven-year-old red setter, was making his way through the covering of fir trees lying on the lower slopes of Dechmont Law. As he approached a clearing in the wood he was shocked to see, twelve yards in front of him, a large circular object. According to some reports it was supported by three thin metal legs, although Bob himself has not verified this. The object was dark metallic grey, and around the circumference Bob noted a distinct narrow flange. It did not move, giving him more time to note that in parts it seemed transparent, in contrast with other surfaces which looked like giant sections of emery paper.

As Bob cautiously approached the mystery object, two small spherical devices, similar to World War Two naval mines with spikes protruding all round, suddenly dropped to the ground. It appeared to Bob that they had come from inside the 'craft'. They rolled toward him making a distinct plopping sound as they approached, one moving to the left and the other to the right. Both arrived at the side of a boot at the same time and simultaneously attached a spike to each side of Bob's trousers. They now tried to drag Bob towards the hovering UFO. At this moment Bob caught a whiff of a pungent smell which immediately made him choke. Over the noise of his dog barking furiously, Bob heard a clear hissing sound.

The next thing Bob remembered is coming to, his face pressed hard against the wet ground. His legs were aching, but through the pain he managed to note that the two spheres and the 'mother' object had disappeared. The barking in his ears confirmed that the faithful Lara had not abandoned him, but Bob was for the moment unable to calm the dog's fear, as he had lost the ability to speak.

In a state of shock Bob struggled to his feet. He was unable to start his lorry so he staggered the mile back to his home in Livingston. His trousers were later found to be torn and his legs cut and bruised, and it has been suggested that it was during this confused period that the damage was done, as Bob scrambled over a barbed-wire fence. The straight, neat line made by the tears, however, would seem to contradict this.

Bob's wife Mary was deeply shocked when she saw the state her husband was in, and didn't know what to think when he told her he had been attacked by a spaceship, assuring him 'there's no such thing'. However, it was clear that Bob had been the victim of some sort of event, even if it had a more down-to-earth explanation. Acting quickly, Mary phoned the doctor, then Bob's boss, Malcolm Drummond, head of the Forestry Department, to report the incident. A quick check round Dechmont Law by other forestry workers failed to reveal anything out of the ordinary. No sign of an alien craft. Nor of a band of marauding thugs, an explanation put forward by some when they heard of the incident.

The local police had been alerted and, from their Livingston base, soon arrived at the scene of the 'crime'. Bob joined the officers, headed by Detective Inspector Ian Wark, having insisted on revisiting the spot where he had been attacked. The police and victim noted extensive ladder-shaped impressions in the ground just where Bob reckoned the 'craft' had been standing. Indentations revealed the path along which, Bob explained, the spherical objects approached him. Marks in the earth supported Bob's claim that he had been dragged towards the larger object before being released.

The police took Bob's account seriously and a criminal investigation was soon under way. This, of course, didn't mean that Bob's explanation of seeing an alien craft was in any way accepted as a basis for the incident. However, Bob appeared to be a perfectly truthful witness and had clearly experienced something which could have been a physical assault. The involvement of the police ensured that the incident received nationwide publicity. However, in spite of the considerable media attention and a widespread search, no clue as to the source of Bob's attack was ever unearthed. The file on Bob's encounter remains open.

The police did confirm in their enquiries that Bob's trousers bore two significant tears which had been made in an upward direction. His legs were cut and bruised in the same area. Someone or something had clearly caught hold of Bob in a grip powerful enough to damage his clothing and mark his body.

Interest in the incident, now one of the most famous in the annals of ufology, has remained high. Bob Taylor has consistently stood by his account. When I spoke to him in January 1998, Bob, in spite of a slight stroke and a heart attack, and the loss of his wife, confirmed to me the reality, as far as he was concerned, of what he saw. He added that up to the time of the incident he had no interest in or awareness of the subject of UFOs. Nor did he have any knowledge of UFO activity or any other strange events in the vicinity of Dechmont Law. Bob has little time for those who try to explain his sighting away as a mirage or other phantom of the mind. Indeed, it is the character of the man (his boss called him 'sensible and straightforward') which has convinced many that an encounter of cosmic significance occurred that day on windswept Dechmont Law.

When the police say of a witness:

> 'I think that what [he] was telling us he actually believed. As far as I was concerned, I had no reason to doubt anything about what he was telling us. I

> spoke to neighbours who had lived beside him and
> had known him for many years [and their view was
> that he] just would not make up a story like that'

then it is clear that they believe they are dealing with an honest man. That was Inspector Ian Wark's verdict on Bob Taylor. So in opposition to those who are confirmed sceptics I would state that I am wholly convinced that Bob saw something weird that November morning. But was it really an alien spacecraft? Given the intense interest in the story, it is reasonable that we should consider explanations given by those who reject notions of alien contact in general or who have doubts about this incident in particular.

In the magazine *Fortean Times* (Issue 56, Winter 1990), Nigel Watson wrote an article entitled 'Livingston—I Presume!' in which he expressed the sceptical point of view that 'it was highly convenient that this event took place when and where it did'. Watson argued that 'It gave a chance to promote the development zone to the nation in a very cheap and rapid manner . . . many people made a "pilgrimage" to the location and a snowman was erected on the landing site. It was a logical step for the local tourist board to capitalise on this; the "selling" of the Loch Ness Monster provided them with a compelling precedent'.

What Watson was suggesting was that the UFO incident might have been a publicity stunt to attract tourism and attention to the area. I think that this is fanciful, because Livingston Development Corporation would not have involved themselves in such a stunt, nor was it necessary for them to do so to sell the area, which was already on its way to becoming Scotland's 'silicon glen', home to computer and associated industries.

But was it staged to attract tourism? As I wrote to *Fortean Times* (based in London) and explained, Livingston is not Loch Ness. This is industrial, urban Scotland which is not really tourist country. With Edinburgh on the doorstep, any local tourist trade is related to the attraction of the capital, and the West Lothian area (in which Livingston is situated) would not function as a tourist magnet on its own. I'd suggest that the Taylor encounter was promoted simply because journalists found it an interesting and credible story, since the police were investigating it. Even relatively staid papers like the *Scotsman* gave it good coverage. I don't think there was any ulterior motive. Bob himself made next to nothing out of the incident and never tried to capitalise on his fame. In fact, he was soon thoroughly fed up with the interest his encounter generated.

Watson, however, finds it 'puzzling that the witness [i.e. Bob] and his family went to see relatives for the weekend. This had already been arranged, but you might have thought that after such an earth-shattering experience he might have wanted to stay at home and rest'. I don't follow this reasoning. If Bob was part of a stunt of some kind, then there would have been more reason to stay at home and make the most of it. Anyone who has met Bob will know that to go and get on with his life, no matter what, was wholly in keeping with the man's character. Bob did go to the local hospital, but he had to wait so long to be examined that he got fed up and left. A not unreasonable reaction.

In Bob's case one of the intriguing factors was that there was a lot more evidence than is usually available after a UFO report. In most instances, even where an alleged abduction has taken place, all that we have to go on is the account given by the person involved. In this case, there were not only the injuries suffered by Bob Taylor, but the physical traces left by the objects which were perfectly visible when the police and journalists arrived on the scene. Did these, however, relate to the actual encounter? It seems an amazing coincidence that at the spot where Bob claimed he saw a UFO there were marks on the ground, yet the marks do not seem to relate directly to the object he saw. These indentations were a combination of ladder-like depressions in the earth and circular or hoof-like marks. The UFO that Bob saw seemed to be hovering above the ground rather than resting on it and, from his description, there doesn't seem any obvious link between the structure of this 'spaceship' and the marks found in the earth. If the object had been resting on three or more supports then the depressions in the ground would have formed a symmetrical pattern which isn't obvious from any of the diagrams made at the time. True, the ladder-like marks exhibit a symmetry, but don't appear to fit in with the shape of the craft or any appendage that Bob describes.

The round or hoof-shaped depressions might have been formed by the spherical objects Bob described as leaving the mother ship, but the track marks don't appear to follow any coherent direction and in fact break into two distinct paths of successive indentations. I don't believe that this was an animal track, but neither does it appear to fit the description Bob gave of the movement of the 'mines'. If you take Bob's account you would expect to see tracks that approach him from a specific point and tracks that indicate that an object returned to a specific point, but the circular impressions don't seem to confirm this.

In his book *The UFO Mystery Solved* sceptic Steuart Campbell completely dismissed this physical evidence, pointing out that there had been cable-laying by water authority workers who had been using an area nearby for stacking ladders and other equipment. He reasoned that they had used this clearing for storing ladders and that this had caused marks in the ground. With his usual diligence, Mr Campbell tracked down the workers involved who 'denied having stored anything there'. Campbell 'suspected that they were not telling the truth, perhaps because they were not supposed to have used the clearing for that purpose'. That may be a correct assumption. On the other hand, maybe they were being truthful, particularly as Bob Taylor, a regular visitor, stated that 'he could not recall having seen anything lying there on previous visits'. The truth is that the origin of these marks has not been solved. They didn't have any odd chemical or other substance associated with them—at least not when tested—so they may well have a straightforward explanation. On the other hand, we might well ask: 'Why there?' Why at that very spot where Bob had his experience? It's one of those mysteries within a mystery.

Bob himself, however, has always been convinced that he saw something extraordinary. So in one way the issue of the physical evidence is a red herring. The matter stands or falls on the basis of Bob's testimony. Various suggestions have been put forward to reconcile the fact that while Bob was an honest person who described what he saw as it appeared to him, what he saw was, in some eyes, an impossibility.

So did Bob imagine it? If so, what triggered his imagination? Was it an hallucination brought on by an epileptic fit? This was the explanation favoured at one point by Steuart Campbell. Bob, however, had never suffered a fit in the past and at the time of writing almost twenty years later hasn't experienced another.

On the other hand, the symptoms that Bob described—breathlessness, a strong smell, unconsciousness, followed by dizziness, disorientation, headaches and dehydration—could be linked to epilepsy. But they could be linked to many other things too, such as the aftermath of a physical assault. Or other situations where the body reacts quickly and strongly. When Taylor's GP, Dr Gordon Adams, examined him in his home soon after the encounter, he noted that his temperature, blood pressure, heart rate and breathing were normal. The possibility of epilepsy was raised, I believe, because it leads to the conclusion that Taylor hallucinated the incident. However, is it likely that a person would suffer such a severe one-off fit without some obvious aftershock or recurrence?

But, perhaps Bob saw a bizarre object which he misidentified as a 'spaceship' or which he found so unnerving that it brought on an epileptic fit. This is another possible solution which Steuart Campbell has asked us to consider. Now, we know that ball lightning (or a phenomenon that goes by that name) does exist.[1] The phenomenon usually appears as glowing balls

1. Although ball lightning remains a controversial phenomenon, it has gained some respectability among scientists. In ball lightning cases, witnesses report seeing a glowing mass of energy up to a few metres in diameter which seems capable of moving through solid objects. The mass is sometimes described as seeming to possess intelligence—to be aware of its surroundings, and to be under directional control. It sometimes explodes with a blinding flash—hence the term 'Ball Lightning'.

of an unexplained nature which at times seem under intelligent control. They can appear anywhere, even inside a house. So it is not unreasonable to suppose that ball lightning could have been present on Dechmont Law that morning. It's also fair to concede that catching a glimpse of such an unusual phenomenon might be unnerving. But why would it trigger an epileptic fit? Why, alternatively, would Bob Taylor interpret ball lightning as a spaceship with mines rolling towards him. I'm afraid it doesn't make any sense. People who encounter ball lighting can describe it for what it is. To say that Bob saw ball lightning seems like seeking any answer to account for the inexplicable. We all suffer frights on a weekly basis when, for example, cars suddenly pull out in front of us. Do we see aliens then?

Critics may be on firmer ground when they look to the planets for explanations of UFO sightings. People often do misidentify heavenly bodies as alien spacecraft. So did Bob round a corner of his regular patch of woodland, see a mirage of Venus and interpret it as a UFO? Steuart Campbell notes that 'two planets were rising exactly in Taylor's line of sight as he rounded the corner and looked across the clearing. . . . Venus (magnitude –3.7) lay at an altitude of only 3 [degrees]' . . . and, to cut a long story short, Bob saw a mirage of the planet which brought on an epileptic fit and . . . the rest is history.

I am not convinced by this argument as many people on many days of the year may see a distorted image of Venus or anything else. Does it bring on epileptic fits or people claiming to be attacked by alien spacecraft? There isn't even evidence that there was a mirage of Venus at that time, so it doesn't seem reasonable to argue for this 'hypothesis', in spite of the scientific jargon that accompanies it.

An interesting parallel to the Taylor incident was uncovered by ufologist Jenny Randles. This took place in Canada on 20 May 1967. The witness saw the UFO, approached it and was then hit by a 'blast of compressed air, filling his nostrils with both . . . sulphurous odours and also a smell like burnt electric wiring'. The witness felt that he 'was covered in a bad smell'.

OTHER DECHMONT SIGHTINGS

Bob was alone when he experienced the event which haunted him thereafter, but there were a host of strange goings-on in the surrounding area that day. Many of these incidents were reported some time after the event, years after in some cases. The incident on Dechmont Law was a part, probably the climax, of a whole series of weird events witnessed during the hours before Bob's encounter.

Mr A Ferguson of Edinburgh was parking his lorry in a lay-by at 8 p.m. on 8 November when he noted a strip of brilliant light, shaped like a ruler, heading for Dechmont Law. I didn't become aware of this incident until October 1992 when the witness wrote to me. He had, as it turned out, tried to report the incident at the time to BUFORA (The British UFO Research Association), but without success.

Another witness at around this time was Mrs E Scott, who claimed that while she was standing at a bus stop looking towards the Pentland Hills she saw a round silvery object with flashing lights. At first she thought that it must be a helicopter, but immediately realised that it wasn't and decided instead that it 'must be a UFO'. She wasn't alone, as there was a lady beside her in the queue, although they were strangers to one another. Mrs Scott drew the woman's attention to the strange object and this second witness expressed the view that it was something out of the ordinary. Suddenly the object shot off at high speed towards Dechmont Law and disappeared.

Mrs Scott only described this incident to me many years after the event, in 1992. She was unsure of the date and placed it either the day before the Dechmont incident or actually on 9 November. Neither could she recall the exact time, only that it was daylight. Given the time of year, the sighting must therefore have taken place between roughly 8 a.m. and 4 p.m., so linking the sighting with reports from other witnesses on the morning of 9 November, the day of the main incident.

An incident which definitely took place on 8 November involved Mrs Josephine Quigley. She and four friends watched from the Livingston area while a circle of lights slowly rotated. It was 5.50 p.m., and in the prevailing darkness it was not possible to make out any particular features. The UFO held the same position in the sky for the time they had it under observation, around two minutes, and Mrs Quigley only lost sight of it when she herself moved away. The object appeared to be too low to be an aircraft, though as it is difficult to estimate altitude when there is no fixed point to compare distances, this can only be speculation.

The UFO spotted by Mrs Quigley has similarities with that seen two hours later by brothers Steven and Alan Little, but there are also significant differences. The object they saw close to their home at Bellsquarry, Livingston, appeared dome-shaped, which fits in with the spherical object seen by Mrs

Quigley. The brothers perhaps had a better view of the UFO as it was around 400 metres away from them over a road. As in the Quigley sighting, the brothers noticed that it hovered, and they estimated its height at 150 metres above the ground. Unlike the other UFO, however, this one had an array of lights, glowing white with pulsating blue and red lights on either side. Alan and Steven kept watch on the object for several minutes, until the whitish glow which gave a clear outline to the object faded. Shortly afterwards the pulsating lights went out. There was no sound at all from the mystery object.

Against this background of incidents the sun rose on what was to be a truly amazing day. By rush hour, strange incidents were already being reported. At five minutes past eight, a driver, Graham Kennedy, heading west on the A89 (see Fig 1), was passing Bangour Hospital when he noticed a bright light above and to the left of his car. It raced towards him a few metres above the ground, on a collision course. Swerving to avoid a crash with the orange-coloured, torch-shaped object, he nearly rammed a car heading in the opposite direction. Fortunately, both cars managed to stop in time, but the driver of the second vehicle claimed that he had seen nothing of the light which had come so close to causing a serious crash. Both men might be forgiven for believing that the unidentified object was a figment of the imagination of someone who, as the day was just beginning, was not quite fully awake.

Curiously, though, a similar event occurred near Warminster in England, back in 1965 when that area was (as the Press named it) the 'UFO Capital of the Western World'. On 10 August 1965 Terry Pell was driving his lorry to Warminster when a ball of flaming crimson light sped across the sky, then floated down to his cab in a head-on motion, threatening to smash through the windscreen. Mr Pell, like Mr Kennedy a decade later, swerved to avoid an impact, and ended up over a bank. There were no witnesses, as his wife and daughter, though in the cab with Terry, stayed asleep through the brief but traumatic ordeal. Luckily, however, there were other witnesses to our mysterious Bangour phenomenon. A van driver, also heading west on the A89 towards the town of Broxburn, saw a bright light in the sky. Though stationary, it struck him as too big for a star or planet. The light flashed intermittently on and off, but gradually grew dimmer. Eventually, as nothing else of significance occurred, the driver moved on, but the memory of the strange event remained firmly fixed in his mind.

Around the same time, a young nurse, Anne MacGregor, stepped from her bus and started to walk along the A89 towards Bangour hospital. As she went, Anne heard a distant, but distinct, hissing noise. Glancing upwards, she caught sight of a bright yellow light that appeared to be descending above the area known as Deans situated close to Dechmont Law.

A few minutes later, a cyclist travelling to work at a tyre factory situated in nearby Newbridge village, stopped to check the traffic flow before making a right turn. As he did so, he spotted a bright yellowish light that appeared to be hovering over the M8 motorway, close to Deer Hill—the local name for Dechmont Law. Were these two incidents linked to the Taylor incident? It would seem odd if there was no connection, given that these mysterious UFOs were seen so near in time to the main event.

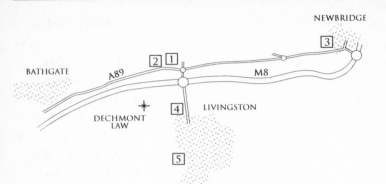

Fig 1. Map showing the location of sightings by witnesses in the area of Dechmont Law in November 1979.

Key: 1. Graham Kennedy
      2. Anne MacGregor
      3. Cyclist, Newbridge
      4. Mrs E. Scott
      5. Mr A. Ferguson

So what was Bob's encounter? Was it ball lightning? Probably not, but perhaps this phenomenon may lead us to a possible answer. A month before Bob's sighting an interesting incident occurred which echoes the Dechmont affair. It was unearthed by Michael Keatman and Andrew Collins who reported it in an edition of the magazine *Flying Saucer Review* (volume 26, number 3, 1980) and throws an interesting light on later events. The encounter took place on October 10 in Dedridge, Livingston. The witness, Mrs Steward, preparing for bed at a quarter to one in the morning, was closing the curtains when she saw a 'large, greyish-coloured, dome-shaped object with six red lights that rotated in an anti-clockwise direction'. The sighting was accompanied by a noise like that of a 'muffled helicopter' which changed into a 'high-pitched diesel engine' as she watched. The UFO, which had been hovering, rose up and gradually disappeared.

In the following weeks Mrs Steward felt very thirsty, particularly in the early morning around the time of the sighting. She also felt very tired and heavy and her body weight increased by several pounds. Was this pure coincidence or, as in Bob's case, did the unidentified object have an actual physical effect on the witness? There are similarities between the incidents: the sighting of a domed object followed by physical reaction, but can we say any more than that? It's noticeable that the object seen by the Little brothers also appeared dome-shaped, so we do have reports that support one another.

Electromagnetic forces undoubtedly have an impact on our bodies and minds. Was there a massive build-up of such forces on Dechmont Law that morning? Did these impact on Bob in such a way as he rounded the corner that somehow his mind was opened up? Some might say yes, he hallucinated, but others would suggest that perhaps a susceptibility to some energy in the area opened Bob's mind to things that the rest of us cannot see. (This hypothesis is discussed further in Chapter 9.)

In 1992 Scottish ufologist Ken Higgins and I were instrumental in having a plaque erected to mark the site of this historic incident. It was achieved thanks to the co-operation of Livingston Development Corporation, and was the first time anywhere in the world that a UFO has been officially recognised. Even at this point, however, controversy dogged the event. LDC chose a controversial wording for the plaque. It ran: 'This is the site referred to in Arthur C Clarke's *Mysterious*

World which describes an encounter between a forestry worker out walking and what appeared to him as an unidentified flying object'. Bob Taylor's name was noticeably absent from the plaque which had been fastened to a large stone or cairn. The inclusion of Arthur C Clarke's name seemed decidedly odd, as apart from referring to the incident in a television programme he had no connection with it. LDC held no opening ceremony, or at least not one to which any UFO groups had been invited.

Pleased though Scottish ufologists were with the official recognition, there was a feeling that a more fitting and descriptive monument would have been appropriate. I asked for and was given permission by LDC to erect something, provided I took financial responsibility for its erection and care, conditions to which I agreed. Well-known sculptor David Annand has produced a design (Fig 2) which reflects Mankind's place in

Fig 2. David Annand's design for the Dechmont Law sculpture.

the vast and endless mystery of the universe. It proclaims no solution to Bob's encounter, but does assume that at this spot a challenge was made to Earth's self-preoccupation.

In 1983, on the fourth anniversary of the encounter, SEMR took well-known medium Katrina McNab to the site to try and see if her psychic ability could uncover any clues to what had occurred. Katrina was in no doubt as she meditated on that famous spot that alien contact had occurred there. One of the most striking sensations that came over her was that of burning. Although Bob did not have burns to his body, this might have been a reference to the dry, choking sensation he experienced as the two objects took hold of him.

The Dechmont Law sighting was a key incident in the development of Scottish ufology. It put Scotland on the world UFO map, while at the same time inspiring various individuals to enter the neglected area of UFO investigation. But the incident has remained controversial. In 1996 science writer Duncan Lunan suggested that the object Taylor saw might have been an RPV (remotely piloted vehicle) of an experimental nature. The explanation did not meet with general approval. However, in 1967 in Nebraska, USA, aliens allegedly 'showed a witness a small object the size of a car hub-cap which . . . was a remote flying sensor that sent back pictures and which they despatched to check out an area before they landed'. Lunan put forward a more straightforward terrestrial explanation— that it was the military testing new technology. On one fact we can all agree: Bob Taylor's encounter has never lost its ability to intrigue.

Close encounters of the fourth kind (see Appendix B), such as that experienced by Mr Taylor, are unusual. The vast majority of UFO sightings involve strange lights in the sky. Weird glowing balls that perform strange movements and sometimes even follow people about as if they were spying on them. But if extraterrestrials exist, why would they attract attention to themselves in this way? Would entities from a distant galaxy fly over Scotland with lights flashing? Why do they need lights anyway? It is hard to make sense of it, yet we can't just ignore these incidents. There is clearly something odd happening. There have been too many reports, too many close-up sightings to dismiss the phenomenon out of hand. But are we dealing with ET or another related mystery?

TARBRAX SIGHTING

In January 1998 I received a phone call from Jennifer Whyte who lives in the village of Tarbrax. On Thursday 11 December she had retired early to bed and was looking out of her bedroom window. On the moorland that stretched before her she caught sight of a blue light, very bright, which seemed to be hovering close to the ground. It also seemed to be pulsating with an inner core and a thin, curled 'tail' which seemed to twist round it. Jennifer fetched her binoculars to get a better look. With the blue light now in focus 'two very bright triangles appeared to the right of the blue light'. The triangles were inverted. The base of the pyramid which resulted from these overlapping triangles was at the top and the point hung just above the ground. The triangles appeared to be made up of many small red lights rather than being one solid object, although it may be that there were sections between the lights which were dark in colour and so not visible. The blue light now began to fade or, alternatively, move directly away until it was out of sight. The triangular UFOs hung around for a few minutes till they too disappeared in the same way as the blue light. Mrs White estimated that the sighting lasted a total of five minutes. (This incident also has significance for the A70 abduction case—see Chapter 6.)

Amanda Royle caught sight of a similar strange blue light from the window of her home in Claverhouse Drive in the Inch district of Edinburgh. This incident took place on Thursday 12 January 1995 at 3.45 in the morning. Mrs Royle had been unable to sleep and caught a glimpse of a light through the curtains of her bedroom window. Curious, she decided to take a look, and witnessed a bizarre sight. Over the roof of the houses opposite there hovered 'a bright blue oval disc with a yellow tinge', which appeared 'as bright as a full moon'. It wasn't clearly defined as 'the edge of the disc was hazy'. Amanda watched the object for five minutes, went to make some tea and returned to the bedroom at about 4.15. The object had now disappeared. It had made no sound during all this time and Amanda was not aware of any after-effects. It is true that there was a full moon on the 16th of that month, but Amanda is in no doubt that what she saw was not the moon in some strange guise.

RIDDOCHHILL INCIDENT

Mysterious lights come in all sorts of colours and move at all kinds of speed. On 16 August 1992 a Bathgate couple, Mr and Mrs Tait, witnessed a strange incident, one which had them rushing to their telephone. At 10.15 p.m. exactly they saw an intense green light travelling from east to west on a downward trajectory and appearing to impact with the earth about half a mile from their house. Convinced that they had been unwitting observers of a plane crash, they rang Edinburgh airport to report the incident. To their relief and surprise, they discovered that there were no aircraft in the area at the time. Whatever they had seen, it was clearly not an aircraft.

A few days later, following a telephone call, I met and spoke with the couple. Both hold down responsible jobs (one is a teacher) and had nothing to gain from reporting the incident. In fact, they emphasised to me that they wanted no personal publicity. In between hearing of this incident and visiting Mr and Mrs Tait, I heard from Nicholas Reid, then a twenty-two-year-old law graduate living in Broxburn. He confirmed seeing a 'stream of green light which was travelling [at an angle of] 45 degrees towards the earth'. Nicholas awaited the inevitable impact and from his window scanned 'nearby fields for any evidence of fire'. To his surprise, however, he could detect no evidence of a crash. At first, he thought that the incident could well have had a natural explanation, although his sighting did not fit in with the timing of a meteor shower which occurred that month.

With Nicholas's account backing up the Tait's description, I was convinced that something strange had occurred that night. Further confirmation came when Ken Higgins, checking back through his files, reported that an almost identical incident had occurred at a bing in nearby Boghall in the 1980s. Several witnesses had observed a green light hit the ground and burst into flames. Mr Tait was certain that he knew roughly where his UFO had come down. I was taken to the spot, called

Riddochhill, where it seemed the impact crater might be found. The area had once been an important coal mining location, but had long been disused and eventually in-filled with a view to long term redevelopment. At one end a black scurry revealed where the old mine workings began. Marks scarred the surface of one slope, produced perhaps by an object hitting the ground at speed. I was so excited by this evidence that I took several pictures for photographic library of SEMR (Scottish Earth Mysteries Research). Apart from these marks, however, there was little else to be seen, in spite of a search which covered a substantial part of the infill.

The reason for this emerged over the following weeks. It is a reminder that no serious investigator should get too easily carried away! The initial incident was covered by reporter Ian Kyle, then of the *Edinburgh Evening News*. As a result, new witnesses phoned in and it became obvious that the object had not come down near Bathgate, but travelled several miles further west. A family living in the village of Blackburn reported that they had seen the object descend from the sky and land to the rear of their house. Again, for fear of ridicule in a small community, the family did not wish to be named. When I visited the family, however, the evidence that came from the grandmother and grandson was very firm. From her bedroom on the first floor of the house they had seen an intense green ball come from the sky and hit the earth behind a line of trees in open farmland, a few hundred yards from their terraced house.

An investigation of this undulating countryside was carried out by Ken Higgins and myself, accompanied by Ian Shanes, a psychic medium from Glasgow. Although this survey turned up many points of interest, it failed to uncover any sign of an impact, or any marks that might conceivably have been made by an object landing. Whatever the object was, it seemed to have disappeared as mysteriously as it arrived.

Some years later, however, a solution was put to me. A number of independent investigators had been scouring the area, convinced that there was an underground base out of which these balls of light (which it was assumed were alien spacecraft) were entering or leaving. As far as I am aware at the time of writing, no evidence has emerged to back up the underground base hypothesis, at least in the Lothians.

Some have asked, however, why a UFO investigator would bring along a psychic. You can only deny the involvement of those with psychic ability if you believe that UFOs are nothing other than solid spaceships travelling billions of miles from other galaxies. However, if there is a chance that they are something else, then we need to have experts in various fields investigating the phenomena. What Ian found, though on the surface not directly linked to the sighting, fascinated me. After tramping across many fields we came to a small wooded area. It looked like an oasis in the middle of well-ploughed farmland. It had that untouched feel about it, almost like walking into another world. Ian immediately felt that we had arrived at a special place. At this point Ian saw many small entities. According to him they were well aware of what we were doing. I could certainly sense something different about this wooded spot, although I couldn't see the creatures he described. Was this somehow linked to these strange lights in the sky?

As I walked back across a field, I headed towards a row of cottages and managed to strike up a conversation with a local farmer. He hadn't seen the green object or been aware of the newspaper coverage. He did tell me, though, that ten years earlier a strange 'yellow' object had travelled over the same farmland visited by the green light.

Interest in the green light continued unabated, and from all over the Lothians witnesses came forward to testify to having seen this type of strange object. Mrs Adriane Goldie, a Mid Calder housewife, reported seeing green lights on 15 October 1992 'darting about in a zig-zag pattern as if they were playing'. Some cases, it emerged, stretched back several years. As long ago as 1981 Marion Findlay from Edinburgh wrote to the *Daily Record*, describing a bright green light travelling across the sky, moving 'too fast to be a plane'. Like the Bathgate couple, however, Mrs Findlay's husband 'thought it might be a plane crashing'.

Returning to the more recent times, William Mackay from Glasgow, who was carrying out lightning tests on the roof of St Cuthbert's Church in Edinburgh on 27 October 1992, saw 'a very luminous green light' moving at speed at around 7.10 p.m. It travelled from 'east to west from Edinburgh Castle to the Usher Hall, where it disappeared into a cloud'. Mr Mackay added that the object 'was brightly coloured and appeared to leave a disappearing green vapour trail'.

ROSSLYN CHAPEL

In passing, it is interesting to note that the Jewish astronomer Flegetanis identified the Holy Grail as a green stone fallen from the skies. Students of Earth Mysteries will note the existence in the Lothians of Rosslyn Chapel and its association with legends of the Grail and hidden arcane knowledge. Strange lights have been seen in the vicinity over many years. Of course, if you are convinced that UFOs are nuts-and-bolts extraterrestrial spacecraft, you will view the connection as pure coincidence.[2]

One scientific explanation put forward for the numerous green light sightings is that they are meteors. However, the quantity of the objects seen and size and intensity of the light rules this theory out in the majority of cases, though certainly not all. And even when a meteorite is seen and its trajectory pinpointed, the timing may not match that of the event noted by witnesses. This was the case on 16 August 1992. A meteor was observed, but whatever it was that witnesses reported to me, it was not that particular (and by all accounts spectacular) meteor entry.

The difficulty in arriving at a solution to the green light phenomenon is shown by contradictory testimony I received from witnesses who observed the object 'landing' near the village of Blackburn. On 20 October 1992 a senior policeman who witnessed the event wrote to me. He had been measuring a window for curtains when at around 10 p.m. he 'became aware of a cluster of bright white and green lights in the sky immediately to the north-east of the town'. He concedes that 'the light formation did look rather unusual' but believes that

2. Rosslyn Chapel has long been associated with ancient mysteries. It has been suggested that it may be the resting place of The Holy Grail, and/or the Ark of the Covenant, which are hidden in a sealed vault beneath the chapel . Whatever the truth of these claims, there is concrete evidence of links with the medieval Knights Templar, while the interior of the chapel features strange carvings, many of pagan origin whose exact meaning remains a mystery.

'this may have been due to the angle . . . I was viewing it [from]'. The light cluster then split in two, one side 'dipping sharply at an angle of approximately 45 degrees, before levelling off and continuing northwards at a reasonably fast speed'. Meanwhile, the 'other half of the light cluster moved off in the opposite direction at a slow speed, but without appearing to change altitude'. Not unreasonably, this observer, viewing from Blackburn, came to the conclusion he had been watching 'two domestic or military aircraft which suddenly changed direction or flight path'.

I put this explanation to the Blackburn family who had seen the green light hit the ground to the rear of their home. They were quite certain that the series of events described by the policeman did not fit what they had seen. They had definitely observed a single bright object which had come down in the vicinity of their village. Could there have been two separate green lights that night? It appears unlikely given that both were seen at about the same time. Yet all the witnesses are adamant about their interpretation of what they saw. The opposing testimony makes it difficult to draw firm conclusions.

1947 SIGHTING

Strange balls of light crossing the skies arouse our curiosity, but to come to a clearer view of what we're dealing with, we need more detailed evidence—evidence of encounters with solid objects. Soon after Kenneth Arnold's report in 1947,[3]

3. Kenneth Arnold was piloting a small aircraft over Washington State in the USA, on 24 June 1947, when flashes of light caught his eye. These turned out to be from the sun reflecting on a formation of nine silver craft which he judged to be flying at over

witnesses in the Lothians were reporting sightings of strange objects which we would undoubtedly describe as UFOs.

Andrew Cherry was a 22-year-old factory worker, employed by Woods Bottle Works in the Portobello district of Edinburgh. It was 5.30 on a beautiful summer's morning in July 1947, as Mr Cherry waited at his usual bus stop close to St John's School in Baileyfield Road. Glancing skywards, he caught sight of a strange object, disc-shaped with what looked like a large glass dome in the style of an observation window. The UFO was hovering about 300 feet above the ground, close enough for Mr Cherry to get a clear view of its humanoid occupant. The 'alien' was wearing dark clothes and was sitting or standing beside a control panel of some kind. He also noted the marked metal texture of the spacecraft—'like rough diamonds'—and the 'orange-yellow colour', which he thinks may have been simply a reflection of the sun's rays.

The area around the object looked hazy, possibly owing to the object's energy source. Mr Cherry could hear a low, smooth hum, which he associated with the flames he could see escaping from the disc. He reckoned it to be 12 to 15 feet in length, but showing tremendous power as it tilted, spun away and disappeared over the Fife coast in a matter of seconds. Mr Cherry describes his experience as 'ghostly, eerie and awesome'.

This extraordinary event made such a profound impression on Mr Cherry that he has never forgotten what he saw. As he

1,200 mph—faster than any known plane could manage at that time. It was in reports of this sighting that the term 'flying saucer' was coined—not from Arnold's description of the shape of these craft (he stated that they had a rounded front, straight sides, and came to a rounded point at the rear, though he also described them as like jet planes without tails), but from his explanation of the erratic way they flew: 'they flew like a saucer would if you skipped it across the water'.

said in 1994, 'after all this time I still have chills run through my body'.

SIGHTHILL, CORSTORPHINE HILL

There may have been a genuine gap after the Cherry sighting, or did witnesses simply not bother reporting their encounters? It was in 1958 that Mrs Lyn Livingston, now a Care Officer, saw 'five or six disc-shaped objects, very high up and travelling at speed'. The encounter, in the Sighthill area of the city, lasted only a few seconds before the objects disappeared from view. In another sighting from the same year, James Black of Balgreen Road, Edinburgh, saw a long silver-coloured object streaking across the evening sky over Corstorphine Hill, part of which has been occupied since 1913 by the capital's famous zoo. We know, mainly from research in the United States, that UFOs seem to have a special interest in animal anatomy, even to the extent of dissecting and mutilating their victims. Was this the reason for their visit at that time? We can only speculate. Mr Black, however, was so impressed by the incident that he painted a picture of the event, which was presented to me by his daughter.

ANIMAL MUTILATION

It is interesting to note that in 1995 claims of animal mutilation surfaced in the West Lothian area. Investigator David Colman videoed the corpse of a sheep which appeared to have died in a strange fashion in a field not far from Edinburgh airport. The farmer on whose land the sheep died claimed that it was killed by a fox. The cause of death, however, seemed to be a huge wound around the throat, which looked as if it had been ripped open. This would surely have been beyond the powers of a fox. Might it have been attacked by another animal, perhaps the mysterious 'black cat' which has appeared in various locations in Scotland? Brian Wood, a self-employed landscape gardener believed that he saw a creature which looked like panther in April 1997. This encounter, which took place near Boghall, West Lothian, so intrigued Brian that he decided to set up a hide in the nearby hills. Boghall is only a matter of miles from Edinburgh airport, so if the creature is indeed a panther or other 'cat' then the two locations are well within roaming distance. The animal Mr Wood caught for an instant in the light of his torch looked about 4 feet long and 3 feet high, but the beast has still to date avoided capture. As have so many other strange animals reported from other parts of Scotland. So are we dealing with 'earth beasts' let loose by some irresponsible owner? Or are these animals roaming our space from another dimension.

BATHGATE VIDEO EVIDENCE

By the 1990s the widespread availability of video cameras meant that UFO investigators could have with them an 'impartial witness'. In November 1995, Brian Curran's home near Polbeth, Bathgate, was 'buzzed by a fireball UFO', according to *The Sun* newspaper. The reporter also claimed that 'the huge blazing craft appeared just yards from them as they cleared up after a party'. Although, in fact, the orange object remained some distance away in the night sky, the video footage clearly shows that something very strange took place. The UFO appeared as a bright orange disc and had the characteristics of a three-dimensional object. It's surface was ruffled and although one commentator described it as like a baby's rusk, I would describe it as identical to the famous gong struck at the start of old Rank films. The most intriguing aspects of the mystery object were the two semi-circular gaps, one at the bottom and the second on the lower right, which in the early frames look like monstrous bites out of a round cheese. However, as the video runs, it is as if a mechanism is in operation, and two smooth coated chunks move out of the main body to fill the empty portions. As Brian and his wife Shirley continued watching, the object disappeared, then re-appeared, then shot off at an amazing rate and vanished. Air Traffic at Edinburgh Airport claimed there had been no unusual sightings that night. Interestingly, in February 1996 a similar object was filmed over Inverness, and days before the Curran encounter an almost identical UFO was filmed over Norwich in England.

Analysis of Brian Curran's video was carried out by SEMR member John Morrison (see Figs 3a and 3b). John noted that analysing the video was difficult owing to the sequence being short. In fact it was only four seconds in duration and only two frames appeared to be in focus. The detailed scrutiny was undertaken frame-by-frame and in slow motion so that the progression of the image on the tape could be properly examined. The changes of structure that the UFO went through proved to be intriguing. Instead of the circular object visible to the casual observer, there appears an arrow shape which in one sequence looks almost like a delta wing. At the end of the

This viewing was done frame-by-frame and in slow-motion so as to give me time to study what was happening to the image. Below is a list of significant changes that occurred in the sequence. The time & frame number when the changes happened are also included.

[S]	[F]	
00	00	Start of sequence. Orange circle visible, semi-circles taken out.
00	09	Camera operator zooms-out slightly.
00	22	Bottom semi-circle starts to disappear.
01	10	Bottom semi-circle disappears altogether.
01	13	Camera operator starts zoom-out, and right side semi-circle starts to disappear.
03	01	This shape appears:

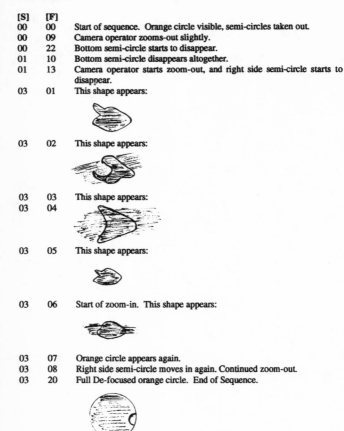

| 03 | 02 | This shape appears: |

| 03 | 03 | This shape appears: |
| 03 | 04 | |

| 03 | 05 | This shape appears: |

| 03 | 06 | Start of zoom-in. This shape appears: |

03	07	Orange circle appears again.
03	08	Right side semi-circle moves in again. Continued zoom-out.
03	20	Full De-focused orange circle. End of Sequence.

Fig 3a. Part of John Morrison's analysis of the Brian Curran video.

The following colours were observed when each of the following frames was paused.

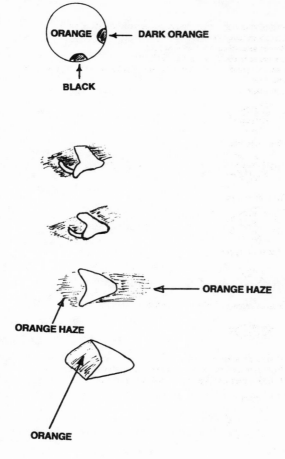

Fig 3b. Analysis of colours observed in the Brian Curran video.

clip the orange circle reappears, which may be due to the lens being out of focus. Morrison's conclusion was that 'an airborne object or light is certainly recorded by the video' but 'the circular image seen at the beginning of the video sequence is almost certainly not the original . . . shape, but a de-focused image of the object/light source'. So Brian Curran had definitely caught something strange on his video, but in reality it was more triangular than round-shaped. Although we had the 'impartial witness', the problems of interpreting the evidence have remained.

Only a few weeks after the Curran incident, more video evidence was made available after UFO investigator Dave Colman caught a strange object on tape in the Lothian area. It was at 10.22 p.m. on 29 November 1995 that Dave spotted an object in the sky and started his camera rolling. The sequence he took covered over thirteen minutes and certainly revealed in the first part something strange.

It should be explained that David filmed a second object the following day which, according to John Morrison's analysis, 'almost certainly depicts an aircraft about to land at Edinburgh Airport'. However, the 29 November footage cannot be explained in these terms. This reveals a nut (as in iron!) shaped object with a dome on top and a disturbance, perhaps a propulsion blast, exiting from the section underneath. Several other objects appear, including one with a rectangular shape and another with a delta wing type structure. They may, of course, be camera distortions of the main object, possibly caused by reflections within the lens. After a couple of minutes the main object 'brightens and releases two small objects/ lights at about the same time. Both descend at the same rate.

One descends to the left and the other appears to descend almost straight down'. Curious stuff, but Morrison also reported seeing 'a small grey object entering the main object' just before the two small UFOs emerged. As he comments, 'This certainly puzzled me as I do not know of any military/ civil aircraft where objects are passed to aircraft in mid-air, apart from in-flight refuelling of other aircraft'. A procedure which is certainly unlikely in the circumstances shown in the film footage. So what we have is a definite mystery. Unfortunately, the video quality is not sufficiently high, and the sequence of events is only obvious under frame by frame scrutiny. It's a pity, as it is footage which deserves a wider audience.

REPEATER WITNESS

UFOs, as has been seen, are not necessarily the traditional round or oval form. In fact, they can come in any shape or size, as Andrew McMichael of Mortonhall in Edinburgh can testify. This case is remarkable, not only in that here we have one of those exceptional cases of a 'repeater' witness,[4] but in the variety of the phenomena. It also raises the issue, which we will continue to review through this book, of the exact nature of the phenomena with which we are dealing.

On 8 August 1996, Andrew McMichael woke up at 2.15 a.m. A fox had been coming into the garden and so Andrew decided

---

4. A 'Repeater' witness is an individual who experiences several UFO sightings or who may even see UFOs on a regular basis. These individuals are the exception, as most witnesses experience only a single isolated encounter. The proportion of repeater witnesses has not been properly quantified, but in Scotland at any rate they are rare.

to poke his head out of the bedroom window and see if their nocturnal visitor had eaten the food left out for him. He had. The plate was clean. As Andrew looked up he was, as he later told me, 'just in time to see an object move in an undulating path across the trees and houses at the edge of Frogston Road to the south of my house. It was completely silent and had a slight round bright red emission at the centre'. The UFO was oval in shape with a small dome. He estimated its size as around 30 feet long and 15 feet from top to bottom. When it first caught his attention it was hovering at around 200 feet, directly above the houses opposite. The object moved away in 'a slightly wavy pattern' then 'rose up as if to clear a clump of trees'. To Andrew, it seemed to change direction twice, as though searching for something, before disappearing behind some sycamores bordering farmland.

Although this was a definite UFO sighting, it was not the first strange incident Andrew experienced. A week earlier, on 2 August, he woke early, at around 3.15 a.m., disturbed by the movement of his wife and her exclamation, 'What on earth's that . . . !' Together they looked out of the window and were almost blinded by 'an unearthly dazzling white light' which, as Andrew recalls, 'was so bright that I couldn't see anything else outside our bedroom window'. He describes 'a slightly buzzy feeling' as if a static charge was present. The light moved off silently in a westerly direction.

About a month later, in casual conversation with neighbours, Andrew learned that they too had been woken by a strong white light, bright even through thick bedroom curtains. The sensation of an electrically charged atmosphere was also present. This incident occurred on the same date as Andrew's, but forty minutes later. So had the phenomenon returned to a nearby spot? It seems the obvious explanation.

Following these events in August, Andrew experienced two other odd incidents. Just after midnight on 23 December 1996, he awoke to find a large snowflake-like object covering the entire glass of the window. It was five-pointed and resembled, to Andrew, 'a bright diamond'. He was transfixed by its simple beauty, but the tranquillity of the moment was shattered when his dog suddenly let out a bark. Abruptly the 'snowflake' shattered into a hundred tiny diamonds which fell onto the ledge of the window sill. When Andrew 'rose and approached the window, there was nothing to be seen'.

A week later there came another strange occurrence, again just after midnight, to disturb Andrew's sleep. This time he saw 'an incredibly beautiful red bright moistness' at the bedroom window. It had the appearance of a swirling red dust with a crimson glow. When Andrew looked up to see where this strange display ended and the sky began, he was amazed to discover that there was no sky to be seen. Gradually, the red glow moved away and clear moon and heavens were revealed. Following this event Andrew told me that his 'health had improved beyond all recognition'.

There is, of course, a recognised state in between waking and sleeping where the individual appears to be unable to distinguish between dreaming and reality. Andrew is confident that this did not happen in this case. He points to the fact that movement in his hand, restricted after a stroke, increased and that generally he felt much better—tangible evidence that something had taken place.

So was Andrew McMichael's experience an extraterrestrial

visitation, or something quite different—a psychic incident perhaps? The proximity of the incidents indicates that they were in some way connected, but in what way? Were they all in Andrew's mind? The testimony of his wife and neighbours suggests that at least one of these incidents definitely took place. That event, then, has independent corroboration.

Of course, any early morning encounter leads to the comment: 'Oh, you must have dreamed it!' Andrew, however, also experienced a fascinating daytime sighting twenty years before the events at Mortonhall.

In late summer 1976, at around 5.30 p.m., Andrew caught sight of what he took to be an aeroplane banking over Clermiston Hill. The 'plane' seemed to be moving in an odd way and Andrew suddenly realised that it was going to crash, into a row of trees on the side of the hill. Just as disaster seemed inevitable, the object flipped onto its edge to reveal a disc shape with a raised central area. The UFO was very large, around 300 feet across, Andrew estimated, 'with a very flat elliptical profile' and 'coloured blue-white', almost as if it was trying to camouflage itself against the background of the sky.

Andrew was not alone when this incident occurred. He had a witness, his colleague Andrew Wood, but as is the case with so many witnesses, Andrew was 'totally amazed that [apart from them] no-one else noticed this quite extraordinary sighting'. The way it moved was also very strange. 'Instead of moving as an aeroplane would, edge on to the airflow, the large disc moved upright, slowly at first, stopped, then just looked as if it switched off . . . or disappeared completely'.

ARTHUR'S SEAT

Daylight UFO sightings often produce more useful evidence as the witness has a better opportunity to note the shape and other details of the object. A 48-year-old jogger, Ian Atkinson, was making a circuit of Arthur's Seat, that lion-shaped hill which dominates the Edinburgh skyline and features so often in descriptions of the city. It was early in the morning of Thursday, 28 October 1992, around ten minutes to seven. 'It was a dark, clear sky', explained Ian, 'no clouds and the stars were visible'. He continued, 'As I was coming round the Radical Road . . . just up from the Pollock Halls of Residence, I saw an oval/round object, white and clearly defined'. Ian is a photographer and has a keen eye for detail. According to him the object was not glowing, but was sharp-edged and definitely solid. Within two seconds it had traversed an incredible distance across the sky. It vanished from sight 'almost as if', Ian added mysteriously, 'someone saw it and the light was switched out'. Time and again key witnesses have reported an eerie feeling that UFOs are aware of the observer's presence.

PORTOBELLO SIGHTING

Pat Macleod of Portobello got much closer to her UFO. Anyone who has had the good fortune to speak to Pat will come away with no doubts as to her sincerity and her conviction that what she saw did in fact take place. Having interviewed Pat several times and videoed her relating these events, I have no reason to doubt her account. Pat's encounter was considered of such significance that it was included in a SKY TV programme on world-wide ufology.

One morning in October 1992, Pat was driving along Duddingston Park, making for the local health centre in Mountcastle Drive to keep an appointment. The time was 9.50 a.m. As she drove, Pat became aware of an extremely bright flashing light in the sky. Half a mile further on, keeping the light in view, she realised that it was getting bigger and the brightness intensifying. In fact it was drawing much closer to her and as it approached she noted that the central sphere of light had a ring or flange round it. This reminded her, Pat told me, of pictures she had seen of the planet Saturn.

At about twenty to thirty feet from the ground, the object slowed down and appeared to hover. It was large. Very large. The length of an aircraft wingspan, according to Pat. Around the circumference, at regular intervals, were squares of light, like glowing windows.

Pat had not been checking her watch while this curious event unfolded, but reckons it was now around ten o'clock. She was due at the health centre at that time, and reckons she arrived not too long after.

As she turned off the main road to carry on down a sidestreet to her destination, the object veered east in the opposite direction and slowly descended, seeming to land in an area of open ground called Niddrie Burn—a valley-shaped expanse of grass with a stream running through the centre. Although it is open land, the ground is, in fact, surrounded by houses and multi-storey flats which have a clear view of the valley. Incredibly, in spite of considerable publicity over the incident, not a single person came forward to testify to having seen the object simultaneously with Pat's sighting. Pat has confirmed to me that there were cars on the road at this time, though heading away from the descending sphere.

How is it possible that something so large and bizarre, so utterly distinctive, was seen by Pat, but passed unnoticed by others. Did Pat misidentify another natural object? Investigation into the possibility that this might be a helicopter proved inconclusive. Although evidence indicated that there had not been any helicopter movement in that area at the time, it is impossible to be certain. But Pat obviously knows a helicopter when she sees one and is adamant that, whatever she saw, it was not a helicopter. She was able to confirm that the craft she saw moved silently, which casts doubt on the helicopter theory. Furthermore, such a noisy machine landing in Niddrie Burn in broad daylight would surely have been spotted and reported. A helicopter as the basis of this incident must be ruled out, particularly if we accept that the object passed within a hundred feet of her car and Pat had every opportunity to make a positive identification. She was so convinced something weird had happened that she called the police to enquire whether any other witness had rung in to report the event. Then, as now, Pat was determined to prove the reality of what she saw. She has said that a number of people came into the shop she owned and confirmed that they too had witnessed strange incidents at the time she went through her experience. Not being an investigator into UFO phenomena, Pat did not bother to take their names, an omission she later regretted.

UFO sceptic Steuart Campbell has a completely different explanation for Pat's encounter. He believes that she 'saw a double-merged mirage of Mercury caused by seeing it enlarged via a temperature inversion'[5]. Mr Campbell points out that Mercury would have been in Pat's line of sight as she drove down Duddingston Park South. He suggests that Pat's description of the object as 'resembling Saturn' is 'a good description of a double-merged mirage of a planet'. Pat's movement in the car may then have created the impression that the object was growing in size and 'landing'. Although this explanation cannot be dismissed, the intense nature of the experience coupled with Pat's detailed observation at close quarters casts doubt on this scientific theory.

Interestingly, however, although no other witnesses directly confirmed Pat's sighting, evidence did emerge of curious events that day which back up Pat's account. Jon Jeromsom, who ran a plumbing business in Duddingston Park, was looking out of his showroom window when he saw a bright object descend to about 50 feet. It hovered for several seconds, then vanished. The time? 10 a.m.—exactly the same time as the object Pat had encountered disappeared from her view. Later that day Mr Jeromsom believes he observed the same light again, poised over a building directly opposite his business at around 4.45 p.m.

The UFO may have returned to the area some months later. On Christmas Day, to be exact. Mrs Ann McGuire of Portobello

5. Stars and planets are all seen through the earth's atmosphere which inevitably distorts our view of them. This causes the apparent 'twinkling' of stars, for example. Changes in the atmosphere, it is suggested, can make a huge difference to the way a planet appears to a witness. This is especially true when a 'temperature inversion' occurs. Normally, warm air rises through cooler air, but in a temperature inversion warm air lies beneath cool air and leads to dramatic distortions in the appearance of planets, sometimes creating two images of a single object which become 'fused' and appear as a single larger object. This, it is claimed, accounts for many UFO sightings. (See Steuart Campbell's *The UFO Mystery Solved* for a fuller explanation.)

High Street looked out of her bedroom window at 10 p.m. that night and became aware of a black oval-shaped UFO in the night sky. She got a good view of the mysterious object as it stood clear of clouds and was sharply defined. She watched it for three minutes, during which time it remained stationary. It made no noise and she was not aware of the object moving away. Later that week when she saw a drawing of Pat's UFO in the *Edinburgh Evening News* she instantly recognised it as the one she had seen.

MOTHMAN

My inquiries into the Macleod sighting uncovered a very curious incident which, although it did not link directly with Pat's encounter, had taken place in a house overlooking Niddrie Burn a few days before. The witness woke up in the early hours of the morning—she isn't sure why—and caught sight of a brilliant white light clearly visible through her bedroom window. She tried to draw her husband's attention to the phenomenon, but he stayed resolutely asleep. Curious and slightly apprehensive, she got out of bed and went to the window to take a closer look. She noticed that the light seemed to be coming towards the window. Her attention was drawn to a tree at the foot of her garden. Poised on one of the thicker branches stood a thing which she described as 'a giant bird' the size of a man or possibly a human-like figure with wings. Was this the only Scottish sighting of Mothman,[6] the

6. 'Mothman' is the name given to a half-human, half-bird-like creature with enormous wings which has been reported on several occasions, particularly in the USA. This entity stands upright when on the ground, but has also been observed, with wings folded, crouching on branches of trees.

mysterious creature which has been encountered across the Atlantic in various parts of the United States? Badly frightened by what she had seen, she tried again to wake up her partner, who would not move and gave the impression of being in a trance. She climbed into bed, and as she did so, a light came into the room and moved along the wall till it had travelled all the way round back to its starting point. The witness remained in a highly nervous state till, as dawn broke, she at last fell asleep.

Could the mysterious object glimpsed by Jon Jeromsom be the same one observed by Pat Macleod? Or, even more incredible, the same one that was witnessed several miles away the year before? There are definite similarities. A couple from the village of Ladywell near Livingston in West Lothian were looking from their back room window when they spotted a bright light in the sky. It was 10.30 p.m. on a clear August night in 1991. They could be sure of the time as ITN's regular news programme had just ended. Both husband and wife were familiar with aircraft lights, as the flight path to Edinburgh's airport at Turnhouse passes close to the house. It was precisely because this sighting didn't fit into the pattern of approaching aircraft that it first attracted their attention. Its appearance struck them both as being completely out of the ordinary. They were so intrigued by the spectacle and the fact that the light made no attempt to move but simply hovered, that Mr John Gartside took out his binoculars to take a closer look.

What he saw fascinated him. He could make out a pyramid-shaped object with a series of lights clustered at each corner. Both he and his wife were now certain that there was a solid mysterious presence hovering over the electricity pylons in the field outside their village. Drawing some strange sustenance, perhaps? As they watched the object for a full twenty minutes through binoculars, there can be no doubt that they witnessed an incident that was outside the normal. A quick phone call to Turnhouse Air Traffic Control produced the startling response that nothing was showing up on radar! The visitor disappeared as suddenly and unexpectedly as it had arrived.

The appearance of the object came within twenty-four hours of another strange incident for the family. The night before, as they lay in bed, a brilliant beam of light unexpectedly illuminated their bedroom. It shone with such intensity that it turned night into day. Both Pat and John leapt from their bed in an attempt to discover the source of the strange illumination. The light, however, having swept the four walls, simply vanished.

An investigation by Ken Higgins and myself soon afterwards revealed no obvious explanation for the event. The position of the bedroom windows and doors made it highly unlikely that the incident could have been caused by something as mundane as passing car lights. They would have had to shine through a landing window before penetrating the doorway and the angle involved ruled this out as a possibility. Nor was there an object from which a light could have been reflected into the room. Again, the direction and intensity of the illumination meant that such a solution could not be seriously entertained. Furthermore, the beam entered *horizontally* and thus an overhead source, such as a helicopter, could be eliminated. It is noteworthy that the family reported no noise at the time of the experience.

The incident, therefore, remains in the 'unexplained' category, despite the testimony of additional witnesses. Neighbours of the Gartsides who live directly opposite experienced the same beam of light travelling through their home. They too could detect no obvious source for this light. But is there a connection between this event and the pyramid shape seen hovering in the area? There is no obvious link, yet it is strange that two such curious incidents should happen within hours of each other involving the same family.

One aspect of the case, however, illustrates a recurring theme. The appearance of a triangular or pyramid-shaped UFO. These objects may in fact be a 'craft' of the same shape viewed from a different angle. UFOs of this type have been reported many times. In February 1996, for example, Mr Willis from Edinburgh spotted an unusual shaped object. He sent me a drawing of the UFO which was clearly triangular with a blue-coloured nose, green body and red tail. However, in his letter Mr Willis also told me that a few days later he and his family 'saw the object again, but this time it was very high up in the sky'. He kindly included a diagram of the second

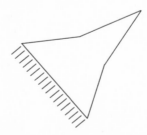

Fig 4. Mr Willis's second drawing of the object seen over Edinburgh in February 1996, showing the unusual shape, and the bright red tail section.

sighting. This second drawing (Fig 4), which Mr Willis believed was the same UFO seen on the first occasion, looks distinctly more pyramid-shaped, or, with its slight bulge in the lower half, might even show a cone-shaped object.

FORTH BRIDGE SIGHTING

This difficulty in determining the shape of an object is further illustrated by a sighting from October 1990. A very well known one, in fact, as it coincided with the centenary celebrations at the Forth Bridge. On 7 October 1990, at approximately 9.15 p.m., Lyn[7] and Alex Livingston were watching a firework display to mark the one hundredth anniversary of the opening

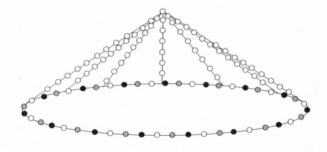

- ●   Red light
- ◎   Blue light
- ○   White light

Fig 5. The cone-shaped object seen over the Forth Road Bridge in October 1990.

7. Lyn was a witness to the 1958 sighting in Sighthill, Edinburgh, mentioned earlier.

47

of the railway link over the Forth. It was a clear windless night. High in the sky Lyn suddenly noticed a circular-shaped object, formed by a battery of red, white and blue lights (see Fig 5). It appeared to twinkle and rotate, changing from a circle to a shallow cone shape. The object remained in view for a full fifteen minutes, growing dimmer as either the strength of the lights faded or it drifted northwards over the Fife coast. Lyn sent me a detailed drawing of the UFO which gives it a cone-shaped appearance. However, it struck me that viewed from a different angle it might look pyramid or even triangular in shape. As in so many cases, however, no-one else came forward to report having seen the object. If they had viewed it from another point, they might well have described it as different in structure. It is certainly possible that, instead of UFOs of varying shapes and designs, we might be dealing instead with similar UFOs which only appear different because of the witnesses' viewpoint.

ALIEN CONTACT

But what of those Scots who claim to have made contact with visitors from outer space? John S is one such person. His experiences, however, call into question the nature of the whole UFO experience: if what John has been experiencing is as he claims, then the 'aliens-from-distant-planets' theory almost pales into insignificance. We are dealing with contacts which almost defy belief. Yet one fact has become more obvious in recent years as the UFO experience has grown and ever more witnesses have emerged—we can't simply talk about UFOs as 'alien entities'. The nature of the contacts made, and the witnesses' descriptions, suggest experiences which are almost religious in nature. This is a theme which is now cropping up with increasing frequency.

John knows he could make his story easier to believe by withholding details, but he is brave enough to give the whole picture.

John is a 45-year-old ex-engineer who lives beside the Forth and Clyde Canal in a small West Lothian town. He experienced psychic phenomena as a child, but strange incidents only started again in 1991. John has kept a diary of the numerous odd events which have occurred. It would not be possible to describe every encounter, but a general picture of the evidence will, I believe, show just what a mysterious world we live in.

John is a tall, thin, thoughtful man who has reflected a great deal on the strange incidents which have centred on him and his semi-detached cottage. On 23 December 1994 he was sitting watching television when suddenly the picture went haywire. Strange patterns formed across the screen before it went blank. In the kitchen, the emergency lighting, running on batteries, failed. The next thing John remembers is being in a room with no windows. Looking him over was a 'human-looking alien'. And John wasn't the only 'visitor'—sitting on a bench were four young men staring blankly as if they couldn't believe what they were seeing. The entity turned to John and, though it uttered no sound, a warning echoed through his head, 'Don't go and investigate'. The being then spun round and walked through a door into what appeared to be a corridor. It struck John forcibly then that *he may not have been in a ship, but in a building*. John was strongly tempted to follow the being into the corridor and open a door, one of several he could see at regular intervals along the smooth contours of the craft's walls. However, he sensed that if he did he would see something that might not be particularly pleasant. Perhaps, some form of alien entity. At this point John 'woke up' to find himself back home with the room bathed in red light.

As a result of another experience John has been able to give a good description of the interior of an alien craft. It was between 15 to 20 feet in diameter and, on this occasion, he found himself standing on a partly raised balcony on the outside edge, which was about a metre wide. The floor of the UFO was formed by shiny metal slats like polished aluminium. They appeared disc-shaped, perhaps even forming a pattern. The walls had been welded from the same material, although here it took the form of panels.

In the middle of the room stood a couch, more like one found in an operating theatre than in the average home. John's recollections are highly detailed, even down to a black cushion lying on some sort of table. The austere atmosphere of the room was broken by a single window, gently curved, which ran from floor to ceiling. Perhaps sensing his curiosity, two creatures, which inexplicably he could not see but could feel, lifted him up to the window and he could look out at the panorama of the universe stretching before him.

When John 'came to' in his bedroom, at around 4 a.m., he noticed puncture marks in his neck. Small red ones, which felt itchy and sore as if a cluster of hypodermic needles had been stuck into his skin.

8. 'Greys' are the small alien entities which seem to have dominated accounts of close encounters for the past twenty years. They are usually described as small, almost child-size, with thin bodies and limbs. Their most recognisable feature, however, is an insect-like head with large, dark, almond-shaped eyes.

On 8 November 1995 John saw 'what looked like a new type of ship. It looked like a giant frisbee. The occupants were like the greys,[8] only with smaller faces and rounder eyes'. John noted that this was around the time of Brian Curran's sighting (5 November), although the incidents may not be linked.

These are the 'straightforward' incidents John has experienced. Other encounters, however, involve pagan religious figures, including the Greek god Zeus and the god of nature, Pan. Their 'spirits' came to John and conveyed a variety of messages to him. Of course, we can suppose that in some way John is psychic, and that for him both the UFO experiences and these more spiritual incidents have a common source. This notion is not new to anyone who has spent time with mediums, as some (though not many) will report receiving messages from—and even seeing—'alien spirits'. Or maybe they're not spirits. We have tended to draw a line between the UFO experience and the spiritual, but perhaps they can't be so easily separated.

From his own encounters, John has been able to establish a possible perspective. 'Let's say the person I have called Zeus is a god, or put it another way, he is a leader of a group of scientists/organisers who arrived on the scene when the world was forming. . . . They obviously don't die like us, and they have engineered the planet. . . . We have mistaken them for deities in the past and are in danger of doing so today. . . . We have called them gods because they have god-like powers . . . but I quote the words told to me: "we are gods but not the creator". Perhaps they do not have any more understanding than us of who or what the creator is.'

I share John's sense of confusion. The more UFO incidents that occur, the more uncertain the scene becomes. Spirits from beyond, all-powerful ETs, or what? Even with his breadth of experience, John remains unsure.

One encouraging aspect is that John feels that the aliens 'if that's what they are' have attempted to heal him. He suffers from a number of maladies, including arthritis. After a visit from the entities John, who had difficulty walking any distance, found that he could walk a mile with ease. Maybe these are friends rather than something to be feared. Indeed, some argue that our government and aliens are already enjoying an '*entente cordiale*'.

MINISTRY OF DEFENCE INVOLVEMENT

In spite of their denials, it is clear that the Ministry of Defence and the armed forces are very much interested in UFO encounters. In April 1995 a commercial airline pilot, Iain Ray, brought his cargo into Edinburgh Airport from the East Midlands. It was a regular run and he had landed well on time at 1 a.m. It had been a clear night and the flight had been trouble-free. As Ray taxied off the runway away from the passenger terminal, he noticed a lot of excitement among the British Airways security staff. He learned that Air Traffic Control radar systems had monitored an unidentified object hovering near the airport. There had also been a visual sighting confirming the presence of the UFO. As Air Traffic Control followed the UFO's movements, a cargo plane from Gill Aviation, based in Newcastle, was coming in to land. Edinburgh asked the pilot to take a look at the strange object but he was unable to confirm the report. On the ground, though, there seem to have been several well-qualified witnesses to the presence of an unidentified flying object.

Or were there? A week later, Ray was back in Edinburgh and asked Air Traffic if they had reached any conclusion about the mysterious visitor. He was met by a wall of silence. The tower denied all knowledge, claiming they didn't know what he was talking about. Mystified, Ray mentioned it to colleagues. And then an even stranger tale emerged. He was told that RAF Kinloss had scrambled three Tornado aircraft to investigate objects which, it seemed, appeared as a bright white light at an altitude of two to three thousand feet. As the aircraft approached, these objects shot straight up and disappeared. My own attempt to confirm this incident met with a firm, but extremely speedy, denial from the Ministry of Defence. Gill Aviation failed to respond to my requests for information, all in all confirming my suspicion that whether or not it was a visitor from another planet, something strange was seen over Edinburgh that day.

THE WEST COAST MYSTERY

THE GLASGOW REGION AND AYRSHIRE

Repeater witnesses, while rare, are not confined to one area of
Scotland. Rita Drummond from Maryhill in Glasgow has seen
UFOs of all kinds for years. Her first encounter took place
over thirty years ago in 1968 when she caught sight of a cigar-
shaped object which was silvery-grey in colour. The incident
took place at a time when Rita was experiencing dreams of an
extraterrestrial nature. In these dreams she would see strange
shapes in the sky and then try to hide from them. It was
impossible to escape, however, as a round object with antennae
would always manage to find where she was. Were these
more than dreams? Was an attempt being made by 'outside
intelligence' to contact Rita through her subconscious mind?

Sceptics might argue that Rita had imagined it all, but several of her sightings include detailed descriptions of the strange objects she has glimpsed. In October 1997, for example, she saw a disc-shaped UFO with a raised cabin-type structure on top travelling at speed. There were dark patches all the way round which may have been windows. A shimmering heat haze surrounding it may have indicated a propulsion system of some kind. Travelling behind were four small objects which also looked disc-shaped. Perhaps the larger UFO was the 'mother ship' which had sent out four unmanned probes. But why over Glasgow? And if so, what were they doing? A few months earlier in August 1996 several witnesses claimed to have seen an orange pod-shaped object with smaller ones moving around it. This happened over Kirkcaldy in Fife, only fifty miles from Glasgow.

Most of Rita's sightings have involved the appearance of strange lights in the sky, but though these encounters make up the vast bulk of UFO reports generally, what makes Rita's case unusual is that she has seen many such objects. These incidents often involve lights of different colours travelling so quickly or in such a strange way that they cannot easily be explained as aircraft or any natural phenomenon. Rita also has a unique sighting in her log. On one occasion she saw something that she describes as looking like 'a squiggly worm'. The object was red and white in colour, jumping erratically and glowing like a fluorescent light. What are we to make of this?

One possible interpretation of what Rita saw is that what may have looked like a worm could also be seen as a snake. Such glowing snake-shaped objects in the sky were a familiar sight to ancient civilisations, and snakes or serpents have worldwide significance as a symbol of life, even in the Bible. Was Rita's vision meant to be a signal? The ancient Egyptians used the snake as a symbol of eternity across the Universe and they too firmly believed our ancestors came from the stars.

1952 SIGHTING

But maybe we have been jumping the gun and should start at the beginning of Glasgow's involvement in the UFO phenomenon.

In 1952 Joan Torrence was leaving Elder Park Primary with her friends. It was 4 p.m., the end of the school day, and a warm summer's evening lay ahead of them. As Joan crossed the playground, a dark shadow fell across the school. The sun had disappeared from sight. She looked up as did a crowd of pupils who seconds before had all been heading cheerfully for home. What Joan saw brought her to an abrupt halt and has been etched on her mind ever since. About a hundred feet up, a little above the school steeple, hung a sombrero-shaped object, tilted slightly to one side. It seemed to be rotating. Joan doesn't know how long she watched for, but she was aware that her teacher, a step behind, as well as the janitor on one side and her friend on the other, were also entranced by the mysterious object. 'Time seemed to stand still', explained Joan. The spell was broken by the sudden movement of the UFO, preceded by a distinct whining sound. It shot off, heading across Glasgow to be seen and reported by other witnesses. Joan ran home to tell her mother what she had seen. A disbelieving parent had to eat her words when she read the reports in the following day's papers!

A quarter of a century later Glasgow school kids were still glimpsing weird objects. In 1978, on a bright summer's day, a group of schoolchildren were distracted from playtime games by a strange sight. Hovering above the fence enclosing St Mark's Primary School in Muiryfauld, Glasgow, was an object which looked like something from Star Trek. 'It glistened in the sun, about four feet across', recalls Euan Riley. 'It looked weird,' he remembers, 'like two fedora hats joined together'. Then it just vanished. The incident was over too quickly for the pupils to summon any adult witnesses. Would they have been believed anyway? 'Miss, there's a UFO outside the school!' Yet Euan's description is too precise to be easily dismissed. It was silver-coloured, he records, like shiny metal and very sharply defined, hovering about twenty feet above the ground. The sighting made a dramatic impact, so much so that Euan contacted SEMR when a case we had been investigating was reported in the *Glaswegian* newspaper in 1993, years after the incident. Euan wrote: 'Although I was young, the memory of the incident has remained vivid in my memory, and I am sure of what I saw.'

CLYDESDALE ENCOUNTER

The earliest sighting from Clydeside was also made by a child. A close up encounter, it dates from 1948, less than a year after the Arnold incident which sparked the modern UFO phenomenon. Linda was nine years old at the time, at school in Greenock. She was heading for home during the dinner break with a schoolfriend when she became aware of a distinct humming noise. Linda glanced up towards the source of the sound and was amazed by what she saw. Not one, but four UFOs. Two were saucer-shaped and two like elongated cigars. The girls were so excited by this that they jumped up and down and waved towards the objects. Linda recalls figures waving back in response, but can't at this distance in time describe them. The objects were very low down, almost at roof height, hovering. The 'saucers' had windows all round the circumference separated by upright flashing bars. The 'cigars', however, had windows only at the front. Linda felt that they were being deliberately watched by the UFOs. Suddenly, one of the cigar-shaped objects which had been hanging back swooped down and immediately all four UFOs rose upwards and disappeared through the clouds. Linda's sighting was very close. She says that she could see the objects as clearly as a car, train or bus.

SILVER DISCS

In May 1976, Allistair McNeil, now an actor in his 40s, was sitting in a flat in Westbourne Gardens whiling away the hours talking with two friends. Glancing at the clock, Allistair noticed that it was 3 a.m. and it was at that exact moment that a movement outside caught his attention. Looking through the window, he saw a large, silvery, disc-shaped object hovering about one hundred feet above the grassy space opposite the flat.

He later estimated the 'saucer' to be 60 feet across with round porthole windows on the upper sections. Through the windows light was clearly visible. Allistair gained a clear impression that the disc was metallic, possibly because of its silvery sheen. As they looked at it, the object appeared suddenly to hurtle towards them, although Allistair thinks that the disc may, in fact, have been moving all the time and only given the appearance of hovering. It soared above them over the rooftops and rapidly disappeared from view.

It is interesting that the disc emitted a buzzing and humming noise as it travelled. Allistair emphasised that it was a clear, dry night, with good visibility. The object stood out against the sky with a sharp and clear outline. There could be no mistaking what the three of them saw.

The unexpected appearance of the disc left a powerful impact on Allistair and his friends. They felt that it was generating a particularly powerful 'aura', one that could almost be touched and tasted. To Allistair especially it seemed almost 'divine' and he remains convinced that 'it was definitely not from this planet'. The three friends were, he explains, 'dumbfounded' and informed me, in that phrase reminiscent of the '60s, that 'it blew our minds'. Sceptics would probably have laughed at Allistair's comment and remarked that the whole incident was a good example of an overactive imagination. However, in this case, sceptics cannot have it all their own way.

Some months later in the same year, another silver UFO was reported. On 5 October 1976 at 9.40 p.m. Ben Goodwin, then a recent recruit to the police, watched a silver ball descend over the city. He was in Drumchapel at the time and the strange object seemed to be, from his vantage point, 'just to the left' of Glasgow Airport. As the UFO neared the ground it swung back and forth like a pendulum, then suddenly shot upwards and disappeared. Ben has now left the force, but told me that many officers had witnessed strange sights in the sky. But, in their formal reports at least, they would always put down a 'rational' solution as they didn't want to put their careers at risk. He said that the standard 'explanation' for inexplicable lights was that it was 'car headlamps reflecting off low clouds'. However, that definitely can't account for Allistair McNeil's encounter.

Quite independently of Allistair's sighting and totally unknown to him, an earlier incident occurred within yards of the same street. In 1955, twenty-one years before Allistair's encounter with the disc-shaped UFO, a child had a bizarre encounter in Belhaven Terrace, which abuts onto Westbourne Gardens. The incident was reported in an issue of *Enigmas*, the newsletter of the UFO group Strange Phenomena Investigations (SPI). Emma Roberts, the pseudonym given to the witness, described the spot where the encounter took place. Today, as at the time, it is wasteland, unused and partly overgrown with trees, shrubs and wild plants. In the summer of 1955 Emma, then eight, was cooking potatoes over a small fire with her sister and a group of older children. Suddenly Emma became aware of strange entities or 'beings' as she describes them. She found she couldn't take her eyes off them. Her sister was frightened by the appearance of these 'visitors' and Emma told her to run home.

Emma, on the other hand, was fascinated by the sight and continued to watch, wondering all the time who or what these people might be. Were they nuns? (There was a convent nearby). Were they engaged in some secret business? But to all these thoughts, even as a child, her mind came back with a clear 'no'. They were something else altogether.

The two entities she had first spotted were now joined by several more. All of them seemed focused on the ground and completely ignored the children. Emma now realised that they were floating rather than walking and that all these beings looked identical. They were tall, thin, very pale-skinned, wearing long, floating, plain white garments with white caps. Emma was particularly struck by their eyes which were noticeably deep and penetrating, within distinctly pointed faces.

All at once, as if a spell had been broken, one of the entities turned towards Emma, almost as if he had 'tuned in' to her presence. He moved up the slope towards her, looking not at her but through her. All the visitors then turned and followed the first. Emma was now convinced they were not human. She turned and ran. She doesn't tell us, but presumably all her friends took the same action. Anyway, there is no record of the beings chasing anyone all the way to their houses. Whatever they were after, it was clearly not their youthful spectators.

SPIRITUAL DIMENSION

It's clear that in both Allistair's and Emma's encounters there is a religious link. Did Emma's experience have a connection with the convent? Allistair felt almost spiritually transformed. In the case of Eleanor Harvey the link is even more direct. The incident which haunted her thereafter took place in 1971 when she lived in Carmunock Road opposite King's Park.

'It was a beautiful early July morning' she records, 'I was waiting my turn to get into the bathroom'. As she stood patiently she glanced out of the window. It was a normal rush hour with heavy traffic pouring by, people standing at the bus stop. Then 'all of a sudden I heard a noise. It sounded as if something had landed on the roof'. Eleanor thought it was maybe workmen sorting her neighbour's TV aerial, though as it was 8 a.m. it seemed rather early to start such a job. Her surprise deepened when 'what sounded like the engine of a small aircraft was switched off', to be followed straight after 'by a broad beam of light' which shone through Eleanor's window. The beam struck Eleanor at a point just above her eyes.

Surprised, Eleanor drew back from the window, then heard a shout. A face appeared, 'beautiful and sad'. The beam was shining through the image but Eleanor could make out 'silver hair . . . cut to shoulder length, a moustache and a neat, square-cut beard'. The eyes were brown, a shade of hazel. The mysterious entity looked at Eleanor and she felt 'as if he was stripping my very soul', although 'no word was spoken'. By this point Eleanor must have been able to see more of this being as she noted that he raised his right hand with his palm towards her in what she saw as 'a sign of peace'. As she watched, the image grew stronger so that eventually she could see all of him. He was dressed in a long gown which shone gold in the still-present beam of light, but which she judged to be coloured white. She noted one odd fact about the gown: there were no obvious joins or seams even though it covered his entire body to the feet. On his feet were leather sandals and around his waist, loosely slung, a gold cord, knotted, which almost reached the floor.

Eleanor was entranced by this scene but the spell was broken by another scratching sound, followed by a noise like a motor being started. Then came the rattle on the roof 'and the invisible machine took off', as Eleanor put it. She rushed to the window, but couldn't see anything to account for her encounter. But then a voice said: 'I am the light of the world. He that believeth in me shall have everlasting life.'

Eleanor believed that she had been visited by Jesus Christ. While she had been watching him, she had even found herself looking for the marks of nails on his hands and feet. But why would Jesus visit a house in Glasgow and use a UFO to do it? On the surface it's hard to make any sense of it, but religious symbolism and UFO experiences do seem often to be inter-twined, although the nature of this link remains a mystery.

Are these experiences 'just' the product of those who are more imaginative, or does psychic ability play a part?

It is significant that Allistair McNeil is an actor, a profession which attracts sensitive people who are traditionally more psychically aware. That is not to argue that the sighting was a phantom of the mind. The UFO was seen by two other witnesses at an identical moment, suggesting that the disc, whatever it may have been, possessed some form of objective reality.

Another example of UFOs and the artistic mind interacting concerns the case of the Glasgow UFO group CEIV. Indeed, it was the sighting of a 'bright amber saucer' in 1985 which led to the formation of the group. CEIV is short for 'Close Encounters of the Fourth Kind', a UFO research classification indicating contact with extraterrestrials (see Appendix B). CEIV used to 'skywatch' (a term used by Ufologists to describe a night survey of the sky for anomalous objects) when they caught sight of a fuzzy, orange-coloured, star-sized object coming towards them from the north-east. The 'saucer' moved noiselessly and clearly did not appear to be an aeroplane of any known type. Some months later, the group were assured by 'experts' that their sighting was of a smoke ring! An explanation which hardly seems likely, given the length of time of the sighting.

CENTRAL GLASGOW SIGHTINGS

CEIV's UFO was observed from a suburban garden on fairly high ground, but some sightings have taken place right in the centre of the historic city. In December 1990, Maria Mortimer was standing at a bus stop outside the branch of British Home Stores situated in the St Enoch's Shopping Centre. At 4.30 in the afternoon it was, at that time of year, already dark, but the skyline stood out sharp and clear. Looking towards a car park, Maria saw what at first seemed an unusual silver-coloured aircraft. Although it was the size of a conventional plane, it appeared to be round, with a belt of amber lights across its centre. Maria pointed out the mysterious object to the lady standing beside her, a complete stranger, and together they watched it as it traversed the town centre at roof-top height. Gradually, it moved southwards, flying very smoothly, Maria noted, until it slowly drifted out of sight. Unusually for such an incident, the sighting lasted for at least five and possibly as long as ten minutes.

Even more astonishing is the fact that this encounter, over the heart of Glasgow's commercial centre, is no isolated incident. In November 1979, just one week before Bob Taylor's

Livingston experience, a man walking near George Square, scene of many a political meeting and the famous 1919 riot, watched in amazement as a football-sized object sped by him. It emitted a high-pitched hissing sound, and after this near collision the witness could smell a strong odour of sulphur hanging in the air. Mr McDougall described the object as being spherical in shape and grey in colour. But the fact which struck him as being of most significance was that the sphere moved as if it were operating under some kind of control. There are obvious parallels here with the Bob Taylor incident which was to occur a few days later.

It should be noted, however, that whilst Bob's sighting was clearly of a solid object, Mr McDougalls's UFO has similarities with that phenomenon known as ball lightning. (See the Livingston case in Chapter 1 for further discussion of this topic.)

George Square has always been a rallying point for political radicals, and for UFO sightings too, it seems. A decade after Mr McDougall's encounter a couple crossing the east quarter spotted an octagonal object hovering in the sky above them. They reckoned it was about 30 feet across, and therefore felt sure that it would have been visible to all around them. Yet, to their astonishment, everyone else seemed oblivious to its presence. Suddenly, in a brilliant flash of blue, it vanished.

AERIAL LIGHTS

Bright lights, white or coloured, are a frequent feature of Glasgow sightings. On 9 November 1979, the same day as Bob Taylor's encounter, a lady in the Easterhouse district watched an unusually bright light in the heavens. The light split into two equally bright objects which moved around the sky before reuniting and, as mysteriously as they had arrived, vanishing into thin air.

The West of Scotland UFO Group have been investigating a mysterious sighting which took place on the evening of 9 October 1994. A British Airways stewardess was driving back to Troon when she caught sight of a strange object. She reported: 'I had just turned towards Lugton when I became aware of a very bright light coming onto the driver's seat. It was this incredible bright light hovering there. The thing must have stayed there for about 10 to 15 seconds . . . then it literally shot off into nowhere and it was dark again'. The witness, who had spent twenty-two years in the airline business, was convinced it could not have been a plane because 'nothing man-made could move that fast'. She added: 'I have never seen anything like that in all my years of flying'.

Occasionally, several lights appear to form a pattern. In the summer of 1987, Mary McShane from Pollok was standing in her front garden when she saw a group of lights moving in formation, high up in the sky. It was 11 p.m. and, as Mary describes it, 'each light was twice as big and bright as the stars which formed a distant backdrop. There were seventeen in total, forming two corresponding arch shapes with an inner and outer arch'. The lights seemed to fade to nothing, then would reappear in exactly the same spot. Was this simply the reflection in the sky of ground-based lights? It might be considered as a possible answer, except that Mary was not the sole witness. A few days later the *Daily Record* newspaper received a letter from a man who had seen an object shaped like a shuttlecock in the same area of the city. Distance being difficult to judge, especially at night, it has to be a guess as to whether Mary saw several single objects or one large one. It would surely have to be big to show seventeen separate lights, but at least one witness reported to me catching sight of an object over a mile long hovering over Bellahouston Park! Furthermore, a separate witness during a full moon spotted a 'large space craft' coloured grey, which eventually turned out to be 'as big as Hampden Park' over the Govan area. The same witness has claimed to have seen several UFOs in the area of the sky surrounding the constellation Ursa Major. This association with one part of the heavens is not one which has previously been reported and may result from the particular individual's perception of incidents. Unless there is a case here of 'channelling',[1] which is not claimed by the witness, there seems no reason why there should exist a link between reported UFOs and a star group many millions of light years away.

Several witnesses reported bright lights hovering over the Maryhill area of Glasgow in July 1988. The lights stayed in the area for around ten minutes, and one of those who watched this display, Mrs Savage, was convinced that there was something mysterious about the incident and that 'it was definitely a UFO'. In this case the phenomenon was viewed at a distance, but Mr Cowan near Cumbernauld not only saw a bright object with a long tail travelling fast, but experienced more direct contact. As the UFO passed by his window, the whole bedroom

1. 'Channelling' is a word used to describe the process by which individuals receive messages from alien entities. These messages are usually passed to the 'channeller' by telepathy, and they in turn pass them on to their colleagues or write them down. There are even magazines devoted solely to messages from the 'Space Brothers'.

was lit up as if by powerful searchlights. No source for the sudden brightness other than the mysterious object could be found.

DUNOON OBJECT

A large mysterious object was also seen by a retired PSV driver, John Maclean. The UFO he caught sight of over Dunoon was, he estimated, 'two or three times full moon size'. That makes it very large, although Mr Maclean judged the object to be up to three thousand feet above them in the night sky. It's notoriously difficult to judge distances without reference points, but Mr Maclean had spotted the object as it moved through a gap in the clouds. He reported that it reminded him of 'dance-hall glass mirror balls' that used to be suspended from the ceiling and reflected flashes of light. The flashes of light were absent, but the object was brightly illuminated on the inside which probably means that it wasn't simply a misidentified aircraft. A similar but smaller object was following behind.

Witnesses like John Maclean have no axe to grind. They are simply reporting incidents as they see them. Anne and Mary McGettigan from Castlemilk are in the same category. They spotted a strange light in the sky and decided to report it. As Anne described it, 'I was driving along Mill Street, Rutherglen, towards Castlemilk, when I noticed a bright white light in the sky above Cathkin Braes. I pointed it out to my mum, Mary, who could also not identify what it was. It appeared to move towards us and got bigger, nearly doubling in size. It then shot behind a cloud and as it did so it created a beam of light as it passed through. It stayed behind the clouds for a couple of seconds and appeared to just disappear'. Anne then noticed two planes flying in the same direction, which she feels may have been looking for or following the UFO.

PILOT'S ACCOUNT

A constant criticism of UFO reports is that the individuals involved are 'untrained'—that they don't, for example, know the difference between a fast moving jet and an alien spaceship. In June 1997 I received a letter from a man who described himself as 'a keen private pilot', but who did not wish to be publicly identified. He was writing to me about a sighting he had had over Glasgow in January 1984. He was working on the seventh floor of an office block in the centre of the city. 'It was one of those crisp, cold, clear days', he told me, 'and I stopped working to take in the view. . . . I was trying to identify landmarks well known to pilots. I identified the VOR Rods Beacon beyond Eaglesham. I could see all the way across to the Dumbarton VRP (Visual Reporting Point). On looking back to the VOR I was left gasping as this pink/silver/grey cigar-shaped object literally shot across from left to right and disappeared somewhere to the west of Dumbarton'.

The witness pointed out to me that pilots are taught 'to keep a good lookout at all times' and to judge air traffic for speed, distance and altitude. Using his experience, he estimated that the UFO was ten miles beyond Eagleston at a height of 1,500 to 2,000 feet. In about two seconds it covered a distance of 25 miles. A simple calculation shows that its speed was around 45,000 miles per hour! Not even the latest marvels of the western world can move at that rate. It's no wonder that the witness, having seen such an incredible sight, does not want to be named. As a self-employed businessman he is not convinced that others will take his account as seriously as it deserves to be taken.

Incidents investigated by the Lanarkshire UFO Group and compiled by Paul Grey provide further evidence of strange happenings. In 1982 Michael and Carol Stafford were waiting for a bus in Bellshill. Carol glanced skywards and caught sight of two bright lights coming towards them. She was struck by the fact that their approach was noiseless, but also by the movements of the lights from side to side as if they were being shaken. Then the object was above their heads shining a light down on them. Clearly something odd was going on. Michael grabbed hold of Carol and the children, pulling them away from the light and heading in the opposite direction as fast as possible. As they looked back they saw the object, yellow in colour and triangular in shape, shoot off at an amazing speed. Intriguingly, in August 1996 a red, glowing object, shaped halfway between a boomerang and a crescent, was seen moving on a zig-zag path above the area.

TRIANGULAR CRAFT

From time to time particular types of UFO appear frequently among those reported by witnesses. In recent years the triangular-shaped object has been seen over various parts of Scotland, although in my experience it has not established itself as Scotland's typical UFO. In fact I would need a lot of convincing that the 'typical' UFO actually exists. However, there is a widespread belief that the triangular craft is one that has become a more common sight in Scotland, although it is fair to say that not all reports of this UFO type are anywhere near identical.

AYR SIGHTING

Typical, perhaps, is a sighting made by Margaret Barrie of Leonard's Road in Ayr, on Scotland's west coast. A former executive secretary, Mrs Barrie considers herself an unlikely UFO witness. She was no skywatcher before her encounter, but afterwards she wrote that the incident had turned her into 'an almost compulsive sky-gazer'. Like so many witnesses, Mrs Barrie felt 'definitely privileged to have seen such a strange sight'. I found her a compelling witness.

On the morning of Friday 6 September 1996, Mrs Barrie stepped into her garden to hang out her washing. It was a good day for drying clothes with the sun shining and a good breeze, and only a small scattering of clouds.

Not far from Ayr lies Prestwick Transatlantic Airport. Several flight paths cross the town of Ayr, and large, America-bound passenger planes and equally large military craft are frequently seen in the skies overhead. Mrs Barrie watched one travel from the airport in a south-westerly direction, probably heading for Dublin. She watched till it became an invisible speck on the distant skyline.

She was still at the washing line, when her eyes were drawn skywards again. She was astounded by what she saw. It was a large, dark object, 'a bit like a delta-wing type plane, but at the same time not at all like a plane as the wings were slowly opening and closing' (see Fig 6). She was certain that moments earlier the sky had been clear of any objects.

The UFO, which appeared to be descending, gradually stopped at around 300 to 400 feet from the ground. Mrs Barrie judged its height from that of the training planes she was used to seeing in the area. But this was no training plane. It seemed to hover. 'There was no sound whatsoever,' Mrs Barrie wrote in her report. 'The object was silent. It was "soft" black in colour and, strangely, there was no glint from it, as when the sunlight reflects off metal. There was no glass, no obvious contours.'

She watched the UFO for around ten minutes, fascinated by its strange shape and the mysterious manner of its appearance. Then, hoping to get a better view, Mrs Barrie ran indoors to fetch a pair of binoculars from the upstairs bedroom. At the same time, she called to a workman, a ceramic tiler, who was helping to install a new bathroom suite. Unfortunately, by the time she returned to the garden the UFO had moved from its last position. It was now much higher in the sky, travelling almost vertically upwards. Mrs Barrie continued to observe it as it travelled through a patch of blue between some clouds, becoming a small dot until it finally disappeared from view. The time was now exactly 11.45 a.m.

There may, of course, have been other witnesses to Mrs Barrie's remarkable sighting, but no-one to my knowledge has come forward. My first thought was that if this object could be identified then it was likely that perhaps some form of experimental aircraft was involved. This has been the standard explanation for many of the objects with a triangular or near

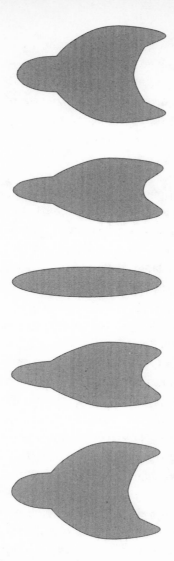

Fig 6. Margaret Barrie's sequence of drawings, showing the changing shape
of the UFO she observed in September 1996.

triangular configuration. However, my inquiries with Prestwick Airport (which houses Scotland's main Air Traffic Control centre) brought a negative response. If it was a new type of aircraft that Mrs Barrie saw that day, it was not one which the powers-that-be are ready to admit to.

PRESTWICK INCIDENT

In the months following the Barrie incident, reports came in from all over the Ayrshire district of triangular-shaped craft. On 7 February 1997 a dark triangular UFO was sighted low down over the village of Burnside near new Cumnock. Three weeks to the day later an identical UFO was spotted in the same area. Two months later, just a few miles away, three lights in the shape of a triangle were reported over the town of Kilwinning. On 18 July in the same year a black triangle was sighted over Kilmarnock, while a similar object was seen the month before over nearby Galston. More surprising than the appearance of black triangles is the unique sighting in June 1997 of a blue-coloured triangle travelling between Dundonald and Saltcoats.

It should be noted, however, that reports of triangular UFOs are not a recent phenomenon. As far back as 1976 a fourteen-year-old boy saw a black object over Carluke, the white lights at each point marking out its triangular shape.

One of the most well-documented sightings, in terms of the number of witnesses involved, took place in May 1997 when callers to Air Traffic Control at Prestwick Airport, and to other official bodies, reported a strange sighting in the sky. Although this was a UFO incident, the magazine *Haunted Scotland* reported details given by Colin Chisholm from the district of Bellfield in Kilmarnock. He described an object 'changing colour, from red to green and then white [which] was very bright'. Mr Chisholm challenged the suggestion that what he had seen was the comet Hale Bopp (prominent at the time) by pointing out that 'it was in the sky to the west and not the north, as Hale Bopp [was]', adding 'I've never seen a star before like that'. Colin's sighting was at around 11 p.m., but an hour later he also witnessed a 'bright red triangular object' travelling at speed across the heavens.

Craig Stewart, also from Kilmarnock, was keeping an eye on the UFO even as he spoke to Prestwick Airport on the phone. He claimed: 'I told them I could see a plane passing the object, and they said they could see the plane but nothing else on radar'.

Craig also reported seeing 'two little red objects shoot off from it'. This calls to mind an incident two years before and not so far away in the new town of East Kilbride. In May 1995, Mark was sitting in his top storey flat looking out of his bedroom window. It was around 9 o'clock on a weekday evening and he was idly watching a commercial plane emerge from behind a tall block of flats in the middle distance. A flight path ran nearby, so evening air traffic was nothing out of the ordinary. But what happened next was definitely unusual. A light appeared to emerge from the plane. Bright red in colour. But had it, in fact, been trailing the jet and come into Mark's view as it dropped down? It descended slowly, hovered for a while, then manoeuvred in a strange snake-like fashion to the left, then down a bit and then to the right. It eventually disappeared into Calder Glen.

This was not the only red-coloured UFO that Mark reported to me. His mother had also witnessed a strange incident. At around 11.15 p.m. her attention had been drawn by a shaft of light piercing the night sky. Looking towards an area called Calderside Farm situated a few miles away, she caught sight of a very large round object, whose inner radius was dotted with round porthole-style lights. On the right section, particularly prominent, were two red lights. We must remind ourselves before we get too carried away that standard aircraft lights include the colour red. But in these incidents it seems highly unlikely that an aircraft was the source of the lights.

STRANGE SHAPES OVER AYRSHIRE

Triangular UFOs are not the only mysterious objects sighted over the Ayrshire countryside. In November 1992, Mr Stewart from Alloway heard what sounded like an engine noise. He went out to look and caught sight of a semi-circular whitish-grey object on top of a disc-shaped object. It was very large and moving low down in the sky. The upper and lower surface of the UFO shone white with a blueish tinge while the area where the two objects joined was coloured grey. The strange disc was heading in a southerly direction and disappeared behind the Isle of Arran a few miles off the Ayrshire coast.

In 1975, Mr Lee from Hamilton observed a 'black sausage-shaped balloon type object' just twenty feet above the ground. He was in Caldercruix near Airdrie at the time and the UFO was about two hundred feet from him. It was moving slowly at around, he guesses, 10 miles an hour, maintaining a constant speed and height and looked as if it was being towed—he could see no line, but neither was there any other obvious means of propulsion. The whole incident, in broad daylight, seems rather odd. Mr Lee has not ruled out the possibility that it might have been a weather or hot air balloon, although considering the shape of the object he believes this to be unlikely. What I found particularly intriguing about this incident is its similarity to UFO sightings at the end of the last century. In both Britain and the USA, witnesses reported strange balloon-shaped structures which moved slowly above open countryside.

HOSTILE ENTITIES

I am often asked if these 'visitors' (if that's what they are) wish to do us harm. One native of Glasgow believes he has evidence that this is exactly what they intend. I have called him Bill, which is not his real name, and altered certain details of his account to ensure his anonymity. Without these safeguards we would not be able to tell Bill's story.

It started back in the '60s when Bill was a mate with the North Sea fishing fleet. On a warm summer's morning in 1969, Bill stood alone on deck watching the sun rise. The beauty of the scene made him wonder if he was dreaming when suddenly he spotted an object which seemed out of place. Too big to be a plane, and above rather than on the water, so obviously not another trawler, it seemed to defy all explanation. Grabbing binoculars, Bill took a closer look. What he saw was a disc-shaped object suspended or hovering just above the water line. It looked like the traditional 'flying saucer' portrayed on countless television programmes, although a humped curvature on top and below gave it an unusual oyster-like appearance. Around the middle gleamed a bright red band.

Bill snapped out of his state of near shock and yelled to his shipmates to come and look. As they arrived on the scene the object raced skywards and disappeared. Several, however, agreed that they had caught a glimpse of the disc just as it vanished. The sea was calm and the weather good, so that visibility was excellent, even for the time of year.

According to Bill, the skipper ordered a note to be made in the log, though in spite of several attempts we have been unable to obtain a copy of this entry.

That encounter was to become a pivotal episode in Bill's life, although he could not have realised it at the time. Bill later became convinced that in some intangible way the sighting had a seriously adverse effect on his life. The memory of the event began to take over his mind so that within a short while he could think of nothing else.

Soon after, Bill's marriage began to fail. He was convinced that his obsession with the sighting and its influence over him wreaked havoc with his relationship with his wife. He began to suffer from nightmares where previously he had been a sound sleeper. Even worse, these nightmares began to haunt him during his waking moments, so that no part of the day was free from the persistent image of an enormous spaceship and its occupants.

By now, Bill had left his seafaring days behind and was enjoying 'landlubber' status at a Welsh radio station. Bright and cheerful on the surface, underneath he was deeply disturbed about the way his life was developing. He kept imagining himself imprisoned by aliens inside a craft from another planet. Bizarre secrets were imparted to him, secrets Bill came to believe. The aliens claimed that thousands of their kind were living openly on the Earth. They looked almost identical to humans and integrated easily into our culture. Several of these individuals had been assigned to watch over Bill, and should he dare to step out of line, they would exact retribution. Bill felt he was being warned to say nothing about his experiences.

By now the pressure on Bill had become intolerable and his marriage broke down. Mentally he was shattered, and a doctor referred him to a psychiatrist, who pronounced him mentally ill.

A period of recuperation followed. Bill never doubted that the experiences he had gone through were genuine, but for the sake of appearances and to calm his own mind he agreed with the doctors that the strained relations with his partner had warped his imagination.

Put on medication and returned to the world, Bill moved to Glasgow and managed to find a job. He knew full well that mentally he was not as he used to be, but somehow he dredged up the resources to cope with life.

Working in a restaurant, friendships developed with his colleagues. Eventually he felt confident enough to confide in one of his workmates, a chef, the history of his troubled past. The man listened sympathetically, though he made it clear he found it difficult to accept the story at face value. Nevertheless, the mere fact of telling it lifted a weight from Bill's shoulders. As he thanked the chef for listening, Bill went on with his work, when he noticed one of the waiters eyeing him curiously.

Bill immediately regretted speaking so openly. He wished he'd made sure no-one had been around to listen. 'Probably has me down as a nut,' he thought. Gradually, as the day passed, the incident faded from his mind.

The repercussions came later. To Bill what happened can never be put down to coincidence. Yet, true to form, Bill will blame no-one for questioning his sanity. That night as he returned home two men grabbed him as he entered his flat. 'They looked just ordinary', explained Bill, 'but what they said wasn't ordinary'. They threatened him in blunt language, told him that this time they would only warn him. But that should he open his mouth again . . . Bill admits that he didn't know what to make of it all, though the incident scared him badly. He was frightened not simply because he had been threatened. Even more terrifying was the possibility that he had imagined the whole thing and his mind was going. But deep down he felt sure that it was fact and not fiction.

The next day Bill turned up for work as usual, only to be sacked. Expensive meats, which he was sure he had placed in the freezer, had been found lying in the store room. As a casual worker, Bill was dispensable. He had no doubt concerning who was responsible—aliens masquerading as humans. To anyone who asks: 'Bill, why should aliens pursue you?' he replies: 'I have no idea. All I know is that they do. They tell me to keep quiet. To say nothing to anyone. Anywhere I try to work they get rid of me. Maybe I've seen something they want me to forget'.

Before Bill's story is dismissed out of hand, reports of similar experiences from the United States should be considered— there have been many documented cases of individuals claiming to have been abducted by aliens, some in horrifying and distressing circumstances. Bud Hopkin, who has written extensively on this phenomenon, has set up a centre specifically to deal with such cases. The whole subject remains highly controversial, especially as the experiences of individual abductees often only emerge following hypnosis. But are these genuine memories of events which actually happened? Or have the memories somehow been created by the witnesses' own imagination? It seems clear that memory 'creation' can take place under hypnosis and thus the extent of the abductee phenomenon—now comprising thousands of individuals— should be viewed with caution. 'False Memory Syndrome' is now a recognised psychological condition which can arise in people undergoing hypnosis when they are asked to recall incidents from their past of which they previously had no conscious memory. It is clear that under hypnosis people do not necessarily recall genuine memories, but may create a false memory based on fictional incidents taken from books, films or their own imagination. Nonetheless, such cases deserve to be investigated, and Bill's account merits serious consideration.

Bill is clearly a candidate for the Hopkins Center. Asked about his mental state, Bill replies: 'I know I'm not normal, but that's because of my experience with the aliens. I'm not lying. There *are* aliens on this earth. The government knows it, but is saying nothing'.

Unfortunately, at the time of writing Bill has disappeared. I hope, however, that he will surface so that at a time when abductions are being taken seriously his case can be assessed by the experts.

There are also many people who have experienced a UFO encounter at close quarters and suffered no ill effects. Allan Kerr, twelve years old at the time of his sighting, is a good example of this. He can vividly recall the event which took place on a hot sunny August day in 1992. It was the twelfth of the month, the start of the grouse shooting season. 'The sky was clear,' he recalls. 'There were no clouds around'. Out of nowhere a 'huge, silvery, shiny, oval-shaped saucer' appeared and hovered over the house (see fig 7). 'I felt all funny inside,' explained Allan. 'My breath was taken away'. Allan's school-friends did not take his encounter too seriously, even though there is no doubt that Allan witnessed something extraordinary. Allan's drawing of the object he saw depicts a typical saucer shape with a clear cockpit on the top and two straight lines along the side.

Fig 7. Allan Kerr's shining silver UFO of August 1992.

Twenty years earlier, Margaret McCulloch saw a similar object. At that time, Margaret was living at Kingsway Court, Scotstoun, and was having trouble sleeping. Rather than disturb her husband, she would go into the spare bedroom and watch the night sky until she felt tired enough to return to bed. From their ninth floor flat, Margaret could get a good view of the Campsies and it was over these hills that one night in the early '70s she saw 'a huge silvery-grey and metallic object'. Mesmerised by the strange sight, Margaret watched the object for several minutes. Nothing happened for most of the time, but just as she was getting used to the sight, a bizarre incident occurred. From beneath the UFO 'a platform like an elevator started to descend with a very bright shaft of light following in its wake'. Margaret rushed through to her sleeping husband to tell him what she had seen. But he refused to listen to her story, so she got back into bed as she didn't want to disturb him any more. It later emerged, through a report in the Glasgow *Evening Times* that two men camping on the hills had also seen the object.

CUMBERNAULD REPEATER

Although almost every witness to a UFO incident is amazed by what they have seen, it is a rare and fortunate person who experiences such encounters time and time again. Individuals who fall into this group are labelled 'repeaters' and, as has been noted, there are very few such to be found in Scotland. Paul, a public sector worker from Cumbernauld, is one.

His extraordinary experiences began in a relatively straightforward manner one October morning in 1996. Paul had set off to work as he did each day, driving by car to the outskirts of Cumbernauld. As he turned left from a junction on to the main Glasgow road, he caught sight of a strange object hovering low down over a clump of trees just opposite. It was before 6 a.m., so Paul pulled the car to the side of the road to watch the UFO. He described the object as shaped like a ship's keel, although a drawing he made of the incident shows an object that might have been a disc shape viewed from an off-axis angle (see Fig 8). At each side of the UFO there was a dull, red, glowing light. He found it difficult to estimate its size.

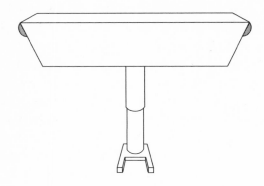

Fig 8. The UFO seen by over Cumbernauld in October 1996.

This sighting had a profound effect on Paul. He was convinced that if he had managed to catch a glimpse of one UFO, there must be others moving around the area, and he became determined to view and photograph these as soon as possible. He was not disappointed. From the balcony of his house, which commands a good view of the valley below and tree-lined hill beyond, Paul began to notice strange balls of light, not only around the sky, but also over the houses and factories within a mile or two of his own home. Paul emphasises that these UFOs are 'not big ones, but small, silver-coloured ones, undetectable unless you are looking for them'. Some of these objects will actually sit on top of buildings, and according to Paul, who has followed them through his binoculars, chase after cars and planes. He has seen them landing in fields and shooting upwards into the sky.

In January 1997 events took a new twist when one of the objects, which had been perched on a factory less than a mile away, flew up to the window of his home. Although the object was small, about two feet across according to Paul, it was a spectacular sight. He had no feeling that this was intended as something specifically for him. Nor is he convinced that they are aware of his presence. He has no sense of having some special contact with an alien presence which makes his claimed experiences all the more remarkable. Although he says 'There is so much happening', he adds that he 'wouldn't mention it to anyone' as he doesn't want his sanity questioned.

There is no doubt, however, that Paul has experienced some very close encounters. Whilst I am inclined to feel that a number of Paul's alleged UFO sightings have a natural expla-nation, such as distortions produced by binoculars, I certainly believe that a number of his encounters fall within the typical parameters of an 'unexplained' incident.

At 2.20 on this January morning, while Paul was lying awake in his bedroom, he caught sight of a cone-shaped object moving in the skies above Cumbernauld. He jumped out of bed and darted downstairs to grab his camera. But when he pressed the shutter release button, the camera appeared to jam. Paul immediately assumed that he had run out of film, but when he looked at the dial he saw that it displayed the number 16, indicating that there were several more frames left. Thinking that the camera batteries might be flat, he swapped them for the ones in the TV remote control. But when he stepped onto the balcony to photograph the UFO the camera still refused to work. (It is worth noting that failure of electrical equipment is commonly reported during UFO encounters. See also the Alien Landing Site case in Chapter 5.)

A number of shining objects were now visible. One had come right up to the house and was hovering just below the gutter. The other objects were rotating above the fields directly opposite the housing estate. Paul found himself fascinated by the one that seemed to have attached itself to his house. 'I couldn't take my eyes off it,' he later reported. As he watched, a funny feeling came over him. He felt his 'insides go completely'. He felt intense vibrations, but these came from inside his body as if his internal organs were being stirred up. Paul suddenly became aware of how alone and isolated he was and stepped off the balcony back into his living room, closing the glass sliding door behind him.

Hardly had he sat down to recover when his wife shouted to him from the bedroom, 'Are you still up? It's half past five!'

Paul glanced at his watch. She was right. He hurried upstairs. Two weeks later the chilling thought struck him: where had three hours of his life gone? Everything that had happened since 2.20 a.m. could only have taken minutes, at the most possibly half an hour. Yet it was undoubtedly true that a whole three hours had elapsed. It was inexplicable. The implications have not escaped Paul, but at the time of writing he has not yet decided on his next step.

One final interesting fact: it was 5.30 a.m. when the experience with the UFO outside his house ended. It was also at 5.40 a.m. when Paul first saw the UFO on his way to work and set off this remarkable train of events.

DIAMOND-SHAPED CRAFT

Those who have had a long-term interest in UFOs will know that when Kenneth Arnold experienced his remarkable encounter with a group of mysterious objects in 1947, he compared their movement to saucers skipping across calm water. On a hot June day in 1995, Pauline Ford was also particularly struck by the way in which the UFOs she witnessed travelled across the sky. 23-year-old Pauline had decided to walk to town from her home in Glasgow's Mount Florida. At around 2 p.m. she came to Eglinton Street and, for some reason, looked up. She was stunned to see what she described as 'a very large white object spinning through the sky'. A drawing she later made shows a clear diamond shape (Fig 9). She thinks there may, in fact, have been two of these.

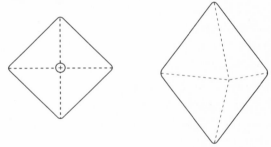

Fig 9. Two views of the spinning white object seen by Pauline Ford in June 1995.

An object somewhat similar to this was seen in October 1996 by Alan, a 34-year-old civil servant, in the Anderston area. It was like a star with four diamond-shaped sections. Alan studied it through binoculars and, although with the naked eye it might have given the appearance of an ordinary star, under magnification it became 'like a hole in the sky . . . it was only a couple of kilometres from me at the most'. It struck him as 'an awesome sight—very beautiful'. Alan was not arguing that this was an alien spaceship, but that whatever it was it had a powerful effect on him, a reaction many who have witnessed UFO sightings have experienced.

FLYING RAILWAY CARRIAGE

Tom Coventry is another whose experience has convinced him that alien spaceships are indeed visiting Glasgow. His close encounter took place on the morning of 15 December 1983. Tom left for work at about 6.25 a.m., his usual departure time, and followed his habitual route down Menock Road in the King's Park district. It was a crisp, dry morning, weather which boosted Tom's spirits as he had a bus to wait for at a stop with no shelter in which to escape from any sudden downpour. As he stood wrapped in his own thoughts, his attention was caught by a distant object moving in his direction at low altitude. At first Tom took it for an aircraft moving in a wide arc. He then noticed spurts of flame issuing from the rear and wondered if it was in some kind of trouble, but as it got close it dawned on him that this was not a plane.

All around him things began to go quiet (ufologist Jenny Randles' 'oz factor'[2]), as if he had entered another world. The

2. The 'oz factor' is a term devised by Jenny Randles to describe the strange sensations experienced by many UFO witnesses just prior to and also during an encounter. Typically, the surroundings become very quiet, while other sensations are magnified almost to the point where the person feels they have left the 'real' world. Although a useful designation, this term has not gained widespread acceptance with ufologists.

object had now come right above his head and stood hovering not more than twenty feet away. It was like nothing he had seen before.

'It was coloured grey', reported Tom, 'shaped like a railway carriage, but with a curved roof'. From it there issued crackling and humming sounds—like electricity. Being so close, Tom could easily recall afterwards the three porthole-shaped windows at the front through which he could make out an interior swirling with yellow smoke.

Slowly the object moved off towards a nearby railway bridge. There it stopped for a second, then shot skywards vertically before heading across the city. Tom watched it disappear in the distance. According to Tom, 'One of the strangest parts was when it did start moving, noise from all around started up again. It was as if it all rushed back!'

Equally strange, however, to Tom, was the fact that no-one else seemed to have witnessed the incident even though a bus arrived while the object was still visible. Passengers on this bus, believed Tom, must have had the chance to see it. Infuriating, too, was the absence of the milkman who Tom always saw at that time on his rounds, except that morning! It was the one time he failed to turn up.

Curiously, Tom's flying railway carriage was not the first such object seen. As far back as 1916 a Royal Flying Corps pilot, on the lookout for enemy zeppelins, spotted 'a row of what appeared to be lighted windows which looked something like a railway carriage with the window blinds drawn.' This incident occurred over Essex on a January night, so the pilot's view of the UFO was nothing like as clear as Tom's. Unlike Tom, he was not fascinated by what he saw, but shot at it with his pistol. The UFO immediately vanished.

Oddly, though he does not describe it as a railway carriage, John Maclean who saw the 'dance-hall light' object over Dunoon, caught sight of a similar oblong-shaped object in the summer of 1991. It was sixty to one hundred feet long and coloured bright red with two bands of light, one at each end. Maclean didn't get such a close up look as Tom Coventry, so we can't be sure that we are dealing with an identical UFO. There was one distinct difference. While Tom's object moved on a fairly straight path, John Maclean's UFO seemed to be weaving about as it moved through the evening sky.

MOUNT VERNON ANOMALY

Perhaps Glasgow attracts unusual shaped objects, from the Bellahouston gargantua mentioned earlier to Tom Coventry's railway carriage. It's not often, however, that a UFO is captured on camera. But that's what James MacLean managed in December 1995. The object he caught on film near his company's headquarters in Mount Vernon was shaped like a flying dumb-bell. Also in the sky at the same time and in close proximity was a long thin object much like a traditional disc-shaped UFO. These mysterious objects were caught on film in bright daylight in full view of anyone who happened to be in that part of Glasgow at the time. No-one appears, however, to have reported seeing these strange manifestations.

This incident does raise a number of important questions. If we are to argue that UFO incidents are somehow psychic phenomena, how can it be that an individual can catch them on a normal camera film? On the other hand, if UFOs have an objective reality, how is it that no-one saw the objects at the time? And this incidentally includes Mr MacLean himself—he saw nothing of the UFOs when he took the shots, and only realised that he had something extraordinary on film when he had the reel developed.

A curious incident occurred at the same time which may or not be coincidence. Mr MacLean himself is unsure. A compass he had in his pocket reversed itself at around the same time that he was unknowingly photographing the UFOs. It had become a perfectly useless piece of equipment. Some might argue that this *was* pure coincidence. Why, for example, wasn't the camera affected? Compasses are specifically designed to interact with magnetic fields, so perhaps it was simply more sensitive to disturbance than other equipment. Alternatively, it may be that the magnetic effect occurred just after Mr MacLean's camera recorded the UFO. Although the effect on the compass may be nothing more than coincidence, as an investigator I'm left in that unhappy halfway house of doubt and uncertainty. But it does seem odd that this should happen at exactly the same time as MacLean photographed these strange objects in the sky. Or are we searching too hard for mystery where there is none? Maybe after all it was simply a remarkable coincidence.

UFO
SCOTLAND
3

THE OUTER LIMITS
ABERDEEN AND THE NORTH OF SCOTLAND

HEBRIDEAN MILITARY ALERT · LEWIS SIGHTING · USOs · LOCH NEVIS OBJECT · ULLAPOOL
SIGHTING · FLAMING GLOBE · ORKNEY SIGHTING · DYCE AIRPORT UFOs · EARLY ABERDEEN
SIGHTINGS · A RECURRING PHENOMENON · BEAMS OF LIGHT · ALIEN ENCOUNTER · FORT
WILLIAM LIGHTS · STONEHAVEN INCIDENTS · REPEATER CONTACTEE · ELGIN ENCOUNTER

It was a clear, cloudless night. Dark with virtually no reflection from street lamps to blot out the natural beauty of the
heavens. An ideal opportunity to observe the sky over Inverness and for one person to witness an unusual phenomenon.
An incident he had not expected and was unable to explain.
He reported seeing 'two large bright lights that looked like
stars . . . sometimes stationary, but occasionally moving at
high velocity'. In many ways a typical, even 'ordinary' UFO
report. True, but what makes the incident stand out is that
it took place in 1848, a hundred and fifty years ago. Surely on
this occasion even sceptics would accept that he had not
been watching that secret American fighter plane regularly
called on to explain UFO sightings. So have UFOs been

visiting the Highlands since Queen Victoria's time?

If we take in the whole of the North of Scotland, we're talking about á large area, bigger than Wales. Yet the countryside is relatively sparsely populated, with people crammed into urban centres of various sizes—from cities like Aberdeen to small towns like Drumnadrochit. If alien beings are travelling to our world, these hills and glens of Scotland would make an ideal hiding place.

But are we dealing with simply an airborne phenomenon? Remember that we live on an island and Scotland alone has thousands of bays and inlets, many of which are rarely if ever visited. Plenty of suitable places for waterborne UFOs or USOs (unidentified submersible objects) to move in and out of without being detected. There has been a suspicion for many years within ufology that these objects, or at least some of them, may emerge from the water. One of the witnesses in the controversial Brooklyn Bridge Abduction case,[1] investigated by UFO expert Bud Hopkins, claimed that the spacecraft they saw dived into the river, after beaming its victim out of a highrise building.

HEBRIDEAN MILITARY ALERT

A more spectacular incident occurred in public view a lot closer to home. Those who believe that there is more going on

1. At around 3 a.m. on 30 November 1989 in Manhattan, New York, a number of witnesses—including two government agents and a high-ranking diplomat—saw a woman in a nightdress, surrounded by three small entities, float out of a 12th-storey window, hover in mid air, then rise up into a glowing oval craft which was overhead. The UFO then flew off over Brooklyn Bridge and plunged into the East River. Despite considerable criticism, Hopkins has remained convinced about these events, citing the sheer complexity of the case as one reason why it is unlikely that this could have been a hoax.

in the seas around the North of Scotland no doubt feel that their position was fully justified by the events of October 1996. A mysterious incident which resulted in a full military alert, but has still to be satisfactorily explained. What is clear is that a massive explosion occurred off the Hebrides at 4.10 p.m. on Saturday 26 October. There were several witnesses to this spectacular incident from the sparsely populated area of the Butt of Lewis. Here, however, another mystery begins. According to the coastguard station in Stornoway (the island's main town), no calls were received from the public until 5 p.m., almost a full hour after the initial event. This is exactly the same time that, according to *UFO* magazine, RAF Kinloss first heard reports of the incident. It appears to have been described as a possible aircrash with a large object (part of the fuselage) seen impacting with the sea. In spite of the report, the evidence is that there followed a two-hour delay before an official air search was launched. It was not until 10.35 p.m. (six hours after the first witness called in) that an emergency message was broadcast to all ships within the vicinity, alerting them to the reported explosion.

It is true, and would have been noted at the time, that the description given by the witnesses did not tally in every detail. All the witnesses, though, did agree that there had been an enormous flash in the sky accompanied by a loud bang and a trail of smoke which led directly into the sea. One witness claimed that just before the explosion he saw an object travelling high in the sky. When the detonation happened the object disappeared but a ball of smoke was clearly visible near the spot where he had last seen the UFO. The explosion was powerful enough to light up the sky in a bright orange flood.

Naturally, those who saw the incident felt that it must have been some kind of aircraft accident. However, an extensive two-day search involving coastguards and the massive, sophisticated resources of the military failed to find any evidence that an accident had occurred. That, of course, was the official verdict. As the military are secretive by nature, if there is an explanation it is unlikely to be revealed to the general public. This doesn't, of course, mean that we are dealing with a crashed extraterrestrial craft. However, the answer hinted at by the Ministry of Defence, without of course being openly stated—that a meteorite was involved—seems no more likely as an answer. This is particularly so as none of the chain of tracking stations across the Atlantic picked up this mysterious object, an admission which is astounding. How is it that an object big enough to produce a major explosion and be seen by at least one witness can enter NATO airspace without being tracked? There are clearly facts in this case which don't fully agree. If this mysterious object was not an extraterrestrial craft, then what in the universe was it?

A variety of explanations were put forward as to the possible source of the explosion, but as investigators such as Tony Dodds of Quest International and John Morrison of Scottish Earth Mysteries conducted their research, some puzzles were solved and new ones emerged. Was it coincidence, for example, that a major NATO exercise was held off the Isle of Lewis a week after the crash, on Monday 4 November? Did a weapon aboard a military aircraft accidentally arm itself and was it then jettisoned to avoid disaster? The substantial number of ships involved would have made it an ideal force to sweep the seas in the area for surviving debris. As might be expected, the military blandly claimed that it was a 'routine training exercise'. You don't have to be of a suspicious frame of mind to wonder whether that was the whole story. The military authorities are experts at concealing information they do not want the public to know. Secrecy is part of the system.

Several air to ground messages were also unearthed which seemed to indicate that a number of unidentified objects had been seen over the preceding months—April, July, August and September. However, as John Morrison shows, not every 'mysterious' incident stays in that classification when looked at by a serious investigator. Considerable excitement was generated by an individual who had been listening to air traffic communications and reported the following comment:

Kinloss (air base): 'Confirm . . . six feet long and three feet in diameter'. Clearly, military air traffic had received a report of an unidentified object seen in the vicinity at the time. Was this the source of the mysterious explosion? Unfortunately, it seems not. John Morrison discovered that further information revealed that a rescue helicopter had been despatched to look at the UFO. We know its exact position: 58°30' north, 7°01' west. We also know the time it was first seen—at 8.03 a.m.— and the time it was reported as 'identified'—at 8.10 a.m. According to the pilot of the helicopter, the strange object was simply a white cardboard box. Now, it might be asked, if the object was nothing more than a box, why did it take seven minutes to identify it? Furthermore, why were they spending time chasing objects in the sea in any case? The sea is full of floating debris. I would agree that these questions may have straightforward answers, but they are puzzles nevertheless.

LEWIS SIGHTING

Intriguingly, this incident is not the first to have puzzled observers of the UFO scene in this area. In the 1950s Lewis coastguards were witnesses to an unusual sight. At 6.15 p.m. on a Friday 'a bright light was seen some 3,000 feet up and about 19 miles south-west of Stornoway'. Coastguards looked at the UFO through powerful binoculars and were able to detect a solid egg-shaped object as the source of the light. According to witnesses 'the upper half was bright yellow. The lower half had a continuous dark red glow like a fire'. The mysterious object descended slowly towards the water and was only lost to view when it came so low down that it 'disappeared' behind nearby hills. The sighting lasted a good sixteen minutes, which, coupled with the fact that experienced observers—the coastguards—were involved, makes this a first rate sighting. It's particularly interesting as the previous week several islanders had reported a red glowing ball in the sky. Perhaps both sightings involved the same object.

The Air Ministry (as it was at the time) confirmed that there were no aircraft movements in the area at the time, but could throw no further light on the nature or origin of the object. Nothing changes!

USOs

So do UFOs enter our water and become USOs? There's clear evidence which points in that direction. On 3 February 1965 in the early hours a seventy-ton trawler the *Star of Freedom* heading for Fleetwood struck an unidentified object submerged near the surface, but out of sight. The trawler was making 9 knots of speed at that time, steaming in 80 fathoms about 15 miles south-east of the Island of Barra. The collision lifted the ship's bow from the water and holed her so badly that a distress call was immediately initiated and the pumps set to work. The crew fought manfully to save the vessel, but it was eventually beached in Castlebay Harbour.

George Wood, skipper of the *Star of Freedom*, expressed the view that he must have hit a submarine. A possible solution, but both the British and US Navies denied that any military vessels had been involved. Of course, it would be wrong to accept such denials simply on trust, but there would be greater danger in the authorities denying their involvement because of the threat to life involved. If there really had been a cover-up which was subsequently blown, the resulting embarrassment would have been catastrophic for the Navy.

But evidence that a submarine might not have been involved comes from the way that the *Star of Freedom*'s encounter follows part of a world pattern. In October 1902, long before the modern era of 'flying saucers', the *SS Fort Salisbury* was cruising through the Gulf of Guinea off the coast of West Africa. At 3.05 a.m., with a clear sky above and a calm sea around, the lookout spotted a large dark object several hundred feet to starboard. An officer was called for and Andrew Rayner responded. He noted that the object was 'between five hundred and six hundred feet in length. It had two lights, one at each end, a mechanism of some kind, or perhaps fins, and was making a commotion in the water'. The USO appeared to be submerging slowly, and as it did so Rayner observed that it had a rough rather than smooth surface.

One thing we can be sure of. The *SS Fort Salisbury* had definitely not—in 1902—encountered a rogue submarine. But is it a sensible leap of logic to argue that the craft was of extraterrestrial origin?

Closer to home, and to us in time, the Aberdeen collier *Thrift* spent several hours on 22 November 1963 searching the area around Girdle Ness. The crew had spotted a flashing red light very low down, perhaps less than 20 feet above the sea, which passed about a mile off their port side before crashing into the sea. Lifeboat stations and RAF Kinloss were alerted and a search initiated, but nothing was found. Frustratingly, the *Thrift*'s radar indicated two objects had 'landed' but the contacts disappeared from the scene as they neared the site.

Perhaps the best known Scottish USO encounter occurred in 1957. The *Avondee* was hauling in a catch near the Bell Rock about thirty miles from the coast. It was around 11 p.m. on a typical summer's night in June. The ship's cook, Mr James Blackhall, was looking at the stars when his attention was caught by two orange-red objects moving at tremendous speed. He pointed out the strange phenomenon to Samuel Noble, whose turn it was to take the watch, and shouted to the rest of the crew: 'Come and see the flying saucers!'

This was clearly jumping to conclusions although they had obviously spotted something out of the ordinary. It is hard, for example, to judge from the account the object's height above the sea. Mr Blackhall estimated their size in the sky from his location as about 3 inches high and 3 feet broad. But that does not tell us whether they were very large objects at a high altitude or smaller objects near to the trawler. UFOs of all shapes and sizes have been encountered—even up to a mile in length! Mr Blackhall explained that 'At first they seemed to be moving together, but suddenly sheered off and disappeared'. The UFOs left behind a luminous trail, but, unlike a conventional jet, when the object disappeared the trail disappeared instantly.

The crew kept watching in hope that the mysterious visitors would reappear, but the sky remained empty. Perhaps the final word should be given to the *Avondee*'s skipper who was the last on deck when the cry 'flying saucer' was heard. 'When I arrived,' he explained, 'there was only one object. It was like a ball of fire'.

So what are we dealing with? Is it a largely airborne phenomenon capable of entering the sea? Or submerged USOs which find both mediums no barrier to travel at mind boggling speeds. Evidence from the lochs of Scotland doesn't, it has to be admitted, clear up this puzzle, but does point to the fact that to look solely to the skies is to grasp only a part of this enigma.

LOCH NEVIS OBJECT

In June 1997 *Saturday Times* journalist Jim McLean reported a strange incident. Microlight pilot Hamish Smith spotted an unidentified object beneath the waters of Loch Nevis as he flew priest Michael Hudson on a photography trip. The pair had been taking snaps of remote churches and other landmarks when they caught sight of the mysterious craft. They were able to photograph the object to confirm that they hadn't been hallucinating.

Hamish claimed that he had 'never seen anything like it. It

was not a shoal of fish and the entrance to the loch is only eight metres deep so it couldn't be a submarine'.

Although coastguards and police were alerted they took several days to check the loch. As might be expected after a lengthy time lapse, they found nothing, although echo-sounding equipment did seem to register an anomaly. Had the UFO left some 'phantom trail' in its wake?

Hamish's photo certainly showed a solid-looking object and the picture he drew depicts a keel-shaped craft, but certainly not a submarine. On the other hand, it doesn't seem like a typical airborne UFO. Separate evidence that something odd had been going on came from a female witness who doesn't wish to be identified. She was walking near the mouth of the loch when she 'saw a weird wave rolling up the loch'. It struck her as unusual as the surface of the water was flat calm. Loch Nevis does have direct entrance into the sea so it would be possible for a small vessel to pass in and out, but it seems an unlikely route given the size of the UFO Hamish reported. If it was indeed a solid object it seems far more likely that it arrived in the loch directly from the skies above.

ULLAPOOL SIGHTING

UFOs are regularly reported down the coast of the West Highlands. In June 1997 the manager of an Ullapool grocery shop videoed a bright object over the summit of Beinn Ghabheach. The UFO flashed beams of red and blue light as it gradually sank behind the mountain. The sighting lasted several minutes and was seen by several witnesses. It should be noted that this area of Scotland is one of the most under-populated in Western Europe. There's no doubt that the reported incidents must represent a fraction of what is going on in the skies over this still little-travelled part of our country.

FLAMING GLOBE

UFOs know no geographical boundaries and whether or not 'hot-spots' exist, one thing can be said for certain. Incidents which stretch our imaginations to the limit can occur at any geographical location. Proof of this can be found in the experience of Arthur Moar, an inhabitant of Sandwick, one of the remoter parts of the remote Shetland Isles. A retired small-farmer, Mr Moar was used to early rising, and the morning of Monday 6 January 1992 was no different from any other. At five minutes past seven—he could be sure of the time as he had just finished checking the dial on the clock—all thoughts of continuing with his daily routine were disturbed by the appearance of a bright, flashing light which lit up the whole room. Mr Moar hurried to the window and observed a strange object on the ground about 30 or 40 yards from his house. The description in Mr Moar's own restrained words says a lot about his ability to remain unruffled by the bizarre sight that met his eyes. The object, he reported, 'was about five or six feet high with flame all around it' and 'in the centre I saw the globe of the world and . . . all the markings on the globe'.

A flaming globe landing from the sky! It is without doubt one of the most incredible sightings ever. Mr Moar noted that the globe was grey-coloured and that the area round the globe was dark red. The object was enclosed by a flange about 4 inches across. From the rear of the object protruded a round, white tube, out of which flashed the intense light which had first caught Mr Moar's attention.

The globe, he adds, was of suede-like material and even appeared to have rumpled up in the manner of a hastily dumped coat. Even as he watched, the UFO flew up into the air, leaving behind the white tube which remained standing on the ground. This tube, which to all intents and purposes looked solid, gradually faded away until it eventually disappeared from view. Although Mr Moar observed the object for only a short time, it is an event he is unlikely ever to forget.

On a scale of strange events listing from 1 to 10, I would classify this as a definite number 10. Why? Because there seems no obvious object in the first place which could provide a justification for claiming a misidentification and secondly, the UFO did not look remotely like a 'flying saucer'. But if it wasn't from outer space, what on earth was it? If further reports are received of a similar object we will, perhaps, be in a better position to find a solution.

Less dramatically, perhaps, but equally intriguingly, in December 1992 dozens of callers in the Shetland Isles bombarded the police, and anyone in authority, with reported sightings of a fireball streaking across the night sky, travelling from north-west to south-east. Other witnesses who contacted Lerwick coastguards described it as a 'bright white light', but it was undoubtedly the same object. Checks with the RAF base at Pitreavie Castle drew a blank. Officially, there were no planes in the area at the time. The phenomenon may have been the same as that seen further south on the mainland by Alistair Donaldson, out walking his dog in Banchory around

8.50 p.m. He reported it as being 'as bright as a star', with 'sparks coming out of the back, and it had a tail. There was no noise'. He explained that he did not believe in UFOs, but that it definitely was not an aeroplane or a helicopter.

ORKNEY SIGHTING

Not to be outdone by their island compatriots, the inhabitants of Orkney have their own strange tales to tell. One January morning in 1994 Stephen Leech of Stenness (close to the famous standing stones of Broghar) was travelling to work with colleague Paul Anderson. They were heading along the A965 to the island's main city, Kirkwall. Suddenly, 45-year-old Steve, a native of Yorkshire, spotted a 'huge, glowing, cigar-shaped object' travelling across the sky at a fantastic speed. Steve noted that 'it was gone in a couple of seconds and was moving too fast for an aeroplane'. Although it was 8.30 in the morning with a cloudy sky, both men were convinced of what they had witnessed, even noting the turquoise colour of the object. Steve and Paul came forward with reluctance to give their account, but felt sure that with all the traffic on the road that morning other car drivers must have seen the strange object. As is often the case, however, they were disappointed by the lack of corroborative responses.

DYCE AIRPORT UFOs

But where we have an experienced 'skywatcher', do we need that corroboration? Isn't the evidence of an anomaly, noticed after years of practical observation, adequate to prove that something odd is going on above us? Andrew Duncan (a pseudonym, as for employment reasons the witness does not wish to be identified) was based at Dyce airport near Aberdeen. On 9 November 1991 (the anniversary of Bob Taylor's sighting) at around 12.15 p.m., Mr Duncan was looking out of his operations' window when he spotted a strange object overhead. He put it in that category as, being used to seeing planes and helicopters from many different angles, he was unable to classify it as any normal airport traffic. Fetching a pair of binoculars from the adjacent room, he focused on the UFO, but was still unable to identify it. Puzzled, Mr Duncan called up Air Traffic Control (ATC) and asked: 'What on earth is that?' From the tower, however, the men could not see the object which appeared clearly visible to Duncan. ATC informed him that they would contact radar and get back to him as soon as possible.

Meanwhile, a light aircraft had appeared on the airport circuit, but gave no indication by way of message or evasive action that it was aware of its mysterious companion. Mr Duncan called two colleagues through, but by the time they had got it within their sights the UFO looked considerably smaller and they were unable to make an identification. They had, however, definitely seen 'something'. ATC now rang back and, to Mr Duncan's surprise, informed him that nothing had appeared on radar. Glancing skywards again, he noted that the object was nowhere to be seen.

Overnight, Mr Duncan had time to consider the matter and by morning was still convinced that he had witnessed an intrusion which he could not easily explain. As a result, he decided to ring up Highland Radar at RAF Buchan near the fishing port of Peterhead. He was again surprised to learn that they had nothing logged for the time indicated. To Mr Duncan the incident remains an absorbing mystery. As he himself notes: 'I have a pretty in-depth knowledge of aircraft recognition . . . and have always tried to keep up-to-date with ongoing developments. This object I can categorically state was not an aircraft'.

Nor does he believe that he witnessed something as 'ordinary' as a hot air balloon, both because of the design of the object and its speed: there was no 'visual sign of a basket suspended below the object and add to this the relatively light wind conditions and I think that you can rule this out'. Furthermore, Mr Duncan described the object he saw as cube-shaped—a most unusual shape for a balloon. Cuboid UFOs are not common, but they are by no means unknown.

Interestingly, on 26 March of the same year at 11.20 a.m., a helicopter pilot on his way to Dyce airport picked up a highly visible trace on his radar screen. Surprised by its appearance, he checked on local shipping and aircraft movements to see if he could locate the source. He was unable, however, to make a positive identification. Mystified, the pilot formally notified Air Traffic Control of a UFO in the sky. ATC immediately informed the Ministry of Defence which rapidly scanned military air traffic to find out if one of its own transports was involved. Again, they drew a blank and, following standard procedure, fighter aircraft were scrambled to locate the intruder which could be anything from ET to a 'mundane' encroachment of UK air-space by a Soviet reconnaissance plane.

Coincidentally—or perhaps not—at around the time that the helicopter first spotted the UFO, a loud bang reverberated over Aberdeen and was heard as far away as the town of Banchory, about 18 miles south-west. Buildings apparently shook under the force of the explosion, and some witnesses claim to have seen flashes of light in the sky. Whether the UFO and the bang were in any way connected is uncertain except in one respect: no solution was discovered for either mystery.

EARLY ABERDEEN SIGHTINGS

Thanks to the efforts of UFO enthusiast James Walker, it has been possible to establish that the UFO phenomenon had reached Aberdeen as early as the 1950s. In September 1952 a 'flying saucer' (the standard term in those days) was spotted by Mrs Robert Smart from her back garden in St Swithin's Street. Mrs Smart first caught a glimpse of the strange object at around 4.25 p.m. Wearing sunglasses, her attention was drawn to 'a white object against the brilliant blue of the cloudless sky' as the report ran. The witness herself describes the object as being 'like a saucer with a chip out of it' (see the description of the Curran video evidence in Chapter 5) and 'flying in a straight line at a great height in the north-north-east direction'. Mrs Smart tried to point the object out to her husband, but by the time he looked up the UFO had disappeared because of the speed at which it was travelling. Mrs Smart admitted that 'it was moving in the same manner as an aeroplane' but denied that she had simply misidentified it, explaining that 'it was moving a good bit faster than a jet'. Whatever it was, the sighting had a dramatic effect on the witness as she immediately made a drawing of the object which she described a little differently from the initial description as 'something like a painter's palette or a heart'. Unfortunately, the witness's drawing of this early incident—early in the annals of modern ufology—does not appear to have survived.

A few years later, in December 1957, a much larger object was seen by several witnesses as it streaked over the Aberdeenshire countryside travelling inland from the North Sea. Mrs J Esslemont, driving with her husband towards the village of Cove, caught a glimpse of the UFO at around 3.30 p.m. She described it as 'a streak of light moving slowly across the sky with a very bright light at the centre'. To some observers it appeared pyramid-shaped with 'sparks streaming from its tail'. Village shop proprietor Jim Thomson thought he saw 'something like fire'. Mr Thomson had been following the object with binoculars and was convinced 'it wasn't a star. It was certainly moving'. Yet another witness, Howard Smith, described the object as 'a pyramid with a ball shape at the end. Bright orange in colour, it seemed to be burning at the point'.

Predictably, sceptics attempted to 'explain' it, with Professor R V Jones of Aberdeen University pointing out that one of the planets was bright at the time (4 to 6 p.m.). It's also true that the Russian Sputnik had been launched that year, but it does seem unlikely that either a misidentified star or wayward Soviet satellite satisfactorily accounts for the details given by the witnesses.

Three days later two Stonehaven police officers driving into Aberdeen also caught sight of a strange object above and just in front of them. Sergeant Ewen, an experienced flyer, 'discounted the suggestion the light might be from an aircraft. . . . There was only one light there and that was big'. His colleague, Constable Sinclair, thought that he saw something sticking out from the centre of the light, but in the dark it was difficult to be sure exactly what.

A RECURRING PHENOMENON

Events in the area around Dunecht link events of the 1950s with today. Forty years ago several witnesses watched a 'gigantic pear-shaped object, something like an electric bulb' hurtle over Dunecht. Walter Ironside and Mrs Mary Reid agreed that the UFO travelled 'at a terrific speed and left behind a long trail of sparks like a jet trail'. Like a jet trail? But in this instance the object, pale blue in colour, was actually seen to land in a shower of sparks several miles further on. The witness, however, was too far away to investigate further.

On 2 August 1997, again at Dunecht, Andrew Frost saw three star-shaped objects also travelling at high velocity over the area. These UFOs appeared white when moving, but red when stationary and, as in the '57 sighting, there were several witnesses to the encounter. The earlier UFO had landed on 'Egypt Hill', a highly symbolic location for all those who see ancient Egypt as the key to the UFO mystery. The UFO that appeared in 1997, however, seems to have simply disappeared as rapidly and suddenly as it arrived.

It is interesting to note that the green light phenomenon also occurs in Aberdeen. A bright green light made several appearances during November 1992 on the outskirts of the city. Is the green glow only the visible manifestation of a much larger object? On 2 December, in the nearby town of Alford, four boys caught sight of a large saucer shape, as big as a double-decker bus across its width. The 'saucer' was itself grey-coloured, but had red, purple and green lights. Far from being afraid, the boys ran towards the object, which took off at great speed. On the following day, again in Alford, a witness saw a large disc-shaped object hover over a nearby hill for several minutes before heading on a southwards trail.

Interestingly, a decade earlier, a similar object, though this time described as ambulance-sized, was seen in Banff. It hovered above a house, and a band of red and green lights around its circumference was clearly visible. After a few minutes the object moved away.

BEAMS OF LIGHT

On 16 December 1990, two bakers on their way to work were approaching the Kessock Bridge over the Beauly Firth when a bright light lit up the interior of their car. The direct beam seemed to be searching them out deliberately. The witnesses were so startled by the abrupt transformation of night into day that the driver quickly brought the car to a halt. The beam of light immediately disappeared. The two men took the opportunity to have a good look around. They could see nothing that could provide a solution to the strange phenomenon, either on the ground or in the sky.

At around the same time, a family travelling in a car between Inverbervie and Stonehaven, on Scotland's north-east coast, experienced a similar event. A pencil of light suddenly emerged from the sky and penetrated the interior of the car. The incident was over in seconds, but left the family puzzled and curious. There was no obvious source for the light. It seemed to come out of nothing. The family, however, had been aware of a mysterious light dancing in a nearby wood as they passed through, though there is no evidence that these two incidents were in any way connected.

Strange beams of light coming from nowhere and aimed at the ground are a phenomenon known to ufologists all over the country. In Kinross, for example, during August 1982, a witness saw a bright beam of light descend from the sky. However, in contrast to the cases described above, he also caught sight of a bright object which seemed to be the light source. It may be that on each occasion the light beam is encountered it is, in fact, being projected from an object in the sky, but that witnesses are not always fortunate enough to catch a glimpse of the object itself.

ALIEN ENCOUNTER

If light beams are sent by extraterrestrial craft, do they land and do creatures then emerge to walk the earth? A lot of 'ifs' and 'buts' are wrapped up in that possibility! And unfortunately—or not, depending on your point of view—there are surprisingly few cases in Scotland to suggest the reality of ET, whether as 'monster' or humanoid.

One that certainly stretches the imagination occurred in Braemar, near Balmoral, the Queen's residence in Scotland. The Territorial Army (TA) were holding a weekend training session and had based their headquarters close to the village of Tarland, about an hour's drive from Aberdeen.

Manoeuvres for the night having been arranged, two of the party were left to guard a hilltop with orders to dig a trench as part of the exercise. It could not have been a comfortable assignment on a cold November night with little to do except watch the movement of the stars. It was with understandable relief, then, that they watched the first glow of the sun emerging above the mountain tops. It also marked the start of a truly bizarre experience.

The soldiers heard a strange gurgling noise which seemed to come from a clump of trees a few hundred yards from their temporary base. At this point they felt no sense of fear and were merely curious, glad of some relief from a night of cold and boredom. They set off to investigate, walking towards the silhouetted pines. Suddenly, in the half-light of dawn, two large figures emerged and headed in a stumbling manner towards them.

The creatures' size, seven to eight feet tall the soldiers later judged, coupled with their strange movements and incessant gurgling, petrified the TA's finest. They managed to note, however, that the strange noises coming from the two 'spacemen' were, in fact, their voices, strongly guttural in pronunciation. The creatures also seemed to be experiencing problems in traversing the countryside, as if they were either unsure of walking or, to those with a more vivid imagination, unused to the earth's gravity.

The two soldiers did not stop to ask questions, but retreated headlong until they gained the safety of a hut a good distance away beside the main road. It was being used as a temporary shelter by Post Office maintenance engineers. As the soldiers neared the hut, still running, they heard a 'swishing' noise behind them. Turning, they saw all too clearly a brilliant glowing object, shaped like a disc, travelling fast up the road behind them. It was moving so quickly that there was clearly no escape.

Its appearance on the road, however, may have been pure coincidence and the 'terriers' involvement purely accidental as the UFO swooped over the men's heads, pulsating and leaving a shower of sparks in its wake. It soon disappeared from sight.

The soldiers now reached the safety of the hut and hammered on the door until they were let inside, where they poured out their unbelievable story.

Seasoned UFO watchers will feel a little uneasy over this encounter. It seems too exciting, with all the ingredients of a good SciFi story, particularly of that period. Though similar incidents have been reported from elsewhere in the world, an open mind on the incident might be the best attitude to adopt. My own efforts to locate a local source for the story met with no success. The Aberdeen *Press & Journal* searched their archives, but could find no report of the incident. I did, however, discover that the earliest published account had appeared in an edition of *Flying Saucer Review*, the leading UFO magazine of the 1950s and 1960s. Beyond that, it has not so far been possible to learn how the story came into *FSR*'s possession, or to discover any clue as to the identity of the witnesses.

FORT WILLIAM LIGHTS

It is true, however, that the mountains of Scotland have long been associated with the appearance of strange phenomena, from the ghostly grey man of Ben Macdhui to UFOs in the form of intense bright lights. It is the last type that has been observed over the town of Fort William situated in the Western Highlands. One incident which occured in the 1970s involved the owner of a hairdressing salon who, with her husband, saw a brilliant light on the top of Glen Nevis to the south of the town. Behind the glow they could make out the definite shape of a solid object. Although at some distance, it appeared to be round, orange-coloured at the bottom with a flashing white light on top.

The couple had been watching a late TV film, so they could fix the time at around 1.30 in the morning. The object had been seen from their living room, but now they threw dressing gowns over their nightwear and, picking up binoculars, ventured outside to get a better look. The object had gradually moved towards the town and slowly passed overhead, allowing the couple an opportunity to inspect the underside with their field glasses.

They now had to modify their original impression of the shape. The underside appeared triangular, with panels through which orange light filtered down. The white light which had first attracted their attention could now more clearly be seen as a strip or panel on the side of the UFO, which itself now assumed a domed shape. The object was seen to be rotating as it moved. The UFO travelled in an uncannily silent trajectory, emitting no noise whatever. Without warning, however, it accelerated in silence and shot north-west in a flash of light. Subsequently, several witnesses to this UFO encounter came forward.

In spite of enquiries to RAF Lossiemouth and the local police, no obvious explanation has emerged, although UFO sceptic and author Steuart Campbell has offered a solution. 'It is possible', he wrote, 'that what was seen was a mirage of the star Antares caused by its light crossing a temperature inversion into an adjoining valley'. Although the idea of a mirage should not be dismissed out of hand, as it undoubtedly explains some UFO sightings, the proximity of the object makes it an unlikely source in this instance.

STONEHAVEN INCIDENTS

Phantom lights have also been frequently seen in the area around Muchalls near the fishing town of Stonehaven on Scotland's east coast. However, in an attempt to find a solution to these incidents and present the evidence, investigator Tom McClintock has spent considerable time videoing activity there. What does the footage show? Certainly, there is something strange happening in the skies over this sparsely populated area. Round objects, gleaming balls of coloured light, dart about the sky erratically or hang suspended in the air. Are these due to the propulsion system of an unknown space vehicle, or the afterglow of a jet seen from an odd angle? The integrity of the investigator is beyond reproach and the evidence freely available for anyone to form an opinion.

It would be fair to say that the view of the majority of those who have reviewed the evidence and visited the area is that natural phenomena may explain the activity. The location is close to both aeroplane and, more significantly, helicopter routes. Dyce Airport, about fifteen miles north-west, is the busiest helicopter base in Western Europe, with constant traffic to oil rigs drilling the North Sea floor. It is this regular movement which, it is argued, accounts for the alleged 'mysterious' light forms.

To counteract that, one must weigh the testimony of the investigator, a person with a responsible job who has everything to lose and nothing to gain by bringing forward his account. He has visited the area many times and holds the view that these lights are not produced by man-made machines. If that is the case, then we are again at the very boundaries of the unexplained, with the opportunity of making a breakthrough, so frequently does the Muchalls phenomenon appear.

It is worth looking into the background of the key person involved and discovering what brought him to such an intense interest in the area's events. Tom McClintock's interest in strange phenomena began on 13 December 1971 when he returned to the village of Muchalls from his weekly violin lesson held in nearby Stonehaven. It was only a short journey from the bus stop to his house, but as he walked along he noticed a red pulsating light to his right. It was soon joined by an identical object to his left and then another appeared. Tom wasn't frightened by the three UFOs, only interested in trying to find out what they were doing. As he turned into the road that led directly to his home, events took a more disconcerting turn. One of the red lights came very low, almost to ground level. It caught Tom's attention for a moment, and he paused before moving forward. Just at that moment a strange figure appeared from nowhere standing right in the middle of the road. It was blocking Tom's path to his front door. The entity was dressed in a long gown and glowed brightly in the black evening of a rural setting. Showing amazing willpower for a young lad, Tom did not, as I suspect many of us might have done, turn and run or shout for help. Instead he moved a yard forward. The figure simply dissolved into nothingness.

Tom blurted out the story as soon as he got in the door and took his sister out to take a look. At first there was no sign of any strange light, but as they reached the end of the road, the red object appeared again. It came towards them without making any sound and hovered above their heads. Although they could make out a small ring of lights, no other details were visible. After a short time the UFO moved away to disappear over nearby hills.

What is particularly interesting and relevant is that Mr McClintock did not interpret this as simply a ghost incident. Undoubtedly, it does have qualities that point in that direction. Even the appearance of odd lights does not mark it as definitely a UFO incident, as mysterious lights have long been associated with spectral encounters. However, in Tom's mind it was within the UFO category, a view reinforced when, in later years, he had other sightings. In September 1988, for example, he again witnessed a pulsating red light, although this time he had a better look at the source. This was a flat-topped object, drum-shaped, with diamond-shaped facets on its circumference. It moved from behind a hill, and as it did so a white-coloured halo appeared, flashed, then disappeared, as did the object itself behind a low cloud. As indicated, Tom McClintock has not only a story to tell, but hard evidence too. I find him a convincing witness.

REPEATER CONTACTEE

Close to Muchalls is a fishing village which must remain

anonymous as our witness would be too easily identified, strange incidents have also been occurring. The woman in question, Jane Freeman, is not a native of the area, but moved in about five years ago, keen to escape the pressures of city life. She didn't come to the coast looking for alien encounters, but nor was she surprised when strange incidents started to happen. Jane had experienced alien contact from an early age and accepted the existence of extraterrestrials in much the same way as you and I would a visitor from a distant land. Different, but still a part of our world.

It's amazing how many people have had a UFO experience as a child. Jane falls into that category and it was while playing in the school grounds in Aberdeen that she spotted a silver, cigar-shaped UFO travelling slowly in a cloud-free sky. She was fascinated by the incident and felt that she wanted to learn more about distant worlds. But, of course, she was still a child and more immediate interests grabbed her attention. The UFO sighting faded into the background, although it was never forgotten.

Several years passed. Jane's family had moved to the south of England, living in a quiet housing estate. Jane had gone to bed, but a growing urge to look out of the window at the front of her house took hold of her. Jane got up and wandered into her brother's room as hers looked out the back. On the road outside, she saw a strange craft hovering a few feet above the ground. It was flat and circular, like a swollen pancake. The circumference was marked by a distinct band and within the band a series of lights were rotating. Jane recalls: 'I was excited. I ran downstairs and went outside. A human(?) alien was standing beside the craft. He was tall (almost six feet), dressed in a close-fitting suit which also covered his hands and feet. He had a human build. I can't remember his facial features, but he looked human. I walked down the path towards him. He held out his hand, which I took and walked aboard the craft with him'. Jane said nothing to her family about this experience until almost fifteen years later.

In the 1990s Jane took up residence at her present address. Her house looks directly over a rocky foreshore, a tranquil view if the day is calm. But strange incidents have been taking place.

One night as Jane looked out of her bedroom window she saw a UFO come down above the high tide mark. Out of this craft strode five humanoid aliens. Jane felt that they had 'come back' for her. A wave of excitement raced over her. She ran downstairs, then opened the front door and raced down the garden path towards them. Thoughts of her children brought her to an abrupt halt. 'They'll be all right' went through her mind. Was this the aliens reassuring her? Wherever the thought had come from, she now felt sure everything would be all right. The leading alien was now level with her and stretched out his hand in greeting. 'He was', says Jane, 'exactly like the one' she'd seen all those years before. She took hold of his hand and allowed herself to be led towards the spacecraft. Then she felt herself standing at her living room window. The aliens and the UFO had gone.

The incident was the start of a variety of strange events. One September, Jane was lying on the settee when several small aliens, between three and four feet tall, suddenly appeared. They had slits for mouths and black eyes like cats. Jane wanted to speak to these visitors, but found that she was unable to move. All around her everything went quiet. But Jane knew what the small entities were up to. She felt waves of light travelling through her, an experience she associated with scanning. The aliens turned her onto her stomach and continued to scan, if that is what they were doing. Jane emphasises that she felt no pain, but only a desire to communicate. Her visitors, however, seemed to have no wish to, or perhaps couldn't, respond.

ELGIN ENCOUNTER

Lights in the sky, or 'LITS' as they are familiarly known, present an intriguing problem, but encounters which appear to involve extraterrestrials are bound to excite the imagination. In the city of Elgin, at 6.30 p.m. on 18 May 1977, and in the middle of a UK-wide UFO wave, Mrs Caroline Maclennan heard a strange whirring noise and remarked to her neighbour that it sounded 'like a flying saucer'. Shortly after, her ten-year-old daughter Karen returned home and told Mrs Maclennan that she and her friend Fiona Morrison (also aged ten) had seen a 'silver-coloured saucer with a bump on top' hovering in the wood. It had been close to the ground, glowing with a red light. Their attention had first been drawn to the object by a strange humming sound which seemed to have no obvious source. They were playing in fields close to the woods and it was from among the trees that the odd sound seemed to be coming. Being naturally curious, they decided to walk over and investigate. They quickly discovered the mysterious disc which they estimated at around 30 feet long. It seemed to be made of polished metal, but had no windows or doors that the girls could see. It had no identifiable marks either, although around the middle of the 'body' section was a red rotating band.

The UFO was not sitting on the ground, but in the air at about the same height as a fence which separated the nearby housing estate from the wood. The estate, in fact, in which both girls lived. It should be borne in mind, however, that the witnesses were, by their own judgement, around 400 yards away and it is possible that the disc was standing on thin legs or some other supports which were hidden by trees or bushes in their line of sight.

It was at this point that the girls caught sight of a strange figure. It was dressed in silver, around six feet tall with short arms. The entity was standing close to the UFO, but they couldn't be sure if it was carrying out any activity, such as collecting objects, for example. The girls were disturbed by what they had seen, and when the figure seemed to move in their direction, they turned and ran. It soon became apparent after they had covered a short distance that they weren't being followed, so they stopped to look back. As they did so, the UFO moved in erratic motions to its left, before starting skywards at a tremendous speed. With that the girls returned home.

Mrs Maclennan took the girls' account seriously because she had herself been aware of the strange sounds, as had several of her neighbours. The police were informed, but didn't seem able to shed any light on the matter. The children were understandably reluctant to revisit the site, but the following day they plucked up the courage to go with Mrs Maclennan and take a look.

Around the spot where the UFO had been seen was an area about 100 yards across in which a large number of trees had apparently sustained minor damage, including scorch marks on the leaves. Grass had also been flattened. It is not known whether this part of the wood was compared to others, as trees suffer from all kinds of 'predators' from squirrels to high winds. The 'damage' may have been more apparent than real and simply coincidental. 'Scorching' on leaves, for example, may be confused with other natural effects. Soil samples were taken some months after the event, but the results of the analysis, if it was done, seem to have long since disappeared. It is doubtful whether they revealed anything of much consequence, as it's a safe bet that widespread publicity would have resulted from the discovery of significant anomalies. Bryan Hartly, who investigated the case at the time, was convinced of the sincerity of the witnesses and that they were being truthful about what they had seen. Several witnesses later came forward to claim they had observed a similar craft emitting a beam of light around the time of the girls' sighting.

Although Mrs Maclennan recently confirmed to me the substance of the report, the girls, now adults, had no wish to discuss the incident. I can understand their reluctance to come forward and reopen discussion on such a controversial incident. But even though more than twenty years have passed since these events took place, it would be fascinating to have their views of the incident from an adult perspective. If extraterrestrials are indeed visiting our planet then anything which can shed light on the phenomenon is to be welcomed, no matter how much time has elapsed since the actual events. Those who have encountered strange entities are vital witnesses, as very few of us will be given such an opportunity.

A STRANGE VISITATION
THE DUNDEE TRIANGLE

There doesn't seem to be any special reason why UFO sightings cluster at certain areas. I have no answer as to why the 'Dundee Triangle' should have risen to prominence in recent years. But for some strange reason people in the area around the River Tay and its tributaries have been witnessing UFO incidents in increasing numbers.

GLAMIS CASTLE SIGHTINGS

Or is it just that these encounters have recently come to the attention of a wider audience? As far back as July 1967 UFOs were being reported in the area. Two fifteen-year-old boys, Andrew Lawson and Methven Forbes, were in the vicinity of Glamis Castle when they caught sight of a round grey object hovering over a wood. The UFO moved towards them, before rising into the clouds to disappear.

It was never identified and the strange objects kept returning. Less than a month later, on 2 August, there were at least thirty witnesses to an 'oval-shaped UFO, light in colour' over the town of Arbroath. Was it coincidence that at the same time 'a large part of the town was blacked out by electricity failure'. Robin Forrester (16) was cycling in Lochlands Drive when he spotted the object. He estimated its size at between twenty and thirty feet. It was moving towards the ground and at one point was less than a hundred feet above him. He described how it travelled 'fairly slowly over the houses . . . there was a constant red glow from the domed upper part . . . this started to flash in and out'. The UFO followed a flight path towards the sea. A plane? Robin was sure it wasn't. 'It was quieter than a glider', he noted, 'and the eeriness was added to by the fact that this part of the town was in almost total darkness due to the electricity failure'. Another witness to the strange sighting was Mrs Grace Laurie. 'It was a constant red light', she explained, 'which came from the north. The object came down fairly low, but once it passed us it seemed to increase its speed and zoomed away'. She too noted its silent passage.

The police thought the UFO near Glamis Castle was 'probably a weather balloon', while the Electricity Board claimed that the power failure was the result of 'boys throwing pieces of piping against high-tension wires'.

But there are some incidents which defy any 'rational' explanation. The village of Blairgowrie is the unlikely location of some of Scotland's most bizarre UFO encounters.

BLAIRGOWRIE—THE FREEMAN CASE

Situated on the banks of the River Tay, during the summer months, Blairgowrie's scenic hillsides attract visitors from all parts of Britain, unaware of the strange events that have periodically shattered the quiet harmony of the countryside and the lives of the local people.

Take Sid Freeman. Sid is a talented craftsman and artist who built up a considerable reputation in restoring antique furniture. It's a down-to-earth occupation, and one that could hardly prepare him for the strange encounter that was to significantly change his family's entire life.

At 5.30 p.m. on 25 April 1984, Mrs Gwen Freeman, Sid's mother, was sitting in the sun lounger in the back garden of their bungalow in Riverside Road, Blairgowrie, weaving a tapestry. Sid, meanwhile, was at the front, working diligently to clear a flowerbed of weeds. Suddenly Gwen noticed the family dog cowering, and stared in amazement as it ran into the kitchen, its tail tucked between its legs.

Seconds later her attention was caught by a strange cloud of light (as she described it) which enveloped and then, for a split second, actually blinded her. A sensation of warmth spread over her body, centred on the abdomen. Then, directly in front, less than five feet from the lounger, a forsythia bush began shimmering with sparkling lights. Pulling herself to her feet, Mrs Freeman stood enraptured by this beautiful sight.

Her attention was caught next by a beam of light which flowed upwards from the bush, travelled between two fir trees and passed over the roof of the garden shed. Gwen followed the beam skywards where it led to a silvery shape, hovering so low down that it appeared to be over a neighbour's house. Stepping to the side she was able to catch a fuller view of the object, realising as she did so that she was confronting a truly awesome phenomenon. It looked like a 'spaceship' of bizarre design. Gwen later described it as a large, bulbous-shaped object with a long tail. Beneath the tail section, a light illuminated five V-shaped projections with the tips pointing downwards. As she observed this, the front of the 'spaceship' lit up and she noticed that a lip or flange surrounded the circular area. Suddenly the port lights were extinguished and the whole object began to rock from front to back.

The shock of witnessing this hovering craft had driven all other thoughts from Gwen's mind, but now she instinctively shouted to Sid: 'You'll never guess what I'm looking at! Come quickly before it goes'.

Anxious to find out what had caused so much excitement, Sid immediately hurried to the fence that separated the front and back gardens. To his regret, he paused for a split second before following Gwen's finger, pointing skywards. The object was rapidly diminishing in size and intensity. A bright flash followed, and the UFO was gone.

At this point Gwen's husband, Sid senior, arrived on the scene. He had not witnessed the encounter, as he had been gardening directly in front of the bungalow, out of sight of both Gwen and the hovering object. From where he knelt the 'spaceship' was hidden from view by a cluster of trees. Sid, however, was intrigued by the incident and together the family attempted to estimate the size of the object Gwen and her son had seen. They judged it to be around one hundred and fifty feet in length, floating about eighty feet above the ground.

Gwen told Sid that in shape it reminded her exactly of a Yale key.

Back indoors the family decided to call in the local police, and two officers quickly arrived. One remarked to his colleague, perhaps not intending Sid to hear, that the 'Yale key' sounded just like an object that had already been reported over an area stretching from Leuchars to Blairgowrie. The officers then moved outside and thoroughly searched the garden, taking soil samples from the area where Mrs Freeman had been sitting, and collecting leaves from the forsythia bush. After about two hours, the policemen left, telling the family that they would keep them informed of the outcome of the investigation. In fact, from that day to this the Freemans have not heard one more word from the police. Why, it may be asked, the secrecy? Attempts in the early 1990s by UFO investigator Ken Higgins to locate police reports met with no success. No-one at the police station claimed to remember the incident, and Ken was informed that any documents relating to it would have been transferred and probably destroyed.

But the family's strange encounter was to be only the start of a sequence of unexplained events. One morning Sid and Gwen heard an unusual rumbling above the house. The noise grew louder until it became deafening, and the whole bungalow seemed to vibrate. Looking from the back door, they were shocked to see a large military helicopter hovering some forty feet above the house. Underneath it were slung two box-like devices, one black and the other orange. They were hanging so close to the roof that Gwen could see a small red light on one of the boxes. It seemed that the crew were filming the area around the Freeman home. From the way the helicopter was moving they gained the impression that it was also testing the air. In the light of the family's recent encounter, if it was a coincidence, it seemed a remarkable one indeed.

Sid phoned the nearest RAF station, Leuchars, to find out just what was going on. After some initial difficulty, he was informed that the helicopter was simply 'on manoeuvres', and that there was nothing for the family to worry about. Two days later, however, they were startled by the reappearance of the helicopter and were struck by the fact that it repeated the earlier tests. Significantly, the RAF had not chosen Blairgowrie previously to carry out exercises, nor have they found it a suitable spot since.

But was this a cover up by the military? Or another example of 'phantom helicopter' appearances? It has the hallmarks of the latter albeit with some variations. Despite the RAF's admission, it is interesting to note that helicopter appearances have been a feature of a number of cases. In 1978, for example, a Kent housewife, Mrs Clark, was stunned to discover that while she had been busily working in a garden, a helicopter had descended from the skies to hover just a few feet over her head. Startled, she glanced up and saw two men in the cockpit, one of them was looking directly at her. Coming to her senses, Mrs Clark made a bee line for her house. When she looked again the helicopter had vanished. Later she realised that the incident had been even stranger than she had first thought. The helicopter had made no noise, in contrast to its usual deafening activity. On top of that it had carried no markings or landing gear. Furthermore, the cockpit glass seemed to be a simple globe rather than the standard design. Yet if this was a 'UFO type' incident it seems a peculiar one.

If we compare it to the Freeman's helicopter, then we should note straight away that their description was of a very noisy approach. Nevertheless, it may be that, as in the Clark case, the UFO and helicopter incidents were more closely linked than we can imagine.

When I visited Sid in the summer of 1991, the events of those days were very clear in his mind. As I listened in quiet fascination, it seemed impossible that Sid could surprise me with any further revelations. I was wrong, however. For the first time, Sid told me of an event the very morning of Gwen Freeman's sighting which, because of its strange nature, convinced me that it could not be 'invented'.

Some time before midday on April 25, Mrs Freeman called her son to the window. Both watched in silent wonder as a group of strangely dressed males walked quietly up the deserted street. The sight was remarkable: some twelve men and children, all dressed in black Yiddish attire, wearing hats of the same colour and several with pigtails stretching down their backs.

An unusual scene for a Blairgowrie resident to witness! Sid's curiosity, however, turned to anxiety when the group of strangers walked up the path of a neighbour's house, then disappeared inside without even bothering to ring the doorbell. Gwen was struck by one other odd fact. The mysterious men in black had kept moving in deliberate single file, a regular space between each one, from the moment they had caught her attention to the time they entered the next-door bungalow. Even more unnerving was the fact that not one word was uttered by the men in black during all this time.

Gwen and Sid were now in a quandary. They had no wish

to be nosey, but as good friends of the woman next door they were concerned for her safety. Just as they had made up their minds to go and investigate, the same black-coated figures came out of the front door, still in single file, and walked back the way they had come. Sid noticed that once again not one of these mysterious figures exchanged so much as a word with his colleague. Convinced that something odd had taken place, Sid and Gwen decided to make sure that nothing had happened to harm their friend.

They rang the doorbell, then waited anxiously. The door was soon opened by their friend, who seeing their worried faces asked what the matter was! Taken aback, Sid explained why he and Gwen had called round, describing the strange figures they had seen on her garden path. Visibly stunned for a second or two, a smile then creased her lips, as if to say: 'Is this April Fool's Day?' It was clear as far as she was concerned that no-one, and certainly not mysterious men in black, had entered her house either that or any other day. Grasping this, the Freemans were in turn staggered, embarrassed and worried. Muttering apologies, Sid and Gwen hurried home.

Of course, accounts of mysterious 'men in black' or MIBs will be familiar to anyone who has the slightest knowledge of the subject of UFOs. In *Fact or Fantasy*, Hilary Evans discussed several such cases. Typical is that of September 1976 involving Dr Herbert Hopkins of Maine, USA, who was acting as a consultant in an alleged UFO case. He was telephoned by a man claiming to be a UFO investigator, who shortly afterwards arrived at his door dressed in a black scarf, black tie and black shoes, wearing a hat of identical colour. The visitor behaved in such a strange way that Hopkins 'was very much shaken' by the incident. The implication of this MIB encounter was that the mysterious caller was not of this world. Although in this case no car was in evidence, a black Cadillac has traditionally been linked to this type of incident. The Freeman case has similarities to Dr Hopkins' tale—a UFO event associated with the appearance of odd individuals in black—but it seems clear that in Blairgowrie we have a different type of encounter. MIBs are usually described as relatively contemporary in dress and seeking out information from the witnesses themselves. What the Freemans saw comes across as being more of a religious or psychic experience. Or even a combination of the two. It does often seem to be the case that aspects of the UFO enigma take on (despite our best efforts to ignore them) spiritual aspects. Furthermore, the men in black were seen before the UFO incident rather than after it. Had they in some strange way made a mistake about the time of the UFO sighting? Were they supposed to link up with the hovering UFO? Admittedly, it is all speculation, but it is even harder to believe that the timing of these two incidents was the product of pure chance.

Over the next week or so the family did their best to push that strange incident to the back of their minds. They wanted to forget it. But fate, it seemed, had determined otherwise.

One evening the doorbell rang. Mrs Freeman turned down the volume on the television and went to answer the door. On the porch she discovered two strangers, a man and woman dressed in old-fashioned, 1920s style clothing. His was a dark pin-striped suit, reminiscent of the gangster era, with a hat to match. She hid inside a long, flowing coat, and Gwen was struck by her headdress which would have done service as a bowl of fruit! Yet at the time Gwen did not find the two strangers the slightest bit funny. A dark air hung about them.

The couple spoke to her in English, but sounded as if they had each 'swallowed a Bible'. They told Gwen that she must not speak more of what she had seen 'otherwise a great evil would befall' her. Other threats followed in quick succession. Alarmed by what was being said, Sid and his father hurried to the door and ordered the unwanted visitors to leave. They swung round to face each other and, without expression or exchanging words, walked down the path, turned and headed towards the village. They never returned and were not reported elsewhere in Blairgowrie on that or any other day. Was it a message devised by the authorities to keep them quiet? Or simply a pair of cranks? Sid asked himself. The alternatives seemed too bizarre to contemplate.

Sid, of course, was not a UFO buff and so was not familiar with similar incidents. The daughter-in-law of Dr Hopkins (whose encounter was mentioned earlier) was rung by a couple who asked to meet them. When they arrived, the first thing she noticed was their strangely *old-fashioned clothes*. Their conversation and manner of speech did not seem normal— and when they left, they both walked in a *perfectly straight line*. This incident does chime with that of the Freemans, but slightly out of tune. There are clear similarities—an odd couple, dressed in unfashionable clothes—but also differences. Are we dealing here with psychic rather than 'real' incidents?

A few days later, Gwen, on her way to the town centre to shop, bumped into Alison, one of her friends. For no obvious reason she could account for, an overwhelming compulsion to grasp and massage her friend's hands took control of her. She felt powerless to resist this unspoken order. Alison was clearly surprised by Gwen's gesture, but it was Gwen who, after a few seconds, broke contact as her normal shyness reasserted itself, her face colouring with embarrassment. She let go the hands with a few muttered words of apology. Both women were aware of an uneasy feeling as they parted.

Later Gwen wondered what her friend would think of her, and experienced a few qualms when Alison arrived at her door. Alison excitedly showed Gwen her hands. It turned out that she had suffered from arthritic fingers for several years. The stiffness had grown so pronounced that it was hard for her to hold any size of object. The attacks were painful, and doctors were unable to offer much in the way of relief. Overnight, however, the pain and stiffness had gone. The 'miracle' had baffled the doctors, but they were forced to confirm the improvement. Alison felt sure that it was all down to Gwen's magic touch.

Gwen was relieved and delighted by Alison's news. Yet somehow it did not surprise her. It was almost as if she had known it was about to happen. The conviction grew inside her that the UFO incident, disturbing as it was, had left her with some form of healing ability.

It is difficult to estimate how often such encounters are followed by the development of this power to help others. In *Without Consent*, Carl Nagaitis and Phillip Mantle describe in detail the case of Elsie Oakensen, who experienced a strange encounter which may have led to an alien abduction incident. In connection with the Freeman case, however, the interesting aspect is that Elsie became a healer, which she believes was as a direct result of her UFO encounter. This ability was of such significance that Elsie, in fact, became a member of the National Federation of Spiritual Healers. Similarly to Gwen Freeman, Elsie Oakensen viewed her encounter as having a strong spiritual element. (The interaction between the spiritual, or religious, aspects of UFO incidents and the 'alien' nature of the entities involved forms a recurring theme in a significant number of witness accounts.) It is surely not a coincidence that in both Gwen's and Elsie's cases a white beam of light played a significant part in the experience. Elsie consciously recalls 'a brilliant circle of pure white light' appearing close by the sides, rear and front of her car. Under hypnosis she said: 'A brilliant white light is shining in my eyes . . .' The light seemed to suffuse her whole body. Of course, there are aspects of the encounter which distinguish it from Gwen Freeman's. Gwen, apparently, did not undergo an abduction experience. Still, as so often happens, the similarities between cases tantalise the mind without offering any solution to the UFO enigma.

Gwen herself had enjoyed good health, as Sid himself described to me during my visit to the bungalow. A few weeks before the sighting she had gone through a medical check, including a cardiograph, prior to a minor operation. Everything was normal. Sid, however, took the view that soon after these April events, his mother's health began to deteriorate. It was a gradual process spread over some months. In April 1987 Gwen Freeman developed a sudden illness and in November died of a heart attack. Sid senior is convinced that his wife's encounter led directly, in some uncertain yet tragic way, to her early death.

One of the paradoxes of this case is that the UFO incident

was witnessed by Gwen rather than Sid junior, when it might have been expected that the opposite would have been the case. There is no doubt that Sid is psychic, evidenced by the fact that he had experienced strange phenomena from an early age. On the other hand, it is noticeable that Gwen, prior to 1984, had not been an obvious channel for any paranormal phenomenon. When Sid was hospitalised at seven years old with a kidney disorder, he felt compelled one day to get out of bed and look out of the window. He immediately became aware of a blinding light and, as if in a trance, stared into the heart of the glowing object. According to Sid, in spite of having suffered badly through illness, his health immediately improved and he was 'miraculously' cured.

It is noticeable that a bright light appears in Sid's and Gwen's encounters, although with opposite effect. Sid's poor health is improved, a direct beneficial effect on him, whereas Gwen Freeman is given the ability to help others, with possibly adverse results for her own well-being.

Sid experienced at least one more strange incident after the UFO encounter. One evening he watched a flaming ball of fire hurtle over the night sky, coming from a northerly direction. Sid described it to me as being as 'big as five houses' and followed its path with awe as it headed at tremendous speed for the nearby Sidlaw Hills. He felt sure, given its trajectory, that it must crash into one or other of the summits, as it definitely seemed to be heading towards solid ground. He waited for signs of the expected impact, but nothing happened. After some minutes, he guessed that the object had been travelling much higher than he had thought.

This event took place in early 1990 and, unless there was a

particular piece of space debris crash landing at that time, Sid must have gone through some kind of psychic vision. Anything as large as Sid claimed to have seen would surely have made newspaper headlines, but we can find no report that fits Sid's description.

Sid looks every inch the sensitive artist: tall, thin, a quiet air, but occasionally revealing a hidden intensity. You might expect him to experience psychic phenomena even if you didn't know that he had. And though anyone can possess psychic ability, Mrs Freeman, from her photos a pleasant, comfortable-looking woman, looks the opposite of the traditional view of a medium. Even so, it seems more than likely that Sid inherited his ability from his mother, but hers lay dormant until that fateful day when a strange encounter brought it into action.

OTHER BLAIRGOWRIE INCIDENTS

Of course, it would be understandable if at this juncture those who have never met Sid would have doubts about the reality of the incidents he was involved in, particularly with regard to his own account of the flaming ball. It should be remembered, however, that the whole family were involved in these events and as to Sid's sighting, incredibly there were a host of bizarre events which lend support to his UFO encounter. In fact, it seems that the village of Blairgowrie has been a source of strange encounters for over two hundred years. The first bizarre incident is reported in the *Annual Register* of 1767. The phenomenon started on the River Isla near Coupar Angus, a few miles south of Blairgowrie. At first 'a thick, dark smoke' rose towards the sky then dispersed to reveal 'a large luminous body like a house on fire'. The UFO then changed shape and became a pyramid. It now started to move over land with tremendous speed and covered several miles till it hit the flowing waters of the River Ericht. For some reason, at this point the UFO appears to have been deflected along the course of the river and followed it through Blairgowrie. The report doesn't state definitely how the object disappeared, saying only that it 'rushed up this river with great speed and disappeared a little above Blairgowrie'. However, the effect of its passage through the countryside was devastating. It 'carried away a large cart', threw it over a field and knocked a rider from his horse. 'It destroyed half a house, but left the other half behind', leaving an almost clean cut, and 'destroyed an arch of a new bridge at Blairgowrie'. Clearly, some incredible force had been unleashed. One that defies definition. Was it an alien spacecraft that had lost control? A natural phenomenon of an unknown kind . . . ? At this late date a solution isn't possible, but it is certainly evidence that this area is a source of strange incidents which deserve further study.

On its own, the Freeman encounters entitle Blairgowrie to be considered a UFO hot-spot ('UFO Capital of Scotland', as the *Scottish Sunday Mail* headlined it in its 19 January 1991 issue). There is certainly something odd occurring in this small area of the country: crop circles; balls of light; cattle mutilations; and UFOs. All making an appearance within much less than a square mile.

To show the odd way coincidence works, my attention was first drawn to Blairgowrie not by a UFO, but by Scotland's first confirmed crop circle. This had appeared in June 1990 on the very fringe of the town in a field of grass bordering the A923 and owned by the Ardblair estate. Unfortunately, the appearance of this phenomenon only came to my attention in late July, and by the time I journeyed to inspect it the owner, Laurence Oliphant, had already harvested the field.

There were, as it turned out, two circles. With the assistance of paranormal investigator Malcolm Robinson, and using dowsing techniques, we were able to locate the position of the circles and take measurements. At this late stage it was not possible, of course, to be exact. For the record, however, this is what we found: the upper circle was 71 feet in diameter, but the lower circle was only half that size at 36 feet across. Both circles had been formed at the west edge of the field beside a thick clump of trees which overhung the edge of a disused quarry. The field itself covered almost the full slope of the hill on which it stood. The formation we went to investigate had been created about one third of the way up. Avoiding the grazing sheep, I tested the site with dowsing rods and was surprised by the powerful response which set the metal sticks juddering in my fists. The existence of an unknown, yet 'natural', energy source might be a clue to explain the circle phenomenon. UFO investigator Ken Higgins, however, with whom I later visited the site, remained doubtful and wanted to know how the two were connected. All I could do was to point out that the area surrounding the two circles was criss-crossed by lines of 'energy' which ran in both south/north and east/west directions. There was something strange in this field, even if for the moment I couldn't explain it.

I was not, of course, trying to connect the Freemans' UFO sighting with the two circles as several years separated these events. However, it is not perhaps without significance that one of the few crop circles in Scotland should occur near a town with one of the strangest UFO encounters ever recorded.

Interestingly, it has been alleged that cattle died in mysterious circumstances in the same field close to the time that the crop circles were formed. According to our informant (who does not wish to be identified) the necks of cattle loose in the field were found broken, with no explanation of how this could have occurred. We have been unable to confirm that this incident took place.

Returning with Ken Higgins to the A923 at the point where it exited Blairgowrie and bordered the crop circle field, we drove on to Ardblair castle to meet Laurence Oliphant, the owner of the land. Mr Oliphant showed us where a spectacular ley transected his ancestral home, confirming our view that the whole area was one tremendous mystery. But could it explain the UFO sightings?

In fact, at this stage I had no idea that any significant UFO sightings had occurred in Blairgowrie. While Ken and I were speaking over the phone some months earlier, he mentioned something about a lady having seen a light in the sky in the village. It sounded interesting, although not particularly attention grabbing. We agreed to make an appointment to visit and it was left to Ken to make the arrangements. It turned out later that Ken had tried to agree a date for our visit, but for various reasons no date had proved suitable. As the weeks rolled by, the incident faded from memory as UFO reports of more recent sightings rolled in.

Now, admiring the towering walls of Ardblair Castle from its surrounding gardens, Blairgowrie's UFO encounters had completely disappeared from our minds. A comment made by one of the Oliphant family, however, started a little cog moving. It seemed that strange balls of light had been seen in the vicinity and their appearance coincided with the paths of energy lines—or leys—on the estate. I had dowsed one myself in the shadow of the castle. The little cog, however, took a while to turn. About a week later, on the way home from work, the faint recollection of past conversations began to gather strength. Reaching the drive, I fairly dived into the hall to grab the phone.

'Didn't you tell me about a UFO incident in Blairgowrie?' I barked at an astonished Ken.

'Which one do you mean?' responded Ken, who appeared remarkably calm in response to my abrupt question.

It was my turn to be taken aback.

'You mean there were more than one?' I said in amazement.

As quickly as he could, Ken told me of various incidents he had uncovered during the past week. And how he had attempted to make contact with the Freeman family while driving through the area, but been unable to do so. In turn, I reminded Ken about the crop circles and strange lights. For a moment we fell silent. It was clear that we had uncovered a remarkable series of events in what appeared on the surface to be a rather unremarkable town. Spurred on by these surprising discoveries we uncovered through diligent investigation a whole series of UFO incidents spanning some thirty years.

In October 1957, at around seven in the morning, a nurse cycling over the Ericht Bridge observed a metal disc hovering over the road bordering the river. This was, in fact, Riverside Road, that same street into which the Freemans were later to move from England and experience their strange encounter. The nurse at the time claimed to have heard a soft humming and estimated the object to be thirty feet in diameter. It 'hung in the sky', as she described it, before disappearing in a northerly direction. Significantly, perhaps, she noted that as it moved it followed the course of the river. It may be coincidence, but it is nonetheless fact, that the flow of the Ericht through Blairgowrie follows a well known fault line. Was this of some strange interest to the UFO?

Exactly two months to the day after the Freemans' encounter, another UFO was sighted over Blairgowrie. There were four witnesses to this event, including a mother and son. None of those who saw the phenomenon, however, wishes to have their identity revealed. The date was 25 June 1984. The time, 9.30 in the evening. The object appeared at first in the distance as a bright circle about the size of a tennis ball, and trailing a red tail. Every so often a beam of light flashed from its circumference. At the same time, although only visible through binoculars, a strange V-shaped object was seen to leave and then return to the 'tennis ball'. This manoeuvre was repeated several times. After a while both objects seemed to disappear into the sky.

The witnesses were so intrigued by the experience that they met up with the Freemans to compare notes. Both families had been left nonplussed by their mysterious encounters and were desperate to find a solution to these strange events. A solution, however, was not readily to hand.

Having observed Blairgowrie from a distance, it seems that the UFO decided the time had arrived to take a closer look. A businessman on a skiing holiday claimed that he and his wife were followed by a disc-shaped object for four miles along the Glenshee road, just to the north of Blairgowrie. As the couple drew near to some houses, the UFO, still glistening brightly, shot skywards and disappeared at tremendous speed. It was as if it did not like being observed and had made a fast exit before the holidaymakers had time to draw others' attention to it.

Over the following months, Blairgowrie continued to be plagued by weird phenomena. One mile to the west of the town lies the freshwater Loch of Rae. Several residents, who do not wish to be named, reported to Ken Higgins that they had witnessed yellow and white lights moving erratically across the surface of the loch on a number of separate occasions. Local lore has it that sightings of strange glowing objects have been noted since at least the 1960s and, it might be suspected, for a good while before then.

Earth mystery investigators have pointed out that the local countryside is rich in ancient artifacts. Standing stones, neolithic monuments and Pictish carvings testify to a long history of habitation. The area was strangely attractive to prehistoric man, who responded by decorating the land with these enigmatic messages to posterity. The enigma continues today with sightings of UFOs which appear to find the area as attractive as did our forebears.

DUNDEE SIGHTINGS

The 'Dundee Triangle' may have a long history, but what of the city which has lent its name to this UFO 'hot-spot'? Analysis of the reports of strange objects in the sky strongly suggests that Dundee may be the focus for sightings.

In February 1996 three schoolfriends were taking a short cut through Orchard Park, Broughty Ferry. All of a sudden, the early evening gloom was transformed into day by an intense light. Twelve-year-old Cameron Steuart, Joanne Leach and Graham Birnie looked skywards and were startled to see a bun-shaped object with a row of flashing lights around the middle. From the underside of the craft shone the beam of light which had so abruptly floodlit the area. The school chums watched frozen as the craft hovered above them, then as if at a signal all ran together out of the park and towards the main street. As they looked back from comparative safety, they saw the UFO float upwards, then fly over their heads and disappear. The young witnesses arrived home in a state of fright at around 7.30 p.m. Drawings made by each of them showed a very similar craft (see Fig 10).

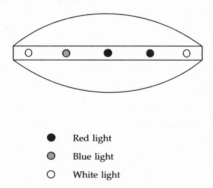

●   Red light
◉   Blue light
○   White light

Fig 10. The UFO seen by three schoolchildren at Broughty Ferry in February 1996.

A similarly fascinating encounter took place in Dundee on 24 July 1993. David Anthony from Edinburgh was staying with relatives in the Menzieshill housing estate situated in west Dundee. At 10.30 p.m., a time noted from a television programme he was watching, David, sitting in an upstairs bedroom, caught sight of a bright light in the sky. He thought at first it must be an aircraft heading for the local airport at Dundee, but quickly realised he was watching no ordinary phenomenon. The light he saw glowed with a strange intensity, and appeared to be moving slowly south, away from and not towards Dundee. The spherical ball of light was low down, perhaps as low as 100 feet above the ground, but began to climb after a time. Mr Anthony could follow the UFO's progress, as from his vantage point he could see a distance of about 20 miles or more. Eventually, after he had watched the object for several minutes, it began to lose its blinding white glow and became hazy. Then, suddenly, the single light split into two, then again into two groups of three or four lights, all blazing white.

When Mr Anthony made some inquiries the following day, he discovered that the airport at Dundee had closed at 8.30 p.m., so he could exclude the possibility of a plane either landing or taking off from there. But what about military craft? The Ministry of Defence refused either to confirm or deny the presence of military aircraft in the area. From Kerry Philpott at 'Secretarial (Air Staff) 2A', he received a standard disclaimer that the MoD only looks at 'reports of unexplained aerial phenomena in order to establish whether what was seen is of defence significance. . . . In this particular instance we are not aware of any evidence which would indicate that a breach of the UK's air defences has occurred but have noted your report for our records'.

Mr Anthony was not satisfied by their response, which took

him no further down the road to solving the mystery of his sighting, and replied to the MoD that he was only trying to find out whether there were any military aircraft actually in the area at the time. The second response he received was more blunt: 'details of flight paths for aircraft operating out of RAF Leuchars in July 1993 are no longer available. I am afraid therefore that it is not possible to answer your question'.

RAF LEUCHARS

In early January 1997, Ryan Milligan was travelling to Forfar from his Glasgow home when he caught sight of a distinctively shaped object in the sky. He told me, 'I asked my friend who was driving to pull over, about 15 miles from Dundee. We all got out of the car at a lay-by and studied the object in the clear sky and [hovering] in the general direction of RAF Leuchars Air Force Base. We stood and watched it for a good half hour giving an erratic and spectacular aerobatics display in the sky'.

The drawing Mr Milligan provided (Fig 11) does indicate a very peculiar arrangement of lights in the sky which doesn't have any obvious coherence.

He also explained that 'this object would sit stationary for about 30 seconds, the lights would suddenly disappear, then vanish and reappear'. Was it a vast craft in the sky? Or light reflections from a ground source? The latter seems unlikely, but not impossible. All in all, it does seem an odd incident.

But when we talk of 'triangles' as concentrated areas of sightings, let's not forget how difficult it is to define geographical boundaries. Does a sighting of June 1997 link with

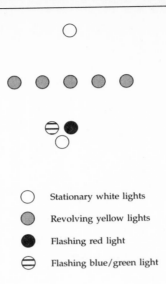

Stationary white lights

Revolving yellow lights

Flashing red light

Flashing blue/green light

Fig 11. The strange arrangement of lights seen by Ryan Milligan over RAF Leuchars in January 1997

the Dundee triangle, or with the Fife-based incidents? A silver disc was spotted by a man out walking his dog in the early hours of 18 June close to Norman's Law (or hill) which overlooks the Tay. The witness was sure that what he had seen was not a civilian plane and that a second object appeared to be hovering above the disc-shaped UFO. But might it have been misidentified military traffic? RAF Leuchars denied that there were any of their or any other planes crossing the area at that time.

But why, then, did a second witness, from her home a few miles east in St Andrews, report an almost identical sighting? She claimed that she had seen 'two silvery objects with no obvious front or back. I watched them for a few minutes flying one above the other. One shot up into the clouds whilst the other kept going dead straight'. They disappeared in a north-westerly direction, straight into the Dundee Triangle. If planes were not involved then is the only answer that the witnesses saw an alien spaceship? Or were the RAF being 'economical with the truth'?

PERTH CLOSE ENCOUNTER

In 1985 in Perth a nurse, Angela Humphreys, was enveloped by a sudden silence while walking across the road bridge which spans the Tay. It was as if the space round about her had suddenly been blocked from the normal sounds of the world. This strange phenomenon is well known to UFO researchers (and, as mentioned earlier, labelled the 'oz factor' by top investigator Jenny Randles). As she became accustomed to this strange experience, Angela slowly became aware of a presence hovering only a few yards in front of her. It was a translucent object about thirty to forty feet long, its shape broken by what seemed to be a window, although more like a viewing deck than a porthole.

Through the window Angela could make out several small entities. One of these creatures placed its hands over a number of levers which it seemed to be using to manoeuvre the craft around and above the bridge. After a short time, seconds only perhaps, the object moved away and vanished. Although it seemed to have lasted hardly any time at all, the encounter left a vivid impression on Angela's mind. She had no difficulty in recalling the UFO's circular shape, as it appeared from where she watched, ending in a thin, streamlined tail at the rear. Angela was completely unaware of the Freeman sighting. All the more remarkable, then, that her description should correspond so closely with that of the Blairgowrie UFO.

When Angela 'came to' she was shocked to realise that pedestrians passing within feet of her had not witnessed the incident which was so real to her. Incredibly, in broad daylight, on a busy thoroughfare, she had been the sole observer of what to all intents and purposes seemed like an extraterrestrial spacecraft. Angela called out to a passing cyclist, for the 'craft' had reappeared just a few yards away! It was moving, but only slowly, making no sound as it crawled stealthily beside the river. Questions rushed through Angela's mind. Was it trying to contact her? Was it searching for something? Trying to abduct someone? Looking for somewhere to land? Angela felt no fear, only an overwhelming desire to learn more about what these unusual visitors were up to. Unfortunately, time was fast running out for Angela. Once again the object's slow movements were taking it gradually out of her sight. Then it was gone; this time for good.

At the moment the UFO disappeared all the normal sounds came flooding back in an overwhelming burst of conscious-ness—the roaring of passing cars, thud of feet on pavements and chatter of fellow pedestrians. Angela's world returned to normal, or as close as was possible after such an experience. But as Angela freely admits, her life could never be the same again. Angela has been on the receiving end of several strange experiences since that encounter. No longer in the Perth area, she went through a bizarre incident involving humanoid entities on a train journey over the Forth Rail Bridge. These entities claimed that they lived under the very Forth Estuary over which they were travelling. The nature of Angela's experience points to some type of psychic awareness having been activated.

REPEATER ABDUCTEE

Karen's encounters, however, may point in a different direction. These had their origin in 1976, almost a decade before Angela's encounter in Perth. And unlike Angela, Karen was many miles away from the city when she stumbled across a bizarre sight. Karen was ten years old at the time, living with her family in a farm cottage close to the village of Meigle—the centre of the 'mysterious north', with its vast collection of standing stones and their still-undeciphered script. If there is one area in Scotland where you might anticipate a strange encounter, it is surely the countryside lying between the River Island and the Loch of Lintrathen. Beautiful, remote, isolated. To a child, however, the land about is simply home, a place to run and play in. So it was for Karen. In the summer of 1976, Karen was recovering from mumps and stayed in the cottage while her brothers and sisters went out fruit-picking, a traditional occupation in the area at this season of the year. She had decided instead to go to a nearby wood, taking a picnic with her. She set off from the old farm cottage at around 9.45 a.m. and arrived at the wood half an hour later, just after ten o'clock. During the walk to the wood she watched a bright rainbow-coloured light in the sky, although any connection with what was shortly to take place is unproven.

Having entered the wood, Karen walked down familiar

paths until she came to a clearing well known to her. Later, much later, as she thought back on the events of the day, she remembered that she had been struck by a strange silence that enveloped her as she made her journey. All bird and animal noises had stopped. The only sound that echoed through the wood came from the dry leaves crunching beneath her feet.

Now even that had been muffled into silence. But it was not out of choice that she remained at this spot. Karen admits that she would have turned and run if she had been given the opportunity. Unfortunately, she didn't have the option. Ahead of her, staring at her, were a group of little figures, four in all, and she, confronted by this strange group, was unable to move. She was, she says, 'frozen to the spot'.

The entities started to come towards her and as they did so she could see that not only their eyes but, more remarkably, their skin was coloured blue. They were small, smaller even than 10-year-old Karen, probably not even reaching her shoulder.

And then she felt hands touching her, cold and slimy. An enormous light appeared from nowhere and the next thing that Karen can picture is lying on a big circular table which had the appearance of hard metal, but felt soft around her, almost as if it had been moulded to the contours of her body. Entities surrounded her, reassuring her everything was all right. Not a word, though, was spoken. It all happened through thoughts that came into her mind. These beings looked human, but she also caught sight of taller entities whose bodies were incredibly thin, like stick insects. She believes that the small entities she first encountered may have been working for these taller aliens.

The place she was in was dark, but she remembers a light shining from somewhere. Drops were put into her eyes which paralysed them for a while. Clearly some form of examination was underway as Karen recalls a 'contraption like a machine' covering her from head to toe and going into her mouth. It may have examined her nostrils as well.

Eventually, Karen was returned to the spot where her mysterious journey had begun. Dazed and shaken, she headed for home. When she walked in, she received another shock. She was sure she had been in the woods only a short while. It couldn't be later than lunch time. In fact it was 6 p.m., way past the usual time for her evening meal. It had been over eight hours since she had waved goodbye and set off with her picnic. Her frantic parents had been on the point of calling the police.

For the next two years, Karen avoided the woods. But in 1978 she experienced a second encounter. The night before the incident Karen had a vivid dream in which she went back to the scene of the first incident and found the small figures waiting for her. It seems that the dream somehow propelled her back into her old haunts. She returned to the picnic site and was once again 'taken up' by the strange entities. She could feel their little hands touching her legs, lifting her as if she was being guided somewhere. She remembers lying on a table and experiencing an agonizing pain centred on her forehead.

Back home she suffered a headache and a high fever and was violently sick during the night. A doctor visited and she remembers him saying that her glands were inflamed.

Once again Karen may have suffered a period of 'missing time'. She left home around midday and returned around four o'clock. Not, perhaps, an unusual length of time for a child to be out playing, but Karen feels that the incident she experienced could not possibly have filled that four-hour gap. What happened during that period? Karen as much as anyone would like the answer.

Until recently, she made no attempt to find one and buried the experience deep within the recesses of her memory. She told no-one of her encounters. Her parents and brothers and sisters were wholly unaware of the incidents. For almost twenty years Karen said nothing. By 1995 she had moved to a large city and had a small child. Memories of her encounter began to surface in her dreams, with the worrying feeling that these entities might have a particular interest in her daughter. It has become accepted by some ufologists, particularly in the United States, that aliens are impregnating female abductees to produce a mixed race of beings. While Karen never claimed that her daughter might be a 'hybrid', she did feel a compulsion to return to the very spot in the wood where the entities had appeared to her. Karen even drove part of the way there before turning back.

Later, Karen did experience another 'missing time' incident. This time it occurred in her own home. She was doing some late studying in the back room of the flat, which doubled as her daughter's bedroom. She remembers seeing a bright light coming in through the window. In the light she recalls catching sight of a dog-faced entity. When she 'came to' an hour had passed. The coffee she had been drinking had gone cold. Karen had no conscious memory of being abducted, but naturally fears that such an event might have taken place.

What are we, as observers, to make of the strange dog-faced entity? What possible link could there be with unidentified flying objects? Or abduction cases? On the surface, it may seem that there is no link, that the vision experienced by Karen does not gel with her other encounters. However, I would suggest that is far from being true, and that this incident can be seen as central to the UFO phenomenon.

This is not a 'one off' incident. In 1997 a witness from Fife, who does not wish to be named, was lying in her bed when the head of a dog appeared. The face, which looked solid, floated in mid air directly in front of her wardrobe. For some reason its mouth was opening and closing although no sound seemed to be coming out. To my mind it's too similar to Karen's encounter to dismiss as pure coincidence.

The link I am going to make may seem far-fetched, but I would ask the reader to bear with me. The dog-faced entity was well known in ancient Egypt—known as the god Anubis. Certainly, Anubis was normally represented with the head of a jackal, and the body of a man, but in some instances he was sculpted with a dog's face. Anyway, at a glance a dog's head looks much like that of a jackal. I would suggest, therefore, that it was this being that Karen saw at the time.

But what is the relevance of Anubis to these recent experiences? How was this entity regarded by the ancient Egyptians? He was, for example, seen as the personification of the summer solstice, the protector of Osiris and the guardian to the dead in the underworld. All these aspects may have had some significance in his appearance to Karen, but if so then the connection is not at the time of writing an obvious one to me. I believe that the incident was a general indication to Karen of a link between ancient Egypt and a present day mystery—the wonder of UFOs. From recent research, some of which has reached the general public in bestsellers such as *Fingerprints of the Gods* and *The Orion Mystery*, it is clear that ancient Egypt was a much older civilisation than might be supposed and also possessed a deeper knowledge of the mysteries of the universe. And it is possible that one of these mysteries was contact with alien civilisations. Why Karen has been singled out for that experience, it is impossible to say, but as time passes the meaning of this experience for Karen herself may become clearer.

To anyone who might think that she is 'imagining' things, Karen can point to the discovery of a strange object in her gums, confirmed by X-ray. She has visited a specialist who has confirmed that an unidentifiable object, which looks hard and metallic, is located in her mouth. Karen was completely unaware of this object until it was noticed by her dentist. It caused her no discomfort and how it found its way there is a complete mystery. Medical investigation into the matter continues and it would be wrong to classify this as an 'alien implant' as there is no evidence which points in that direction, as yet.

It may be relevant to note that less than thirty miles from the area of Karen's encounters lies Aberfoyle, home to the Reverend Robert Kirk, the seventeenth century church minister who accepted entities from the 'other side' as a normal part of life. His favourite meeting place was at a spot now called the 'Fairy Knowe' (or hill), a mile or so from the present town. From his own experience and those he gathered from acquaintances, Kirk compiled a dossier of these beings from other worlds which he published under the title *The Secret Commonwealth* in 1692. The beings described by Kirk were very much part of the woods and hills of the time (and, of course, it was in such an environment that Karen experienced her encounter). These beings also seem to have some of the abilities we associate today with alien entities. They could, according to Kirk, make their bodies 'appear and disappear at pleasure' and 'enter houses' at will. They are like us in appearance, but can take on other shapes if they want to in order to confuse or impress humans. They had lights which shone from an object shaped like a lamp, but which needed no fuel. They had fires which burned continuously, but without wood or coal. This astonished Kirk, but it would not surprise us with our use of electricity and other power sources. These entities also possessed weapons which 'somewhat of the nature of a thunder-bolt subtly and mortally wound the vital parts without breaking the skin'.

But the comparison between Kirk's denizens and present day alien entities should not be drawn too closely. There are probably as many differences as similarities, but there does appear to be a connection of some kind, although as with so much in the world of ufology, the exact relationship appears intangible. However, the blue colour of the beings Karen confronted, a feature which makes a difficult story even harder to accept, was, in fact, a colour traditionally associated in Scotland with the 'other people' of the woods. Stranger still, in the context of Karen's later experience, is that the colour blue was also that of the clothes worn by the Pharaohs, rulers of ancient Egypt, a fact of which Karen was completely unaware until I informed her, and of which I was ignorant until I researched her strange mixture of experiences.

UFO BASES TO BONNYBRIDGE

FIFE AND THE BONNYBRIDGE TRIANGLE

It began as another visit to her brother's house, but ended in terror bordering on hysteria for Eleanor Harper. Eleanor, a telephonist in her 30s, made regular trips to see Brian whose house lies in isolated countryside off the A961 near Struthers in Fife, just a few miles from her own home in Methven. It's only a short drive there and back, so Eleanor would often drop by for a chat, as she did on the evening of 13 October 1997. However, it was now approaching 10.20 p.m. and Eleanor was keen to make the return journey. 'I know it was 10.20 when I set off because I asked my brother,' she explained, 'as I had been there for quite some time.'

She set off in her Audi along the A961, a winding country

road, heading for the B927 turn off. Eleanor, however, was familiar with the route. She drives her son to school on the A961 every day, and reckons she could normally manage the trip in under twenty minutes. There was no reason to expect that anything out of the ordinary might happen. The occasional car passed, going in the opposite direction, but there was no-one following behind, so, as Eleanor explains, 'I drove along the road at a steady fifty miles an hour'. A sensible speed for a road which hardly deserves its 'A' classification. Suddenly a bizarre, unexpected incident occurred. 'Just before I reached the woods past Montrave', Eleanor explains, 'a flash of light came across the bonnet and windscreen of my vehicle. The night was dark although the moon was very bright, but I knew it was not the moon as the light crossed at just above windscreen level.' Eleanor got such a fright that she swore out loud.

CHASED BY LIGHTS

She now felt understandably apprehensive. She'd caught a glimpse of something odd which it was hard to explain and, alone in her car on a quiet road with still a few miles to go to get home, she had no wish to confront the object again.

Eleanor now turned on to the B927 which would take her back to Methven via the town of Leven. It's a narrow road, but very straight at first with a pronounced dip. Suddenly, as if a switch had been flicked, four lights appeared in a row behind her. 'They were first at a distance but very bright. I knew it was not another vehicle of any kind. I became very frightened at this point'. Eleanor realised that there was nothing else to do but to keep going. The lights seemed to disappear but then 'the lights came again and this time [they] were closer'.

Just another car close up which Eleanor in an agitated state mistook for something else? No—from Eleanor's description, this encounter was far from straightforward. As she describes it, 'suddenly bright lights appeared in my vehicle. The whole of the car was lit up very brightly. I became frightened, almost hysterical. I was shaking—my hands, my legs, my whole body. I began to cry. I travelled down the road at 90 to 100 miles an hour. Very fast indeed. I don't know to this day how I ever managed to drive down that road at such a speed, but I did. I thank God that no other vehicle passed me on the road that evening or I don't know what would have happened to me.'

Just as the B927 enters the town of Leven there is a very sharp bend. Eleanor somehow managed to negotiate it without injuring herself and at last came upon the reassuring glow of street lighting, just before the first row of houses. At this point the mysterious lights simply vanished, but the fright Eleanor received led her to drive through a red traffic light on temporary roadworks and continue home as fast as she dared. She arrived back at 10.50 p.m. She remembers the time because her mother enquired about it when she got in.

I'd emphasise that when colleague Brian Wilson and I visited Eleanor we were both struck by her self confidence, and the calm manner in which she detailed the incident. She had clearly been though an ordeal at the time, but it was obvious that she was not someone who would be easily frightened. Eleanor told us that she had no belief before in the paranormal, but that the events of that night had changed her mind. She confirmed to me that there had been no further incidents after that of 13 October and no strange dreams or memories.

There are a number of aspects of this encounter worth further consideration. Eleanor is an HGV driver and, through her involvement with the Territorial Army, has become familiar with land vehicles of all types. She is, therefore, adamant in her belief that there was no vehicle following her. She points out that power lines running close to the scene of the incident would make it impossible for a low-flying helicopter to have been a possible source. The lights, which were all white, were spread across the road in a line, too far apart to belong to a vehicle or even several motor bikes.

There was also the matter of missing time. Eleanor had taken thirty minutes to cover the distance from her brother's house to her own home. According to her own estimate it should have taken half that time, especially as she took the B927 at a much faster speed than normal. If should be re-membered that Eleanor takes that particular route every day so she should be reasonably accurate about the time taken to travel the distance. Arguably, it's a case for regression hypnosis, but the issue of false memory syndrome raises considerable doubts over the usefulness of material 'retrieved' in these circumstances. At the time of writing Eleanor has not ruled it out as a possible avenue, but has taken no steps to enlist the services of a hypnotist.

Although no chase was involved, train driver Mr G Waugh caught sight of a UFO which had a similar appearance to the one which followed Eleanor. Mr Waugh, from Bridge of Earn, was looking out of his front window on Tuesday 9 February 1993 'before retiring to bed'. What he saw immediately attracted his attention and he hurried to get his binoculars for a closer look. He focused the optics on the summit of Moncrieff Hill where 'six white lights' were shining, but, as Mr Waugh noted, 'unusually they were in a straight line about 6-8 feet apart against the matt background'. After he had observed the lights for about fifteen minutes, they suddenly went out.

It does seem a bit more than coincidence that straight lines of lights should be seen in the same general area, even though a few years apart. Is it also coincidence that Eleanor's terrifying ordeal should take place only a few miles from the location of a controversial alien encounter case just the year before?

THE FIFE INCIDENT

Like Eleanor's encounter, the remarkable series of events which occurred close to Kennoway near Leven in 1996 didn't start in any dramatic way, but developed from a simple car trip by two friends, Lyn and Jean, and ten-year-old Peter, to a local shop to buy a jar of coffee. It was around 7.30 p.m. (timed by the start of a television programme) on 23 September, dark at this time of year, although it was a clear and dry night.

In an opening scenario reminiscent of the famous Barney Hill case,[1] Lyn, who was in the front passenger seat, spotted a bright oval-shaped light low down in the sky. She watched for a few seconds, wondering what it could be, then turned away. When she glanced back, the single light had become

1. The Barney and Betty Hill case of 1961 has become a key event in the history of ufology. It was the first abduction case to receive widespread publicity. It was also the first time that hypnosis was used as a tool to reveal hidden memories. This case is now recognised as a reference point for all subsequent abduction incidents.

two circles of light. Lyn was now intrigued, as the object did not appear to be moving and so, she was sure, couldn't be a plane and seemed too big to be a helicopter.

Lyn drew Jean's attention to the light and both agreed that it was difficult to account for. A UFO, then, although neither described it as such at this point. Jean, who was driving, slowed the car to a walking pace so that they could get a better view. The object was now to their left and seemed to be hovering behind a farmhouse whose silhouette was visible against the gentle glow. Beams of light seemed to be travelling from the sky to the ground.[2] Suddenly, the field below the UFO was lit up like a firework display, the intensity of the light turning night into day all around them.

The explosion of light ended as dramatically as it had begun. The object, which had remained stationary for so long, now started to move and as it did so Jean and Lyn noticed its triangular shape and that there was a dome on its uppermost section. The UFO then moved away swiftly, rotating slowly to display small red dots of light.

Understandably bemused, Jean and Lyn nevertheless drove on to the local shop. Jean bought the coffee and they set off on the return journey. But on the way back they were again confronted by the strange object as they passed the site of their original encounter at around 8.20 p.m. They first spotted red lights ahead travelling at speed, before the object turned and headed directly towards them. A whole battery of lights came on for an instant, and was then extinguished. And then,

2. Generally, if there is a light beam, witnesses tend automatically to assume that it is directed downwards. But, of course, the beam would appear the same if it was travelling in the opposite direction—could it be that in some cases UFOs are being guided in?

as suddenly as it had arrived, the UFO disappeared into the night. Lyn noticed that three cars were travelling behind them, although there was no indication that any of their occupants had seen the mysterious object.

Having returned home, the witnesses decided after further discussion to revisit the area of the incident. They were both nervous and intrigued, not to mention anxious to resolve an incident which they could not explain. So, at 9.45 p.m. they drove back, and as they approached the site their attention was caught by a blue glow which was visible just above a wood. A star-shaped object could also be seen pulsating and emitting coloured streaks of light—alternately red, blue and green—in a rapid sequence. Lyn described them as being like torch beams, narrow at the base and widening as they reached upwards. Strange events were taking place, but no-one could have been prepared for what happened next.

Moving among the trees were several small entities, and whatever they were, they were definitely not human. Above them towered a tall individual, its height estimated at around seven feet, which seemed to be in charge of its smaller companions. Understandably frightened, Jean and Lyn turned the car round and drove home.

Although frightened, they were still intrigued by what they had seen, and they decided to return and have another look. This time they took a pair of binoculars, lent by Lyn's brother James. As they reached the place where they had last seen the UFO, the blue light was still glowing but with the binoculars it was possible to get a much better view. They could see a shimmering ball which appeared to be emitting heat and energy of some kind. It looked amber in colour, with an

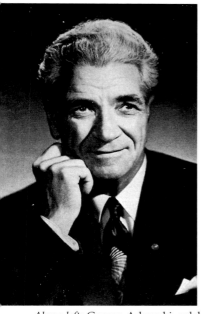

Flying Saucers Have Landed

Desmond Leslie & George Adamski

Above left: George Adamski, celebrated alien 'contactee', who visited Scotland in 1958 and addressed a packed meeting at Tollcross in Edinburgh

Above right: Adamski's 1953 bestseller, which detailed his encounters

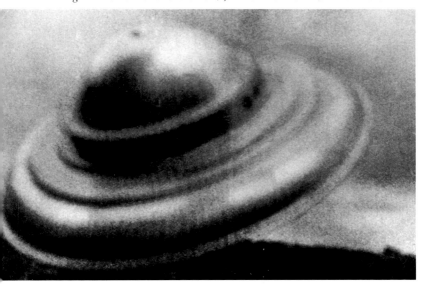

Above: The notorious 'Lossiemouth UFO' of 1954

Above: Cedric Allingham's 'UFO', photographed 'during landing', 18 February 1954

Left:
Cedric Allingham: once thought to be the enigmatic pioneer of ufology, in Scotland—now known to have been a master hoaxer

Above: The 'Lossiemouth Alien', photographed by Allingham in 1954

Opposite above:
Bob Taylor at the site of his definitive 1979 close encounter on Dechmont Law

Opposite below:
Artist's impression of Bob Taylor's encounter

Right: Bob Taylor identifying tracks made by the strange spherical objects which emerged from the Dechmont UFO

Below:
Andrew McMichael's drawing showing the path of a UFO near his home in Edinburgh, on 8 August 1996

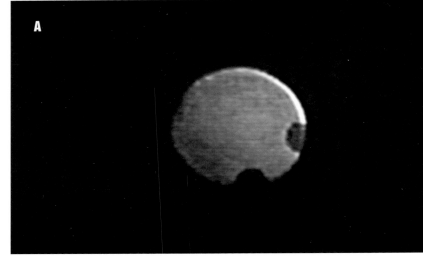

The Brian Curran UFO, November 1995:
(A) The bright orange disc, with two missing sections;
(B) The disc moving away from the camera—the two semi-circular
     gaps have now been filled;
(C) The disc glowing intensely as it moves away at speed

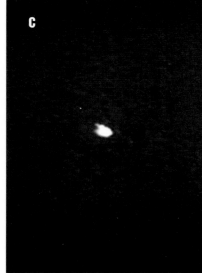

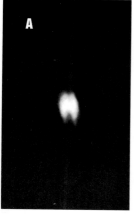  

Above: The Alec Bell UFO, November 1996:
(A) The white, glowing UFO as it appeared in the skies over Fauldhouse;
(B) The object moving closer, with the missing sections of its rim
    remarkably similar to those of the UFO seen on the Curran video;
(C) Now clearly visible as a white disc-shaped UFO with a raised rim,
    again similar to the Curran UFO

Below: The Margaret Ross UFO, October 1996:
(A) The object beginning to transform itself into a half-moon shape,
    with glowing bars of light emerging;
(B) The final appearance of the object—with intensely bright diagonal
    bars across its surface

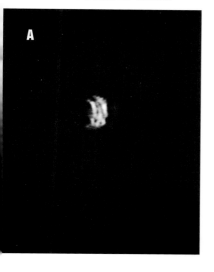 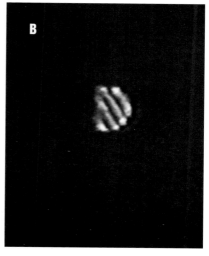

Above: Two UFOs (circled) captured on film by James MacLean over Glasgow in December 1995, as he was photographing a rainbow

Below: Close-up view of object A

Below: Close-up view of object B

Above: Mr Black's painting of the UFO he saw over Corstorphine Hill, Edinburgh, in 1958. The painting was later given to the author by Mr Black's daughter

Right:
The Corstorphine UFO: a close-up view, enlarged from the painting above, showing a classic cigar-shaped craft

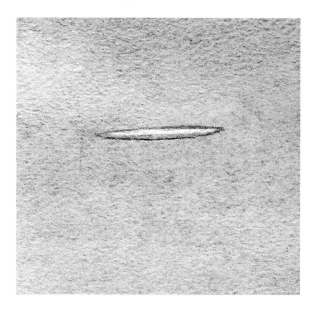

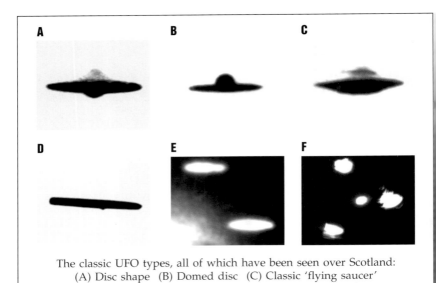

The classic UFO types, all of which have been seen over Scotland:
(A) Disc shape (B) Domed disc (C) Classic 'flying saucer'
(D) Cigar shape (E) Intense white lights (F) Triangular

Below: The crop circle found at Corpach, near Fort William, in August 1995

Above: A simple family photo, taken by Jim Templeton on the Solway marshes. At the time, he did not notice the strange figure in the background

Right: Close-up view of the 'Solway Spaceman'

Above: A classic 'flying saucer'—the Macpherson UFO, spotted near Craigluscar Reservoir, Dunfermline in February 1994. *Inset:* Close-up of the UFO

Below: The investigation at Riddochhill, near Bathgate—site of a suspected UFO crash-landing in August 1992

irregular surface and dark patches. One of these darker patches, situated near the base, could be identified as an opening. The craft didn't appear to be resting on the ground, but was hovering or possibly held up by thin supports. It appeared to be rotating and tilting rhythmically.

To the right of the object, but definitely on the ground, lay a circular disc, coloured dark red but possibly reflecting the amber colour of the ball-shaped craft. All around was the proverbial hive of activity. Groups of the small creatures were transporting boxes and tube-shaped objects from the wood towards the craft. Lyn described these beings as having 'very big, dark eyes and with heads too big for their bodies. They didn't appear to have mouths'. The taller 'supervisor' was still visible and, say the witnesses, they could make out his brown skin and narrow eyes.

The incident had a terrifying ending, described by Jean: 'suddenly dozens of bubble-like things came out of the woods and flew across the field towards us. Then they were all around us, about four feet away, motionless. They were all alike. We could see through them and each one had one of these small creatures inside. They had big black eyes and big heads.'

Later, weeks after the incident was over, Lyn began to have dreams about being taken into the craft. Were details of an abduction experience emerging? The witnesses, quite correctly, were wary of undergoing hypnosis. Their conscious recall of events is the very best type of evidence as it allows investigators to examine the evidence without the worry of 'false memory syndrome'.

After the incident, strange events were alleged to have taken place which have little, if any, parallel in documented

UFO cases. Peter, for example, the ten-year-old who was present at the original incident, claimed (as reported in the *Daily Star*) that a shiny grey alien was in his bedroom and went down to the breakfast table with him. An alien also accompanied him to school in a taxi and shared it on the way back. As Malcolm Robinson, who looked into the case, said: 'because information can sound fantastic, does that mean there is no truth in it?' Children do make strange claims about invisible friends and the reality of these particular events depends, in my view, not on the later accounts by young Peter, but on the initial incidents themselves.

HOLLOW EARTH THEORY

Cases such as that in Fife are a real challenge to our belief systems. This is no doubt why the scientific and other establishments are quick to sweep reports of such incidents under the carpet in the hope that they will be rapidly forgotten.

Ufologists might be on stronger ground with science if they could give an explanation of the intended destination of UFOs. Where do these mysterious objects go when they disappear from a witness's view? Find the answer to that conundrum and you may well have the key to the whole UFO phenomenon. Some UFO buffs have argued that there must exist a dimension parallel with our own whose inhabitants may or may not be aware of our existence, even though the dimensions somehow interact. UFO visits are, consequently, either intended as a deliberate investigation or an accidental intrusion into our world.

Other explanations are no less difficult to comprehend.

Authors have claimed that there are UFO bases located deep beneath the seas or hidden inside the interior of the earth itself. A name has even been coined for this last hypothesis— 'The Hollow Earth Theory'—and the idea has gained a considerable following among the more extreme ufologists. Compared to these solutions to the UFO enigma, the belief that these objects may be spaceships from a distant planet, capable of far exceeding the speed of light, appears almost straightforward and level-headed.

ALIEN LANDING SITE

But would UFOs, even if they truly are alien spacecraft, regularly use an area of Scotland as a base to land and take off? There is one man who is convinced through his own observation that they do. He is David Evans, an active 70-year-old, living near Dunblane, a few miles north of Stirling. From a hill directly behind his home, Mr Evans has witnessed the movements of dozens of 'flying saucers', as he unashamedly labels them.

Mr Evans's story is an extraordinary one, even in the annals of ufology, which is itself a history of the bizarre. Aware that there are many who are only too willing to ridicule his claims, David has made a great effort to obtain evidence to back up what he has witnessed in the surrounding hills. He has taken dozens of photographs of the alleged landing site, several of which, he claims, show UFOs and the methods used by the 'saucers' to defend themselves.

David Evans continually shows willingness to exhibit his collection of UFO snaps to anyone with sufficient interest to travel to his house. He is always ready to discuss his claims. He will even take you to the alleged landing site if you are fit enough to stand a walk of several hours over rough and boggy terrain.

David's experiences started during 1992 when he was involved in a close encounter with a 'spaceship'. The alien craft travelled from the hill overlooking his patio garden, and continued over the village rooftops, before disappearing from view behind the high ground beyond. Because it passed so close, Mr Evans had a good view of the object. He was struck by the grid-like 'mesh' that seemed to form a protective skin enveloping the vessel. It was metallic, or appeared so, glistening in the sun as it sailed over his head, clearly under the control of some form of intelligence.

David Evans, being the character he is, was not one to let the matter rest there, nor did he run to the press with a sensational story. Instead, he decided to carry out his own investigation to see if he could find out where this UFO had come from. He was to be staggered by the facts that emerged.

Perched on the summit of the hill overlooking his home, David kept a watch on the mountains which surround the village where he lives. One particular peak soon attracted special attention. It was a ben situated about ten miles away, but through the binoculars David usually carried it could be brought into perfect view because of the clear Highland air. He watched and waited, certain that sooner rather than later an object would reveal itself and confirm what his instincts told him.

It was, however, an incident much closer to home which convinced him that he was without doubt on to something extraordinary. One night in his sitting room he became aware of a strange glowing light. It seemed to be penetrating far into the kitchen from the paved backyard. David knew immediately—though he is not sure why—that the object responsible for this interruption was not of this earth.

Gingerly, he made his way into the kitchen and, standing well back, looked through the double-glazed door into the yard. Unfortunately he could not make out clearly the source of the mysterious light. Its intense beam, however, he could quite plainly discern—as he had sensed, but hardly dared to believe, there was 'something' out there, fairly small yet solid and emitting a powerful pulsating light.

Cautious enough not to open the door for a closer look, David had a brainwave and crept into the bathroom from which a window overlooked where the UFO stood. He flicked on the light then headed back for the kitchen hoping that he might now get a clearer view of his visitor. However, the object had in that short space of time disappeared. This unexpected visitation convinced David that in his surveillance activities he was on the right track. The watchers knew they were being watched.

Tactics adopted by the UFOs, if they were deliberate, didn't worry David. They intrigued him. Even when a UFO entered his house he wasn't put off his pursuit. Although he didn't see the object on this occasion—'they were too smart for me this time', was his verdict—the UFO left telltale signs which David was quick to latch on to.

He had left the window of his front room open and, while in the garden, heard a strange humming sound come from the interior of his bungalow. When he looked inside, he discovered a round depression had been formed in the carpet, with the pile distinctly pressed down. It seemed as if a small yet heavy object had recently rested there.

Perhaps, he reasoned, the object had not actually made contact with the carpet, but moved on a cushion of pressurised air. The force might be strong enough to make a permanent impression on a soft covering. Whatever the explanation, there was no doubt in his mind that the mark had been produced in some extraordinary way. Living on his own, David knew that he had not been responsible for it. And if he was not, then who—or what—was? An object, he felt sure, of extraterrestrial origin. Its visit to his house had not been an accident.

The point that bothered him was whether it was intended to 'warn him off' or a friendly indication that he was on the right track and must continue his investigation. Later incidents would not resolve this issue, which even today after so much has happened remains obscure.

From then on, David made frequent and increasingly determined efforts to photograph the 'flying saucers'. He succeeded, he believed, on a number of occasions. The photos, however, revealed an even more tantalising glimpse of our alien visitors, according to David—the UFOs deliberately 'spiked' his photos, so that the pictures of the mysterious objects he had caught on film were blotted out by a peculiarly shaped, multi-coloured form. From one end of this sprout pink fingers of flame, as if the UFO had rushed by just as David's finger pressed the shutter.

To David, the fact that his pictures were deliberately obscured was further proof that he was dealing with an intelligence of some kind. The objects, he argued, had been sent by a controlling 'mother ship'. As in the Bob Taylor case (the Livingston Incident is discussed in Chapter One), they could have been remote-controlled devices, sent out to protect the UFO from prying eyes.

Whilst no-one can doubt David's sincerity on the matter, it has to be said that others have offered straightforward explanations to account for the photos David has taken. To at least one professional photographer, the prints show only a reflection caught by the lens. Mr Evans vehemently refutes such a mundane solution and points out that it appears on the negatives neither before nor after the ones on which it is seen.

David also argues that the UFOs have the ability to merge into the background, and can adapt their form to that of the surrounding area. That explains why it is difficult to spot a UFO which may be sitting on a hillside—because it can camouflage itself to an extraordinary degree. A report of a UFO incident which occurred in July 1975 near Machynlleth, Powys, shows that Mr Evans' explanation for a UFO's invisibility may not be so far-fetched. According to the witness to the 1975 sighting: 'the light on top of the object and inside the base began to glow and pulsate in a strange mixture of colours that exactly matched the scenery . . . it simply went into the background like a chameleon camouflaging itself . . . after a few moments it was not there any more!'

HOSTILE ACTIVITY

If there truly are alien craft using this remote glen as a base, is it possible they could be aggressive and even be prepared to destroy one of our terrestrial aircraft? David Evans has no doubt about this.

One May morning in 1993 *The Scotsman* newspaper reported: 'The crash of an RAF Hercules near Blair Atholl, in which all nine on board were killed, was caused by a low altitude stall, an accident report said last night'. But Mr Evans had a completely different view of the matter.

On the afternoon of the disaster he had been out walking in the hills near the town of Comrie. An ex-army man, he claims familiarity with aircraft sounds.

'A big one went over,' he later told me, 'I could tell by the noise it was making. I knew it wasn't a jet'.

As the sound of the propellers receded, David watched as one of the disc-shaped objects, by now well known to him, passed above the hill-tops. Late that evening David learned of the Hercules crash and guessed its cause. The UFO, suspecting that the plane had been sent to monitor its activities, had downed it to warn off further interference.

That night, David rang to inform me of his experiences. Initially, I was sceptical. It seemed too incredible a story to be true, and more out of a 1950s science-fiction comic. However, given such a mind-bending story, it was necessary to do it justice and, consequently, I did enquire at Glasgow Airport, who referred me to Prestwick, about plane movements in the area. I was told that there weren't any that couldn't be properly accounted for. Whatever David had seen, it could not have been another aeroplane.

Through investigations carried out, it emerged that there had been three Hercules aircraft travelling in the same direction, but each following a separate route. One of the routes did seem near enough to Comrie for David to have heard the noise of the engines. I was startled by this revelation. It seemed that here was independent confirmation that David could possibly have heard the Hercules passing at the location and at the time he claims. A hillwalker caught David's attention as the plane roared over, although he did not think of taking the man's name. If he were to come forward now, it would provide additional evidence in support of David's strange encounter.

SCOTLAND'S AREA 51

There is one other possibility. The NATO air base at Machrihanish used to be one of the biggest in Europe, with a runway reputed to measure over one mile in length. For several years rumours have circulated regarding the nature of the secret activities that were carried out at this site and the experimental craft that may have landed here. In 1993, for example, there was a spate of UFO reports over Argyll, leading to speculation that this was somehow linked to secret projects there.

Most people will have heard of the top secret Area 51, an air force base and nuclear testing site in the heart of the Nevada desert, in the United States. It is a key military installation where, it is claimed, devices including alien spacecraft are kept and tested. Was Machrihanish Scotland's Area 51? Interestingly, in his book *Covert Agenda* Nick Redfern doesn't deal with the issue of Machrihanish's involvement in the UFO phenomenon. Perhaps its absence is a testimony to the success of governments in keeping the lid on Scottish UFO reports. There is no policy of releasing Scottish reports as a separate batch, as I learned from the MoD. Yet Machrihanish would be an ideal spot from which to operate aircraft technology that the government wanted to keep secret—including devices allegedly developed from captured alien discs. Or, so the conspiracy theorists argue, even brought to fruition with the help of extraterrestrials, with whom our generals have supposedly made contact!

Far-fetched, certainly, so let's keep our feet firmly on the ground. It is definitely possible, even probable, that the latest in aviation technology has been brought to Machrihanish. With a long runway and its isolated location, it is a useful testing ground. It's not easily accessible and so is protected from prying eyes.

It is likely that some UFO reports have occurred because of sightings of these advanced machines. But would they have led to the crash of a slow moving Hercules? Did an accident occur which was hushed up because of the involvement of secret, state-of-the-art aircraft? David Evans would no doubt disagree. He firmly believes that he has seen alien machines. But, given our government's notorious secrecy, no explanation can be ruled out.

LOW-FLYING SAUCER

About 50 miles to the east, and north of the Forth Estuary, Ian Macpherson, a 45-year-old resident of Rosyth, also believes that he has photographed a 'flying saucer'. 'Is it a hub-cap, a hoax or a UFO (Unidentified Fife Object)?' ran the less-than-serious *Daily Record* headline of 28 February 1994. Ian himself, however, appears perfectly straight-faced about his encounter and upset by the manner in which the tabloids have treated his pictures of the UFO.

Ian tells a credible story about his encounter. While walking one February Saturday round Craigluscar Reservoir near the town of Dunfermline, he heard a peculiar humming sound. It was 3.15 p.m. Glancing skywards, he caught sight of a strange object. According to the *Dunfermline Press* the object moved around for about 15 minutes and came quite close to Ian, but Ian only thought to grab a couple of quick shots as it moved away.

'The craft's acceleration was phenomenal,' reported Ian. 'By the time I wound the film on it was a dot in the sky'. He estimated its size at around 60 feet. The paper quoted him as saying: 'I was holding my camera, but felt unable to use it. I have never experienced such feelings before'.

Ian generously handed over the photos to the *Daily Record*, which was sufficiently impressed to print them for its readers and also forward a set to the Ministry of Defence.

UFO investigator Malcolm Robinson commented: 'It is the most exciting photograph I have ever seen in this country. These pictures are really remarkable. I have never seen anything like them in this country before.'

It was stated that Ian watched the 'craft' for around fifteen minutes, although in conversation with me he has said that it was difficult to be clear about the time involved. He described the UFO as 'definitely metallic' with 'several points of diffused light on its underside inside a darker coloured rim'. The points of light do not appear evident in the photograph. However, Ian drew a sketch of the craft before the photos were developed. The sketch and photographs are similar although, probably as they were viewed from different angles, not identical. The upper section of the UFO as drawn in Ian's sketch appears larger in proportion to the remainder than in the photo. The underside and prominent grill-like flange are not seen in the shot though clear in the sketch, which shows the lower portion of the UFO tilted away from the viewer, whereas only the upper section is visible in Ian's photo.

Oddly, the *Daily Record* published a blown up and rather fuzzy version of the UFO. In contrast the local paper, the *Dunfermline Press*, published a very clear picture which included background against which the UFO had been seen, that is the reservoir and surrounding trees. As the *Record* version appeared before the *Press* publication I was thrown by the clarity of the latter and what it depicted. The snap in the Fife paper seemed remarkably like a clay pigeon used in target practice and competitions: a similarity which had been masked by the *Record*'s close up and consequently less clear image.

UFO investigator Ken Higgins visited Craigluscar reservoir soon after Ian's picture appeared. The background in the picture certainly matched that at the reservoir. Ian had definitely snapped the UFO at the spot he said he had. Ken noted that the area was one used for clay pigeon shooting. It was littered with broken and unbroken clay pigeons. Ian, however, appears perfectly sincere in his story and readers will have to be the judge of the matter. The balance may be in Ian's favour, particularly as Nick Pope has stated that the Ministry of Defence were unable to identify the object.

IN THE SKIES OVER FIFE

Certainly, Fife has had its share of UFO reports. In May 1996 bar stewardess Margaret Mellon saw a mysterious object pass over Saline Hill. It was around 3 a.m. when Margaret was woken by her sister-in-law Janet Duffy, who drew her attention to a bright orange light tinged with blue which seemed to illuminate the whole of the distant peak. Suddenly, a massive craft appeared and sailed slowly towards them before disappearing over the rooftop of their house. Margaret's view of UFOs was dramatically transformed by the incident. Before, she had been sceptical of the whole phenomenon, but her own sighting convinced her that something strange was taking place in the skies over Fife.

Local investigator Sharon Coull has unearthed at least a dozen previously unknown incidents in the 'Kingdom' (as Fife is often referred to in Scotland, because of its historic independence). One, for example, dates from 1988. Sharon reports that 'a woman living at Simon Crescent, Methil, was cooking one night when she saw a bright light in the fields at the back. There was also a loud noise which made her think that a harvester was at work. She became concerned when the noise drew closer and the kitchen was brightly illuminated. As she opened the back door to investigate, there was an object in her back garden which then shot straight upwards and out of sight. The woman's parents who were in bed also heard the noise, and their room was also lit up.

More familiar, perhaps, was the sighting of a triangular UFO. This incident occurred on 15 September 1995 when a businessman, Edward, observed what he described as a 'perfect triangle, moving from west to east over Glenrothes. According to Edward's report 'a triangular object appeared overhead at 9.05 p.m. under perfect night viewing conditions.

It was not giving off light [nor] emitting any noise. It was travelling . . . at about 2,000 feet'. He observed the UFO for about ten seconds and noted that it moved at about jet plane speed although he is sure it wasn't an aircraft. He was also struck by what appeared to be a 'shimmer or air distortion' as it moved. Edward had no idea as to why he saw this object or what it was. All he knows is that he observed something out of the ordinary. Like many witnesses to the UFO phenomenon he does not wish to be publicly identified.

PRISON SIGHTING

Why should an extraterrestrial spaceship visit a Scottish gaol? I can think of no good reason, but evidence of a sighting at Glenochil Prison suggests that at least one such visit has taken place. On the night of 15 May 1994 a brightly lit object was spotted hovering around the perimeter fence surrounding the complex. This wasn't the chance glimpse of a human witness. The prison surveillance cameras had caught the object while scanning the huge mesh fence—escape-proof according to the authorities. The UFO was then seen to move backwards and forwards above it. The prison officer who witnessed the object explained: 'It was a bright white light with a big hole in the middle, like a giant polo mint'. A curious fact is that two officers sent out to investigate what was going on claimed that they could see nothing. Yet back in the control room the white light was still plainly visible on the video screen. The spokesman for the Scottish Prison Service responded to enquiries by stating that the 'logical explanation' was 'camera fault'. Reasonable, if the only evidence was the view of the UFO via the surveillance equipment, but evidence has come to me that other prison officers did see the object with their own eyes, which might explain why the original video footage disappeared. Videoed over, it was claimed, in order not to waste tape, although I don't feel that the saving of public money was justified in this case! It must be asked, why was the tape re-used if it was considered faulty? If the surveillance camera was not working properly, why was it not reported? There is no evidence that any action was taken to repair or replace the allegedly faulty instruments.

ALLOA INCIDENT

Overall, the lands north of the Forth have seen their fair share of UFO incidents. In 1986, the town of Alloa, for example, witnessed a bright circular-shaped object circulating in the night sky. It was the peak summer month of June and so even though it was 9.30 at night the witnesses had a clear view in the brilliant sky. The UFO was never identified.

On the same day a few miles west, in the village of Menstrie, a blue circular object was observed for ten minutes hovering (perhaps watching?) high in the sky. It was a similar object which appeared six years later to a witness in Sauchie, a community to the north of Alloa. Travelling along the A907 which connects both towns a driver saw a bright hovering light. He stopped the car for a better view and noted the UFO made no noise as it moved. It travelled slowly, drifting towards a farm, then suddenly vanished as if a cosmic finger had switched a light off. This was presumably the same object which appeared over the nearby village of Fishcross on 22

July 1986. A blue circular light was seen by a male witness. It hovered over the area for a few seconds, again as if watching, before moving off.

In 1989 Alloa resident Graham Sharp spotted a multi-coloured diamond-shaped object moving over the former mining village of Cowie lying on the south side of the Firth of Forth. It was an April night at around 10 p.m. when Graham and his wife Shelley caught sight of the UFO. The object appeared to be moving slowly, and they were able to follow its manoeuvres for almost half an hour as it changed colour from red to yellow, then green and blue.

'At first I thought it was a planet', admitted Graham, 'but it was definitely moving'.

As a former soldier familiar with aeroplane silhouettes, he knew it could not be a conventional craft. He was so convinced that he was seeing something out of the ordinary that he called out his neighbours to take a look.

They were sure that the object required further investigation. However, when the police arrived they could see nothing unusual! Inspector Alec Brown was reported as saying: 'We had Air Traffic Control check the area and they reported that nothing was flying over Cowie and they saw nothing untoward.' The policemen suggested the sensible explanation that huge lights on the cardboard factory in the area, coupled with weather conditions, caused the light to appear to be moving, and confused the witness. Graham, while conceding that the factory illumination sounded a plausible cause of his sighting, was adamant that the lights were moving. If that was the case, then the Sharps certainly saw a UFO.

In March 1997 the police were again called out to investigate a reported UFO. The witness, Geraldine McNeill, was out walking her dog on the sloping ground above Lornshill Academy on the outskirts of Alloa. It was an early morning exercise Ms McNeill carried out dutifully every day of the week. At 5.25 on this morning, however, her black labrador stopped suddenly and 'started whining with fear', she recalled. The dog simply refused to go any further. Wondering what could be causing the problem, Geraldine spotted a strong beam of light shining through a row of trees directly ahead of her. It seemed to be pulsating 'on a regular rhythm' and at the same time changing colour 'from pale cream through to yellow, to deep yellow, and back to cream again'. Ms McNeill estimated that the light beam was about 30 feet across. Clearly, a large object must be at the source of the glow.

Baffled and concerned, Geraldine, after watching the light for about ten minutes, decided to call the police and walked over to a nearby phone box. As she dialled she glanced at the UFO where 'the light stayed constant, neither changing shape nor size'. The policeman who took her call sounded sceptical, but agreed to send over a couple of men, who arrived shortly after. Ms McNeill had suggested meeting at the back of the Academy so they could get the best view of the strange light.

However, by the time they met up the pulsating light had disappeared and all that could be seen was a pin-point of light to the right of the original. 'If we're not back in five minutes, call the polis!' joked one of the officers as they headed up the slope, watched anxiously by Geraldine. She saw them reach the spot where the light source had been situated and then walk about waving their torches in every direction. After a few minutes they gave up the search and returned down the slope. It was at this point that Ms McNeill noticed a very strange occurrence. At the spot at the top of the slope where the police had been standing seconds before were two odd figures, walking methodically backwards and forwards. Ms McNeill describes what happened next: 'When the policemen came back beside me, they said it had only been a burning log, but that they would arrange for the firemen to come and check the log later in the morning. As they spoke the two figures were still clearly visible at the edge of the trees. I said to the policemen, "If you are back here, who are the two figures up there?" and I pointed to where the policemen had been'. The two young officers seemed taken aback by this and quickly departed, stating that they would have to write up their report!

It's perhaps significant that Ms McNeill's labrador would not go near the trees on Friday, but by Saturday willingly went up to them. Whatever had frightened her had now clearly left the area. Geraldine is adamant that 'whatever caused the light was not a burning log, nor a reflection from a street light'. If that is the case, what did she see? Two entities from another dimension? And why did the police miss these 'people' when they were so close to them? It is a puzzle to which we are still seeking the answer.

HILLFOOTS HOT-SPOT

The area along the Hillfoots, comprising a series of towns and villages (Alva, Tullibody and Menstrie, for example) has become something of a minor 'hot-spot' in the last few years.

In May 1996 company director Ralph Davies and his wife

Kathy saw a bright white light over the Wood Hill near Tullibody. Their house in Benview Terrace, Fishcross affords an excellent view over the slopes and summits of the Ochils. Fetching binoculars they managed to get a good description of the UFO. 'It was like a round light', Ralph said. 'It kept changing, oscillating, then it went smooth and then jagged'. Mr Davies likened it to watching bacteria through a microscope. His wife compared it to a jellyfish although when after about thirty minutes the light moved on it seemed to split in two and change shape becoming oblong rather than round. Both objects, one above the other, headed north lighting up the area as they moved along.

By February 1998 the *Sunday Mail* was labelling Fishcross the 'new UFO hot-spot' because of a steady stream of sightings in the area, although it was a video taken by Kate and John O'Hare which UFO investigator Malcolm Robinson described as 'remarkable'. He claimed that 'The object looks nothing like a conventional aircraft. No sound was heard from it and it didn't display any regulation lights'. Henry Schreiber also saw the UFO and watched it through binoculars. He said that the object 'zig-zagged too fast to be either a helicopter or plane. The shape changed and then the colour changed—first to green then to bright red'. Another strange sighting which will simply never be solved.

CASE SOLVED

An alleged UFO, however, seen over the naval base of Rosyth, was tracked down. Several witnesses on an Edinburgh-bound Loganair flight spotted a fast-moving diamond-shaped object in the night sky. It certainly struck those who observed it as something out of the ordinary. Research by Ken Higgins revealed just how wary we should be of the most dramatic-seeming event, and reports from even the most honest witness. He discovered that the UFO was actually a group of Phantom jets from nearby Leuchars RAF base flying in formation. Although it turned out to be an IFO (Identified Flying Object) it should act as encouragement for serious investigators. It shows that it is possible to explain what looks at first sight to be inexplicable, and thus adds strength to those cases where the identification of a UFO is not possible even after the most meticulous investigation.

Rosyth lies on the north shore of the Firth of Forth. On the opposite bank lies South Queensferry, the departure point, before the road bridge was opened in 1964, for travellers to Fife. Unlike the Rosyth sightings, however, several incidents from the south side of the Forth are still unexplained. Perhaps the strangest emerges from a photograph allegedly showing a strange blurred object beside the yacht *Lady Barbara* snapped at the same moment as a distinct splash was heard as if a large object had entered the water. The estuary was calm at that time and there appeared to be no natural explanation for what was seen and heard.

UNDERWATER BASE THEORY

Such events are food and drink to those who argue that UFOs are not extraterrestrial in origin. There are those who suggest that these alien visitors are less 'alien' than we think, and have their homes underground or underwater, where prying terrestrial eyes find it impossible to locate them. Deep water sites in the Pacific, for example, are obvious areas where detection would be difficult. However, the relative frequency of reports of UFOs emerging from shallow water suggests that they do not necessarily choose to hide at great depth. In Puerto Rico, for example, bizarre shaped objects can be seen emerging from shallow water well within sight of land. The Forth would provide a comparatively safer hiding place. It would also provide a solution both to the many sightings in the Forth area and why UFOs seen there seem to disappear so suddenly without trace.

And yet, with the volume of sea traffic ploughing the Forth, wouldn't *someone* have seen *something* definite? Of course, a lot of the lane movement is military, and you wouldn't expect anything to be revealed in these cases. Others might have seen incidents so incredible they would be afraid that no-one would believe them. And who could blame them? Some have argued that, in any case, the 'visitors' can cloak themselves using some form of stealth technology, so that they can operate very close to our shores and escape detection, all the while spying on our military installations. But that, surely, would be stretching credulity to the limit.

Any object seen on 5 November naturally raises the question, 'Was it a firework?' Particularly when the UFO in question appears as a green light, as it did to one witness on that day in 1992. The witness, however, is adamant that the object she saw had no connection with Guy Fawkes celebrations. On the contrary, it is the very fact that it contrasted sharply with coloured explosions that so obviously were a part of the festivities which attracted her attention. The object moved high in the sky at, she guessed, around 500 feet and, though it was the green glow which caught her eye, the witness got the clear impression that it was somehow solid. Perhaps she meant that the light originated from a solid object which was also using a beam as a means of concealment.

On 2 February 1992 a woman in South Queensferry was woken by a bright flashing light. Gingerly, she opened her curtains and saw what she could only describe as 'a big block flying'. Although it was 12.50 a.m., she immediately phoned the police. Interestingly, the flashing light could be explained as the local coastguard searching for a suspected suicide. The Forth Road Bridge and Rail Bridge are well known launching points for those seeking a quick end to their problems. However, neither the police nor the coastguards could explain the large object witnessed by the terrified woman.

The blue light seen by witnesses in the Alloa/Clackmannan area may have returned in 1992. A witness noted a bright blue object travelling between Kincardine and Grangemouth. The UFO appeared to be moving at speed and headed in an easterly direction. On this occasion, no solid object could be connected with the light. However, a solid object *was* seen moving in a similar direction on two separate occasions in 1992. A witness in Kinghorn on 24 November 1992 spotted a strange low-flying UFO which did not look like any conventional aircraft. As it moved, it did so silently. Was it a secret government machine? A few months previously, in August, a family saw a brightly coloured object moving southwards. The UFO was the traditional circular or disc shape. In the same month and in the same area a man saw a bright beam of light descending to the earth and soon after a bright object could be seen moving slowly north.

A more elaborately shaped object was seen by a witness in September 1992. A young girl observed something she described as being similar to 'a long Christmas decoration'. From her account the UFO clearly had a flange running around the outside. The object was sufficiently out of the ordinary to interest RAF Leuchars. It clearly was not a sighting of one of their planes which led to the report and they, in their turn, forwarded an account of the incident to the Ministry of Defence in Whitehall. So far the mysterious UFO has not been identified.

Around the same time, 69-year-old William Clelland witnessed a 'rugby ball shape of flame travelling at speed'. It was moving parallel to the ground in a direction from Kinghorn to Burntisland. The Forth basin has continued to be a source of UFO reports right up to the present time. In November 1997 Mrs Celia Roach (44), a careworker, watched 'a cigar-shaped bright orange object travelling slowly across the sky'. Mrs Roach noted that the UFO left in its wake 'a small vapour trail'. There was a second witness to the incident as Celia had driven round to a friend's house to give her a lift to work. It was in fact the friend, Jean Cassidy, who first drew attention to the object. Intrigued by the sighting they followed its general direction to try and get a closer look. At one point the UFO seemed to stop, but then headed off in the direction of Grangemouth where it disappeared from view behind smoke from the chimney stacks. Both Celia and Jean had the object under observation for around twenty minutes and Celia described its brightness as 'like the sun'.

THE BONNYBRIDGE TRIANGLE

If the UFO did head over Grangemouth it might have crossed the notorious 'Bonnybridge Triangle'. No discussion of UFO cases in Scotland's central belt would be complete without a reference to Bonnybridge, labelled (like Blairgowrie before it) the 'UFO capital of Scotland'. Although in recent months the excitement generated by sightings in the area has declined, it has gained a reputation as the alleged heart of a UFO 'triangle'. A triangle which, it is suggested, covers an area of intense UFO activity stretching from the Forth estuary to the borders of Stirling on the west and reaching to the fringes of Edinburgh on the east. There is certainly an element of truth in this designation in that West Lothian, for example, has experienced repeated incidents out of all proportion to its size and population density.

If, as local councillor Billy Buchanan has claimed, Bonnybridge (population 5,500) does indeed have over 2,000 witnesses to UFO sightings then it truly is a world hot-spot. A similar proportion of witnesses to population in Edinburgh would mean about 200,000 people had seen a UFO in Scotland's capital.

The recent spate of sightings in the area started quietly enough with a number of interesting although typical UFO reports. These incidents began in January 1992 when Mr James Walker witnessed a cross-shaped formation of stars hovering above the road as he was driving along. He stopped his car and looked back, noting that the lights had now assumed a triangular shape. Mr Walker was understandably mystified by the incident which he felt could not be put down to any obvious source, such as an aircraft. However, perhaps the best known incident took place in March of that year. At around 7 p.m. the Slogett family were walking towards Bonnybridge when Steven Slogett caught sight of a circle of light. He drew the attention of the rest of the family to the strange phenomenon. The light appeared to land in a nearby field. The family walked on, but were halted in their tracks by a football-sized blue light hovering above the road ahead. Isabella Slogett later reported: 'My daughter Carole and I saw a UFO land right in front of us. A door opened and there was a howl-like sound. I screamed and ran off terrified'. According to Carole, 'There was a flash of light as if we were being photographed'. When they reached their home at Leonard Drive, Bonnybridge, the mysterious object was still visible and, it was said, was seen by several other witnesses.

According to the February/March 1993 edition of *Enigmas*, the newsletter of Strange Phenomena Investigations, the Slogett family had a second encounter with an object which flashed its lights at them, although Malcolm Robinson expressed the view that this 'could well have been a car or large vehicle containing a courting couple'.

Reports continued throughout 1992. In November, for example, a Mr Anderson reporting a 'bluish-white light, very bright, which disappeared behind clouds', and a father and daughter witnessed a triangular-shaped UFO.

Another interesting report occurred in 1993 when Ray and Cathy Proceck, driving to Cumbernauld to visit friends, spotted 'an elliptical shape with bright lights around the edge'. As they passed beneath a viaduct they opened the sunroof of their car to get a better look. When they reached the other side they were rewarded by witnessing 'an identical craft'. Both objects were completely silent. Before the incident neither Ray nor Cathy were interested in UFOs, but both were convinced that they had seen something they could not explain.

It was not the nature of the incidents, however, which attracted media interest in the area, but rather the sheer volume of sightings which were relayed to the media by the local councillor, Mr Billy Buchanan. He explained that his constituents were coming forward with reports of UFO encounters and that it was his duty, therefore, to seek an explanation for the incidents. No solution, however, was forthcoming, in spite of the efforts of UFO investigator Malcolm Robinson.

By the end of December 1992 over 200 witnesses to events were being cited by Billy Buchanan, and a public 'skywatch' was announced and broadcast via the television network. Naturally there was considerable public attention as a result, although to the disappointment of those who turned up, including the TV cameras, no UFO activity was observed. The attention, of course, generated more reports of UFO sightings and some ufologists began to question whether it was now possible to disentangle the genuine reports from the sightings inevitably generated by media interest. It is well known that individual reports of UFO incidents increase when existing incidents are highlighted: what previously was simply a light in the sky becomes a UFO.

In order to calm the situation, a public meeting was arranged at the Norwood Hotel in Bonnybridge by Billy Buchanan for Sunday 31 January 1993 at 7 p.m. The *Sunday Post* newspaper reported that 'A town plagued by UFOs has called in the experts as concern grows among residents'. Councillor Buchanan was amongst those claiming to have seen a UFO and added: 'I've had around 400 calls in the past few months'. The article revealed that some of the town's residents would 'be hypnotised in a bid to find any subconscious memories of being taken aboard an alien spacecraft'. In the event the hypnotist did not turn up—although an audience of nearly 300 did, to hear Malcolm Robinson lecture on worldwide UFO incidents, including alleged abduction cases.

At this point Scottish Earth Mysteries Research, in a radio broadcast, urged caution over the Bonnybridge sightings until a proper investigation had been carried out and the number and nature of the sightings could be accurately assessed. As events moved rapidly along, however, it was clear that media interest was not going to be side-tracked by the concerns of any UFO investigators!

The arrival of a Japanese film crew provided the opportunity for some interesting speculation on the Bonnybridge sightings. In the *Stirling Observer* Malcolm Robinson was quoted as 'being convinced that Bonnybridge is one of the world's few "windows" to another dimension'. Meanwhile, according to the reporter, Councillor Buchanan had more than UFOs on his mind. The story ran: 'Councillor Buchanan seemed to have a well thought out game plan. . . . He said he hoped the crew would have relatives back in Japan who could pull some weight. "Hopefully," announced the Councillor, "one of the crew will have an uncle called Mitsubishi who might want to build a factory in Bonnybridge." ' The report continued: 'Councillor Buchanan denied that it had been his intention from the start . . . "Why shouldn't Bonnybridge benefit? We have a superb setting here and Central Region is a friendly and inviting place."' The article concluded with the revelation that 'Councillor Buchanan has a special surprise in store for the Japanese group—a massive cake shaped like a flying saucer'. The Japanese were suitably impressed by this display of Bonnybridgean hospitality. However, attempts to secure financial backing for a 'giant glass mushroom-shaped visitor centre', intended as a UFO tourist attraction, failed to get off the ground, according to the *Daily Record*.

Meanwhile, as Bonnybridge was staking its claim to the title of a 'world hot-spot' for UFOs, the same description was being applied to Edinburgh, a mere twenty miles down the road. Were the UFOs seen in Bonnybridge identical to those appearing over the Lothians? Disappointingly, as Scottish ufologists argued about the nature of the Bonnybridge sightings, the opportunity for a comparison, for piecing together the jigsaw, was overlooked.

Meetings arranged in Falkirk, whilst attracting huge attention and raising the profile of ufology in Scotland, did not really move the investigation forward and, by encouraging people to consider every odd light in the sky a 'UFO', may have muddied the waters rather than cleared them.

Some aspects of the Bonnybridge experience degenerated into farce, as writer Edward Talisman noted in *Phenomenal News*. Describing the controversy over a supposed alien called 'Zal-us', Mr Talisman wrote:

> Sceptics of the Bonnybridge "hot-spot" were given added fuel by the unfortunate antics involving "Zal-us" and the "Council of Nine". Zal-us, according to some newspaper reports, was an alien who had an

important message to give to the world. The message was going to be revealed at a meeting in Falkirk Town Hall, one evening in October. The hall had been booked for the affair by Councillor Billy Buchanan, no less.

So Councillor Billy was at the centre of this enigma? The tabloids seemed to think so and one, (the *Daily Star*, I think) labelled the unfortunate Buchanan "Bonnybridge's Crackpot Councillor". Indeed, to be fair to the press, someone, somewhere seemed to have put words into Billy's mouth which appear to suggest that he had personally met an ET who claimed membership of some galactic body which was overseeing the development of the earth (obvious, isn't it?).

All in all, it made a great read, and, caught up in the excitement, I was devastated to learn that it had all been a load of . . . nonsense. Billy Buchanan had never met an alien, and the name Zal-us was alien (all right, completely unknown) to him. Mr Buchanan was, it transpires, utterly blameless, and bemused and justifiably annoyed at his name being taken in vain.

So where did "Zal-us" come from? Without revealing all the twists and turns of a murky plot, it seems that another UFO group had somehow picked up the name. But where from, I don't know. Anyway, according to *The Scotsman* the name originated with ufologist Malcolm Robinson in his newsletter. However, claims Malcolm: "I don't know how the name Zal-us crept into the article. . . . I would never put in some false data . . . just to jazz it up!" An enigma indeed!

Meanwhile, genuinely odd incidents were taking place in the area. In October 1994 three cleaners, while on their way to work at the Union Chemical Factory at Carronshire, saw five UFOs. Beatrice Campbell reported that she had first noticed the UFOs at around 5.40 a.m. She described one large object which had a light orange glow and four smaller ones sparkling on and off. The larger object appeared to be sending out beams of light to the smaller sparkling objects. Beatrice reported her sighting to their manager, Bill Downie. Soon other employees were coming forward to give their accounts, which seemed to indicate that strange objects had been appearing in the area for some days. The previous Wednesday at 7 p.m. Diane Keating from Camelon had witnessed a reddish-coloured ball which disappeared and then reappeared. She was sure it could not have been a plane because she saw one fly under it. At the same time Steve Lewisham saw a 'bright white' object which moved in a direction away from them, then 'came back and began to glow red and orange. It was going really fast. We saw a passenger plane with its landing lights on underneath it. The object was very much faster than the plane.'

On 28 December 1996 a university lecturer was driving past the slip road which leads from the M80 to the Kincardine Bridge at around 10 p.m. when a light in the sky caught his attention. He described it as 'like a laser beam moving from side to side. My first reaction was that this must be the beam of oncoming cars reflecting off the clouds, which were very low-lying. I thought that this was odd because I had never noticed this effect before, and then I realised there were not sufficient on-coming cars on the road for this to be the case. I then thought that it must be some laser beam coming from Stirling, but thought it strange that it could travel such a long distance'. The witness continued along the motorway to Stirling, but could find no source for this strange nocturnal light. A few months earlier, in July 1996, according to *Northern UFO News* a couple in Stenhousemuir saw 'a brightly coloured object hovering over some nearby fields and surrounded by lights'.

There's no doubt that the 'Bonnybridge Phenomenon' was grossly hyped-up, but it is also true that if we take in a broader area, covering the towns of Falkirk, Grangemouth, Larbert and Stenhousemuir then the number of reported incidents represents a disproportionate number of all Scottish UFO cases.

VIDEO EVIDENCE

One fascinating aspect of the UFO sightings in this area is the extent to which UFOs have been caught on video. According to the *Falkirk Herald* one was even captured on police video cameras in the early 1990s. This was an object reported by Catherine Penman of Hallglen, near Falkirk. Her husband, Scott Penman, first spotted the UFO at around 10 p.m. According to Catherine: 'It was a really bright light which was down quite low. At first, I thought it was a star, but it was ten times bigger than a star and was really close to the house. There is no way it could have been a helicopter or a plane because of the length of time it hovered in the air. I contacted the police because it was so unusual.'

Even greater publicity was given to film footage caught by sixty-three-year-old Margaret Ross of Stenhousemuir. Her video of an object seen in May 1996 shows a bright light criss-crossed by stripes of different colours. Margaret and her husband Alex (72) spotted the UFO as they were preparing for bed. It appeared to them disc-shaped and brighter than a star, and struck both witnesses as being of really strange appearance. As they videoed, the UFO appeared to zoom toward the house. There is certainly no doubting the unsettling nature of the couple's experience, although some UFO investigators believe that the camera may have unintentionally distorted the image of a natural object.

However, in October of the same year Margaret Ross caught another UFO on video. At first the white object which she was videoing to the south of her house pulsated for about 15 minutes. Then it gradually changed, transforming into a half moon shape with intensely bright bars travelling diagonally across and a glowing outer shell. Mrs Ross caught sight of the UFO after she got out of bed at around 6 a.m. By a strange coincidence, her daughter Alison had also spotted the same object from her front room window a couple of miles distant. She watched it for some time before ringing her mother at 7 a.m. to draw it to her attention. Mrs Ross, who had by then already been videoing the UFO for an hour, was delighted to have independent confirmation of what she had seen.

Some of the best video evidence may be found on film taken by father and son Jim and Craig Malcolm from Larbert. From their restaurant just outside the town they have made a determined effort to capture the UFO phenomenon on camera. Amazingly, they now have several hours of video tape documenting strange activity in the skies at the heart of the 'triangle'. Typical, perhaps, is a sighting of 21 October 1997 when Craig videoed a 'spinning orb' and a minute later also caught on film a military jet travelling over the area of the sighting. Coincidence? One piece of tape shows an object taken during daylight hours which even the Ministry of Defence has been unable to identify!

It was stories such as this which encouraged people from all over the UK to visit the area, some with the intention of establishing intergalactic contact. The leader of one such group, Poraig Maille, commented that 'the aliens like to keep us guessing right up to the last minute'.

In October 1996 one of the most remarkable clips of video footage was taken by Hallglen resident Barry Macdonald. Barry was driving along Windsor Road in the Camelon district of Falkirk when he and his girlfriend Jane Adamson spotted a mysterious object hovering in the sky. It was around 6.40 p.m. when they stopped the car and got out to take a clearer look. After they had watched the object for several minutes, Barry remembered that he had his video camera on the back seat. Barry is a keen angler and to prove the size of his catch he makes sure he has the evidence on tape. This time he was going to use his camera to even greater effect. He managed only 30 seconds of film before the object disappeared, but what he managed to get caused a worldwide sensation, and featured on TV programmes across five continents. The UFO appears as an orange oval which appears to change shape to a white disc—in fact the classic 'flying saucer'. It seems to glow again, then turn white once more before disappearing in the blink of an eye. Whether it simply 'vanishes' or moves away at an incredibly high speed is impossible to tell—it is there one second and gone the next. Checks with local airports indicated that no aircraft were in the vicinity at the time.

Events in the Bonnybridge area have certainly kept us in suspense. If Nick Pope, the Ministry of Defence executive officer turned ufologist, is correct, there have been over 8,000 witnesses to UFO sightings in this area. A truly staggering figure. Councillor Billy Buchanan, who played such a key role in bringing the attention of UFO experts to the events in his town, claimed a figure of 2,000 witnesses. It may be that Mr Pope, with his insider's knowledge of the UFO situation, was aware of a large group of reports which has not yet reached the public domain. It is very much to be hoped that in the not too distant future the full extent of UFO sightings in the Bonnybridge/Falkirk/Larbert area will be revealed, and fresh light thrown on a genuine Scottish mystery.

CLOSE ENCOUNTER IN CRAIL

Hot-spots seem to move around and are a constant aspect of the UFO scene. But alien abduction has only come to the fore in recent years. Yet is it really a recent phenomenon or is it that individuals are only now prepared to discuss their experiences? Recently I learned of a possible abduction which took place over twenty years ago in Fife which I hope will show sceptics that we are not dealing with an issue which can simply be dismissed as a contemporary 'myth'.

In the summer of 1975 James Battison, along with his brother and two cousins, was holidaying in the seaside village of Crail. It is a former fishing village on Fife's east coast (or 'East Neuk') and a popular destination for Scots holidaymakers. It was just a little before 12 midday, but the children were too busy on the foreshore searching for crabs to be worried by the first pangs of hunger. Alex (12), Angela (12), George (9), and James, the youngest at eight years old, got on well together and were sharing a caravan with James's mum who was looking after them over the holiday fortnight.

I didn't hear the account from James till early in 1998, long after the events he described. One would expect that the memories might fade over time. However, to James the memory remained fresh in his mind and he readily suggested to me that I contact the other children present to verify his story.

James distinctly remembers that as they were playing 'it was very peaceful', but something in the sky caught his attention. 'I went "Look",' James told me, 'and then it went black. But the blackness wasn't scary. It was peaceful'. However, as James described it, this was no ordinary blackness. 'Everything around went black. I couldn't see anything at all'. Then, as suddenly as it had arrived, the darkness went and it was light again. James assured me that he was 'fully conscious all the time this happened'. He guessed that the incident lasted only four seconds.

Fig 12. The two intensely bright metallic objects seen by four children at Crail in 1975.

Admittedly, it is a bit odd, but is it enough to lead us to classify this in the UFO category? It's at this point that James becomes both hazy and definite. He is sure that he and the other children saw and experienced other things. Yet he is not sure exactly what. He also has doubts that the incident only lasted the fleeting seconds that it seemed to at the time.

He has a clear image in his mind of what first attracted his attention. It was a strange object overhead, but he can't quite focus on what it was. 'It looked beautiful', and—puzzlingly but intriguingly—'it looked like a symbol'. He is also sure that 'there were two separate objects. They were the same size, but one was higher than the other. They looked like biplanes' (see Fig 12). He adds that 'it was metallic, brighter than our aircraft although there was no haze around it as you often get with aeroplanes'. James didn't notice anything like portholes in the craft or any kind of projections from it. It just looked smooth. The picture he drew me shows a long, featureless object, a bit like a metal container for an individual cigar.

Remember that the incident was witnessed by four youngsters aged 8 to 12. Four children who then ran back to the caravan to tell James's mum what they had seen. As might be expected of an adult, however, she didn't take their story all that seriously.

After the incident James seemed to have bad sunburn, and links that to the fact that he was standing directly beneath the object. He also remembers that although there was no noise there was an electric atmosphere which was quite different from what they normally experienced. He likens it to the air just before a thunderstorm.

What has continued to draw James' attention to the incident

though is the thought that he might have seen 'somebody'. He has that feeling that he did and says that Angela saw what appeared to be an old man standing next to them moments before the incident happened. Could it have been one of the 'greys', misinterpreted as an 'old man' by a child's brain?

There's clearly a memory in James's mind which could be unlocked through hypnosis. It's a fascinating incident which seems a prime candidate for regression therapy, but if that path were to be followed, can we be sure, in view of the possibility of false memory syndrome, that a true and accurate picture would emerge?

INTERRUPTED JOURNEYS

CLOSE ENCOUNTERS, CHANGED LIVES

PSYCHIC CONTACTEE · AMERICAN BIAS · THE LOSSIEMOUTH INCIDENT · ALIEN ENCOUNTER AT LOCHORE · MISSING TIME · THE A70 ABDUCTION · GREEN GLOW NEAR ABERFELDY · A70 SIGHTING · PSYCHIC DIMENSION · PIZZA MYSTERY · REPEATER ABDUCTEE · HYBRID ENTITIES · TWO-WAY COMMUNICATION

Maybe it's the media, but there's a general view that alien abduction cases start with a car journey. On route, a strange object confronts the vehicle and its occupants. Perhaps they stop for a close look or are so frightened that they accelerate away but find themselves enveloped by a mist or a strange blackness. Suddenly it's clear again and the witnesses find themselves driving down the road as if nothing has happened, but when they reach their destination they discover to their astonishment that their journey has taken hours longer than it should have done. Time is missing from their lives. Eventually by various means including hypnotic regression they learn that they have been taken up by alien entities.

It's certainly true that this pattern does occur right across the world including Scotland. The abduction incident which sparked off the phenomenon in the USA, the Betty and Barney Hill case of 1961, followed exactly that course and, if the whole thing is simply imaginary, created the pattern which others copy. In England the Aveley abduction incident of 1974 followed a very similar course[1]. But there have also been plenty of abduction incidents which do not conform to the standard scenario and, in fact, fit into no pattern at all.

PSYCHIC CONTACTEE

Andrew Hennessey's encounters certainly don't fit the Betty and Barney Hill scenario. Well after the first cases in the United States, but long before the abduction scene was widely reported, Andrew went through a series of strange experiences. As he described it, 'In April 1980 in my bedroom in Portobello [a suburb of Edinburgh] at around 11 p.m., I was looking at the bookcase when I saw tiny green balls about the size of a one pence piece bouncing slowly over my books. I watched in fascination and horror. I turned over in my bed and hoped they would go away. A while later I looked back but they were still there. Around midnight my parents went to bed and after the lights had gone off I realised that there was a strange light in my bedroom. I saw above the coffee table a hovering silver ball. It moved over to the foot of the bed and I heard a voice

1. The Aveley abduction case has had the same impact on British ufology as the Hill case had in the USA. It was the first abduction case in the UK to become widely known. As in the Hill case, it was also the first example of the use of hypnotic regression in such an incident in the UK. The case involved a family who drove into a mysterious mist and experienced a period of 'lost time'. Hypnosis eventually uncovered memories of having been taken on board a UFO by alien entities.

saying "Don't be afraid." I pulled the cover over my head and tried to get to sleep'.

When Andrew who was twenty-three at the time of the incident awoke the next day he found that he was very tightly tucked up in his bed. Too tightly for him to have done it himself. It was also very late, the clock showing two in the afternoon. He had slept way past his normal waking time. There were vague memories too of grey aliens and that 'something wonderful had happened'. Andrew, in fact, believes he had been floated through the bedroom wall and into a spaceship above his house.

Andrew later trained as a spiritual medium, but felt that spirit contact couldn't explain some of the imagery that was coming through. In 1995 Andrew, now a professional medium, experienced another major alien encounter. 'In 1995 we played a gig at Glencoe. It was New year. After the gig I was lying in my bunk bed when a grey appeared and embraced me. It took me underground and showed me a whole city inside a cavern. I though that it was maybe under Glencoe'.

Through his experiences Andrew has developed considered views on the nature of alien contact. 'I think the human race has been sharing this planet with other alien races for millions of years. The human race was an experiment. We didn't originate on the planet'.

AMERICAN BIAS

But if we do share the planet with other 'aliens' (I've put in the inverted commas because in Andrew's scenario we too are 'aliens') why are they abducting us? And why do they concentrate their abduction efforts on one part of the world. It's undeniable that the United States is by far the main source of abduction reports. From New Hampshire to California there are thousands of individuals claiming memories of forced encounters with aliens. American ufologist Bud Hopkins, at his centre for abductees, claims to have personally dealt with 500 individuals who have had such experiences. This case load on its own is more than the total number of reported incidents in the United Kingdom.

It does seem then that the abduction phenomenon is culture influenced. How else can we explain the frequency of abduction experiences in the States compared to, for example, Great Britain? Or are we prepared to accept the argument that Americans are inherently more interesting to alien intelligence than the average European? Can any sensible person be persuaded that alien contact is a reality and not a kind of modern myth, a re-awakening of the ancient tales of contact with fairies and similar alleged mythological entities? If the whole saga seems less than credible, then, I would suggest, that does no justice to the individuals who have, in all honesty, strange tales to relate. There is little doubt in my mind that inexplicable incidents have affected the lives of a number of people, incidents for which these witnesses to the bizarre still seek an explanation. Their experiences cannot, must not, be dismissed out of hand, as sceptics in America and Britain would dearly love to do. There is certainly a case to be answered.

THE LOSSIEMOUTH INCIDENT

First, however, a note of caution. It may surprise UFO

investigators recently arrived on the scene that Scotland was the alleged location of a very early alien contact case. In 1954, hard on the heels of George Adamski's meetings with Venusians in America[2], Cedric Allingham drove to Scotland for a holiday. He had chosen February for his annual break, so Mr Allingham was either ignorant of the climate beside the North Sea or was a hardy type who could ignore the cold. His destination was the area around Lossiemouth, a well known fishing centre, for a spot of hiking and birdwatching.

On 18 February, while taking a walk on the coastal path from Lossie to the nearby village of Buckie, Mr Allingham caught sight of a saucer-shaped object. It moved away but returned a short while later, at which point Mr Allingham took some photographs, though these showed only a distant speck in the sky.

He had by this time realised that here was a truly mysterious craft. His thoughts were confirmed when the object reappeared yet again, low down, and landed a few hundred yards away. Mr Allingham, meanwhile, was again busy with his camera.

The door of the spaceship slid open and a humanoid alien stepped out. Cedric Allingham was able to communicate with the alien, who turned out to be from Mars, using drawings and gestures. After learning several amazing and previously unknown facts about the red planet—for instance that the 'canals' of Mars did indeed contain water—Mr Allingham

2. George Adamski was the USA's earliest and most famous 'contactee'. In 1952 he claimed to have met beautiful, humanoid aliens who informed him they had journeyed from Venus. He also claimed to have been taken aboard their spaceships on several trips around the galaxy. Later, he toured planet earth, recounting his adventures with these friendly 'aliens'.

reluctantly wished his visitor goodbye as the space traveller indicated it was time for him to leave.

As the disc became a dot in the sky, Mr Allingham wondered who on earth would believe his story. Fortunately, the whole incident had, it turned out, been witnessed by a local fisherman, James Duncan, who testified to the truth of the events. With this sworn statement Cedric Allingham published a book, *Flying Saucers From Mars*, which caused a sensation. Here was documented evidence, with photographs, of contact with a person from another world. Or so it seemed for a while.

Unfortunately for the credibility of ufology in Scotland, the whole series of events was later exposed as a huge hoax. However, it took over a dozen years for the truth to emerge and at the time of the event its accuracy was widely accepted. People wanted to and were ready to believe Cedric Allingham. The revelation that it was fictitious adversely affected the public's attitude towards Scottish close encounter cases. It was not until 1979, twenty-five years after the Allingham affair, that the media in Scotland paid serious attention to incidents involving alien contact.

Since 1954, however, encounters with entities have taken a more sinister turn. Nowadays we talk of 'abductions' rather than 'encounters'. The idea of 'abduction' implies being taken against one's will, rather than the friendly face-to-face chat that Cedric Allingham claimed to have taken part in. This change in attitude as well as the cultural context have affected our perception of what alien contact involves. I would suggest that these variable factors should encourage us to be cautious about abduction reports. There are many disturbing stories, but in assessing such incidents we must try always to locate the wood rather than be spellbound by the trees. We must try hard to be careful and control our enthusiasm, because abduction incidents are at the heart of the UFO mystery and should be objectively assessed.

Bob Taylor's encounter has already been discussed in depth. Arguably, although he was unconscious for a period of approximately twenty minutes, this does not count as missing time. On the other hand, there was clearly a time gap between Bob's physical contact with mine-like objects and his 'coming to'. Bob, to my knowledge, has never indicated that he remembers anything of what happened during this period. It remains to this day a complete blank. Bob, however, has experienced no bad dreams, no frightening afterthoughts and no wakening in the middle of the night in a sweat. He remains what he always was: the calm Scotsman with his feet firmly on the ground.

One fact that, perhaps, separates Bob's experience from most abduction cases is that Bob was unconscious for a comparatively short time and has always been clear about the sequence of incidents as they happened to him. Nevertheless, there is no getting away from the fact that, for at least a twenty-minute period, Bob was unaware of anything that was going on around him. Given the dearth of other evidence, we can only speculate as to what happened to him during that period. Probably he did, in fact, simply lie unconscious on the ground till the barking of his dog brought him round. Whatever the truth, Bob has never shown any signs of worrying about the missing period. Unlike Christine.

ALIEN ENCOUNTER AT LOCHORE

Details of Christine's remarkable encounter, which took place in 1973, did not emerge till the 1990s when she confided the incident to a friend, Brian. He himself had witnessed a UFO in the 1960s and was soon convinced by the account Christine gave that she had experienced something unusual. He wrote to leading ufologist Jenny Randles, who passed the matter on to Scottish Earth Mysteries Research for investigation.

Clearly, after 20 years there were going to be problems establishing what had actually taken place, but it nevertheless represented a challenge which we did not wish to refuse. Intrigued though we became the more we absorbed the broad details of Brian's letter, we did not realise at this early stage just how remarkable, and at the same time frustrating, the investigation of Christine's experience would prove to be.

At our first meeting with Christine in her comfortable first floor flat not far from Dunfermline, with Brian present, it soon became clear that her strange experience still haunted her.

I have visited the spot of her encounter and, in spite of the passage of time and the impressive scenery, a dark cloud can still descend on your mind as you picture the events of that evening. Christine, with her friend Margaret, had visited Lochore Country Park on a warm August day. They had been taken there by Margaret's parents in a car. The evening passed quickly until, shortly before 9 p.m. when it was still light, they packed up and headed for home. Following a lane out of the park they came to a junction where the green ended and a housing estate began. From the car radio they learned that it was now right on nine o'clock. A car drew up quietly behind them.

At this point two things happened simultaneously: the radio went dead and the car engine cut out. As if her eyes were drawn by a magnet, Christine, in the back seat with her young friend, looked to the left across an area of open ground. Heading towards them strode two veritable giants moving in a rather mechanical manner—like machines rather than living beings. Both wore one-piece silver suits, emphasising their over-large heads. Christine cannot be sure how long it took the entities to cover the space that separated them, but she does have a vivid memory of the strange beings getting closer and closer to the car, and the car simply refusing to start. When the two beings were almost up to the window, within yards of where Christine sat frozen and unable to move, she experienced a choking sensation and, it seems, passed out. What happened next remains a mystery.

When Christine came to, she saw the backs of the two 'giants' as they returned in the direction they had come from. Moments after they had disappeared from view, a cone of light spread around the trees at the edge of the field, as if marking the path of an object heading skywards. At this precise moment the car engine roared into life, as did the radio. A human voice was also heard—the driver of the vehicle behind had rushed up and shouted: 'What the bloody hell was that?' Christine doesn't remember if anyone gave an answer. All she recalls is sitting in silence as they continued their interrupted journey.

When Christine walked in the door, her mother's first words were: 'Where have you been?' Her mother reminded her sharply that it was after 11 o'clock. She should have been in long before. Margaret's mother explained apologetically that they 'had been held back'.

After the shock of the parental rebuke had worn off, it dawned on Christine that a ten-minute drive had taken nearly two hours. Or, to be more precise, there were two hours missing out of Christine's life, for neither then nor since has she been able to account for this lost time.

The day after the incident Christine mentioned it to her friend's mother, naturally curious and looking for reassurance as any child would be. Christine has told me that the lady point blank refused to talk about the event, telling her in clear language to forget it. It is hard for a 12-year-old to be persistent when faced with a wall of adult silence and so Christine did not forget, but kept silent about it, for nearly twenty years.

Nevertheless, Christine wanted to find the answer to the question which nagged and ate away at her. What had happened during those lost hours? Could hypnosis uncover the solution? She was willing to try anything and so a first session was arranged with an authority on the subject who, for professional reasons, does not wish to be named.

The hypnosis session proved dramatic. Christine turned out to be an excellent subject and was gradually and carefully taken back to the day of the encounter. Up to that point Christine had been very calm and relaxed, but as she relived the memory of the car engine cutting out a dramatic change took place. Christine became visibly distressed and started choking, putting her hands to her throat, apparently unable to speak. Immediately the hypnotist took action to calm Christine and, sensibly, informed us that he thought it better not to carry on with the session because of Christine's severe reaction. I agreed completely. I didn't think that anything useful could be gained, and Christine's distress had been enough to prove that she had been through a traumatic incident at the time she claimed.

In spite of what had seemed an upsetting few moments to those who had watched, Christine emerged in a remarkably calm frame of mind. She suffered not even a single disturbed night and even said that she was willing to continue with the hypnosis sessions. She remains determined to get to the bottom of what happened to her.

MISSING TIME

Hypnosis does not appeal to everyone and has so far been resisted by Andrew Swan. He too has experienced 'missing time' although he, unlike Christine, believes that there is a simple explanation. Andrew's experience began late in the evening of 30 July 1994. A violent electrical storm was lighting up the night sky, and, in order to get a better look at the lightning strikes, he drove to a vantage point beside the playing fields at Armadale Academy, a secondary school a few minutes' journey time away. Parking his Audi coupe beside the football pitch Andy, a cable-layer with Scottish Power, caught sight of a large object hovering behind a row of trees a few hundred yards opposite. He noted that the UFO was pyramid-shaped and saw the time by his watch was 11.45 p.m. Andy later commented: 'I thought it was going to crash'.

But the object made no attempt to move and hung motionless as if suspended on a thread in mid air. Puzzled, but intrigued, Andy jumped back into the driver's seat and followed the road which took him to a viewpoint on the far side of the mysterious visitor. As he cruised along the route, however, either the UFO he had been watching or a second object flew low down at head height, almost seeming to scrape the roof of his car. The UFO halted abruptly and Andy did an emergency stop. Standing at the road-side, Andy could clearly make out the UFO, shaped like an inverted pyramid, floating either just above or in front of a bing. He estimated the object as being nearly 40 feet long.

The stand-off between the UFO and Andy continued for about 20 minutes, till Andy decided he would, literally, shed some more light on the problem. In his vehicle lay a powerful halogen spotlight and Andy reckoned that this could be put to good use without his having to get closer to any possible danger. Unfortunately for Andy, events didn't work out quite as he had planned.

As soon as the beam hit the UFO, the halogen bulb exploded. Andy took it as a definite signal that the object did not wish to be observed. As he stared at the 'dead' spotlight, the exposed situation that he found himself in dawned on him. He was in the middle of nowhere with not another person in sight. It was high time he left the scene of his encounter. Unfortunately for Andy, when he turned the ignition the car refused to start.

Andy had already had the presence of mind to call the police, but had been frustrated by the delay in their arrival and had taken it on himself to shine his torch towards the UFO with the result described. Locked in an immobilised car, his nerves were stretched to breaking point. Then, as he renewed his efforts to get under way, the enigmatic object shot into the air and flew over him at breathtaking speed.

Andy grabbed his mobile phone and dialled the police a second time. As it turned out a patrol car was already on its way in response to the first call, but had been delayed by taking the wrong road. Andy had hardly finished his second call when the blue flashing light came into view.

Andy quickly explained what had happened and was breathalysed at his own request (with a negative result). He certainly had not been drinking that night. On the other hand, the strange craft had gone and so the police were left with a mystery and a car that wouldn't start. The last problem was far more easily solved, so the AA were called out to get Andy back on the road. I was fortunate enough to be able to locate the man who answered that call, a Mr Donald Macandrew. According to his records, Mr Swan's call was logged at 2.42 a.m. and the AA were informed that the police were in attendance. By the time thirty-four-year-old Mr Macandrew arrived on the scene, over forty-five minutes had elapsed and he noted the time as 3.36. These timings were to assume a deep significance in due course. For the time being the AA man took note of the fact that his 'customer' gave every appearance of having suffered a real fright. To Donald, Andrew explained how he had arrived at his present situation. Mr Macandrew was struck by the fact that his client repeatedly stated that he had been watching the UFO 'for forty minutes' although, if the times given were correct, three and a half hours had gone by since the mysterious object had been first seen.

Donald Macandrew tried to get the car started, but without success. He turned the ignition and flicked the side lights. Nothing. He poked the fuse box. It looked good. No fuses blown. But the car was definitely dead. It was clear that the only way the car would be getting home was at the end of a tow rope. Then, job done, as he pulled into gear to take his charge away a remarkable event occurred. Andrew's side-lights, previously as dead as the proverbial dodo, sprang into life. Thinking a miracle had occurred, Donald turned the car engine over, but the machine obstinately refused to move. As a baffled Mr Macandrew told me when I interviewed him, 'The side lights coming on doesn't make technical sense!'

The following Monday Donald returned to Andrew Swan's house in Armadale, partly intrigued and partly as the conscientious officer who wanted to see if the 'dead' car could be made to rise from the grave again. His astonishment was still obvious some months after the incident when he told me that the car had started as normal later that very Sunday morning of the incident. Andrew had decided to give it a try and, like magic, the motor sprang into life. Both he and Donald expressed themselves baffled by the car's unexpected response.

In fact, in this strange case, there are not one but two mysteries to clear up. What influence was it that led the car engine to stop, then start again wholly on its own? And how do we account for the missing time in Andrew Swan's life? He insists that he made a phone call to the police before midnight. But no phone call was logged by the police computer till 2 a.m. What happened during that gap? Andrew Swan claims that there is nothing to explain. The police, he adamantly repeats, must have made a mistake. Officers, however, equally vehemently deny there has been any mix-up, asserting that their version of the timings is undeniably correct. Intriguingly, Mr Swan refuses to undergo hypnosis as he has no wish to discover that even stranger incidents may have taken place during his encounter.

THE A70 ABDUCTION

One case, which has received a great deal of media attention, is largely based on testimony which emerged when the two witnesses later underwent hypnotic regression.

On 17 August 1992 Gary Wood and Colin Wright had a close encounter of a very strange kind. The two men were delivering a satellite TV system to a friend in the village of Tarbrax, 15 miles outside the city of Edinburgh. They set off at around 10 p.m., expecting the journey to take no more than half an hour. But it was to take them well over two hours to reach their destination.

The A70, once it passes through the outlying suburbs of Currie and Balerno, almost immediately enters a bleak expanse of moor that stretches the length of the Pentland Hills all the way to Carnwath. This desolate and often inhospitable road is known as the Lang Whang. Tarbrax lies off the main road and is itself an extremely isolated place.

As they drove towards Harperrig Reservoir, about five miles from Balerno, the car was approaching a blind bend in the road when Wood heard Wright call out: 'What the hell is that?' Looking up, he saw a very large object that seemed to be hovering 20 feet above the road. By his reckoning the object was about 30 feet wide, black in colour, and resembled the classic 'flying saucer' shape familiar to him from science-fiction films. Windowless, it looked as if it were made of a solid metallic substance.

Terrified, Wood put his foot down on the accelerator in an attempt to drive underneath the object and get away from the scene as fast as possible. As the car passed under it, they were plunged into what Wood later described as 'a void of blackness'. He also described a 'shimmering curtain' falling around them, rather like the picture on an untuned TV set. In the darkness they felt a shunt on the back of the car and then, what seemed like only moments later, they were back on the starlit road once again.

Wood immediately drove off at high speed, arriving at Tarbrax at 12.45 a.m. He had found the experience deeply disturbing, and his only concern had been to get away as quickly as possible. Both men were amazed to learn that they had arrived about two hours later than expected. They had set off at 10 p.m. It was now 12.45 a.m. the following morning. Their 30-minute journey had taken, inexplicably, five times as long.

After the encounter, Gary began to experience various unpleasant symptoms, including headaches and bouts of extreme nervousness. He quickly connected these sensations with his strange vision on the A70. Having tried, but failed, to contact Scottish Earth Mysteries Research (which had changed address), Gary eventually contacted UFO investigator Malcolm Robinson. Soon afterwards, the two witnesses decided to undergo hypnosis in an attempt to account for the 'missing time' on their journey. It was a brave decision, as BUFORA, Britain's leading UFO research group, had long since abandoned the practice because of the unreliability of the testimony produced.

Following sessions with experienced hypnotherapist Helen Walters, details of an abduction by small grey extraterrestrials emerged. In his account of what took place on board the alien craft, Gary described one of the 'greys' as having 'a translucent bone-shaped arm with long fingers'. While he was inside the spacecraft he saw a hole in the floor filled with some kind of thick, sticky fluid. As he looked, he saw 'a head appear out of it with a body and two arms. The creature must have been pretty big, bigger than me. It was like a skeleton with flesh around it. It had long arms, really long arms. It had a long body, really skinny, with the skin tight to the bone'.

He described the entity as having a large head with two prominent, but non-human dark eyes. Its flesh appeared discoloured. These strange beings communicated with Gary using telepathy. Their purpose in abducting him appeared to be to carry out some form of examination. These remembered incidents were far from reassuring for either abductee, although Colin Wright seemed less concerned about the incident than his friend Gary. Indeed, Gary has said that he continues to experience visits from alien beings, visits which he finds disturbing.

The crucial issue in all such cases is whether the details of the abduction incident would have emerged without the patient being hypnotically regressed. Can we be absolutely sure that the account that emerged was genuine, or was it simply the product of a subconscious reworking of a thousand images collected from television, films, books and magazines? It is a long-established fact that hypnosis can lead to witnesses recounting details that are manifestly incorrect. So how do we separate fact from fiction? False memory syndrome may not be the answer in this case, but it has to be considered as a possibility.

Both witnesses remain adamant about the reality of their encounter, the strange craft they came across and the time missing out of their lives. Neither witness contacted the police because they felt sure that the story would not have been believed. How do you start telling such a story, in any case? The delay in reporting it, however, meant that certain vital evidence was not examined. What, for example, happened to Gary's car during the period of the abduction? If they were taken from the car and returned to it at least an hour later, then that vehicle must have been stored or kept somewhere. We will never know what happened to the car during this time, as it was sold on soon after the incident and no testing or inspection was carried out—a real loss to ufology.

Nevertheless, we can be absolutely sure about one thing: something very strange happened that night on the road to Tarbrax. Exactly what it was remains to be determined.

GREEN GLOW NEAR ABERFELDY

An intriguing incident took place in January 1969 near Aberfeldy. Bill McGuire, at the time a student at Jordanhill College of Education, had been attending an in-service training course at Aviemore. The course completed, Bill set off on the return journey by car to his home in Blackburn. He takes up the story, 'I was sober and aware of the cold, bright evening as I travelled in my car. The road back from Aviemore was at times more like country lanes, so I had to be careful and alert. As I reached Aberfeldy . . . I suddenly became aware that my car appeared to be engulfed in a bright, green glow. I drew my car into the side of the roadway, thinking there must be a helicopter above my car. I could not hear any sound, so I switched off my ignition, and put off my car lights. The car remained engulfed in the green glow. I decided to start my car engine again as I was completely at a loss to explain what the glow was. I then travelled about 20 yards and the green glow continued to engulf the car. I again stopped my car. I switched off the ignition and I could hear no sound of engines or anything above my car which could account for the green glow. I was feeling scared, but lowered the driver's side window and looked above my car'. Again Bill noted that there was no obvious source of the strange green light which continued to shine. He got back into the car, turned the ignition, flicked his lights on and at that moment the green glow disappeared. The incident, which he reckoned had begun at 9.30 p.m., had lasted five minutes. Bill also recalls driving by a fir plantation just before the incident which may or may not be significant.

On its own this would rate as a very interesting and unusual experience. However I would like to raise one particular point. At the time of this incident in 1969 abduction experiences were not well known or publicised. But what if they had been? Would Bill have wondered about 'missing time'? Would he have considered going through hypnotic regression and if he had what might have been the outcome? It's significant, to my mind, that whilst Bill was intrigued by the incident he was never worried by it which was probably due to the fact that he did not have to consider the 'alien abduction' factor.

I'm not trying to play down the A70 incident. In fact evidence recently came into my possession which backs up Gary and Colin's account or at least the validity of the initial encounter. This came in the form of a report from Jennifer Whyte of an incident that took place in 1983, several years before the abduction encounter.

A70 SIGHTING

One day in January of that year, at around nine in the morning, Jennifer was heading along the A70, on her way to work, and had reached Crosswoods about a mile from the turn off to the village of West Calder. The spot is about two miles west of the location of the 1992 incident. Jennifer describes what happened next. 'I had just cleared the bad bends and trees of Crosswoods when I noticed a very bright white ball of light coming up the line of the road towards me about 100 feet above the road. I pulled into a lay-by and the object came to a stop above and slightly in front of my car at a height of about 30 feet. It hung above me . . . and then started to move off to the west, It travelled slowly for about 50 yards then came slowly back to where it had been in front of me, paused a few seconds, then shot off at high speed eastwards and disappeared over the Pentlands.' Interestingly, Jennifer was very disappointed when the UFO vanished, going so far as to say that she 'felt bereft'. One odd fact is that Jennifer says that the UFO 'must' have hovered above her for 30 minutes as she was late for work, yet while the incident was taking place she says that she 'did not notice the passage of time'. If the sighting did last that long then at that time of day the encounter *must* have been seen by passing traffic. It's inconceivable that it wasn't.

As to the object itself, Jennifer refers to it as a 'bright white globe with soft edges' and felt that 'it always kept the same face towards me'. Jennifer also noticed what she calls 'some sort of spatial distortion', as she seemed 'to be able to see the road for a couple of miles in front of me [as from above]', yet as she notes: 'from the lay-by . . . I should only have seen a few yards to the next bend'. The UFO was absolutely silent. In addition, although it was a grey winter morning, the country-side around was lit up as if under bright moonlight.

PSYCHIC DIMENSION

Before recounting the next experience, let me say first of all that I condemn the use of all banned substances. I want to make this clear because the witness, Stuart, told me straight out that he has been a user of marijuana. On the night of his terrible experience in 1989 he had smoked some earlier that day. He has assured me, however, that his experience was not related to the effects of his habit. He felt confident in the reality of what took place to put this down on the record. I appreciated his honesty on the matter.

The incident began when Stuart returned to his friend's basement flat in West Edinburgh in the early hours of the morning. Stuart did not have a good relationship with his father, he told me, and therefore at this point in his life was sleeping in a pal's spare bedroom. He spent quite a lot of time staying with friends.

A strange atmosphere seemed to envelope the room. Stuart felt as if a heavy presence was hanging over his body as he lay with his eyes closed on the bed. The room was in darkness and in the dark Stuart could hear the pounding of his heart as fright took hold of him. He felt he could not move properly although he knew he was not paralysed in any way. Summoning up all his strength Stuart threw himself out of bed and flicked on the light. Nothing. The room looked perfectly normal. He clambered back into bed and lay down. Classical music started to play. He could hear it clearly, knowing right away that something odd was happening as it was not the sort of music that appealed to him at this particular moment. 'What the hell is going on?' he muttered, opening his eyes to gaze at the ceiling. By now the music had stopped and Stuart allowed his eyes to wander down from the ceiling. It was then that he saw it. A 'living vortex of energy, like a swirling mass'. He was fascinated yet repelled by the sight. Something then led Stuart to glance in the direction of the window. The curtains weren't fully drawn and in the gap between he could make out a large almond-shaped eye staring at him. The gaze was one of power almost as if an invisible beam of energy was being directed at him. He was fascinated by the eye, yet at the same time he could not hold its gaze. The energy emanating from it forced him to look away. Yet Stuart did not feel that his mysterious watcher was in any way threatening him. All the while this was going on, Stuart could clearly hear the sounds of passing traffic on the road outside. Then an astonishing incident occurred. The disembodied head of the being floated straight through the glass and into the bedroom, where it hung suspended in mid air. Stuart stared in sheer disbelief. It looked exactly like the traditional grey. Insect like with large, dark eyes. Then it simply vanished.

When Stuart examined the window the following morning he noticed nothing exceptional. There were some scratches on the frame, but that could easily be explained by the attention of a local cat. He did notice, however, that the distance from the ground to the pane through which the entity had stared at him was very short. Only a few feet, in fact, so whatever it was was well below human height in stature.

One aspect that has to be considered is to what extent these experiences arise from psychic ability rather than relate to the current 'alien agenda'. I put this point to Stuart when I interviewed him in his Edinburgh flat. Stuart has wondered about this himself so my query didn't come as a surprise. He did often sense a presence either in his room or just outside it. He had seen a door open apparently of its own accord and other similar incidents. He was particularly prone to sensing that 'something' was there at night when he was trying to sleep. He found this disconcerting and often slept with the light on. Some time before his alien encounter he stayed alone in a friend's house in West Preston Street in Edinburgh. During the night he would hear strange sounds drifting from the direction of the wardrobe. Mice? Of course, it might have a simple explanation, but the persistent aspect of this phenomenon points to another conclusion.

All this typifies the 'medium' who is unaware of his ability, or who does not know how to control it. If Stuart is psychic does this rule out the validity of the experience with the alien 'grey'? It does only if we hold to the belief that what we are dealing with is a flesh and blood entity who has travelled across space. (The question of whether the UFO phenomenon has a physical or psychical basis is discussed further in Chapter 9.)

PIZZA MYSTERY

You don't have to be abducted by greys to have strange experiences. Brian Wilson's encounter while working in a pizza parlour has all the trappings of a farce, except for the sinister implications lurking just beneath the surface. Let Brian, a no-nonsense individual, tell of the incident in his own words:

'In the summer of 1990 I was working as a full-time pizza chef in a chip/pizza shop in the New Town in Edinburgh. It was a busy shop, full of tourists who would come in for a home-made pizza. The pizza part of the shop was well decorated with a large display cabinet where most of the ingredients were kept, mushrooms, onions, peppers etc. We would make the pizza of the customer's choice there and then in front of them. Most customers found this exciting to watch as we would toss the pizza base in the air, pour on the tomato sauce and anything else they wanted on it. It would then be put in the oven for a few minutes, and "hey presto!" you had your freshly made pizza.

'One night in August, I was working with my colleague Doug. Two rather small adults came in, about 5 feet in height. They both came and stood behind the counter facing me and with their right hands raised and their palms facing me announced that they were Americans. Their precise words were: "Hi, we're Americans". I thought this rather an odd thing to say as you can always tell Americans by their accents. Anyway, I said "Good evening, what would you like?" They asked me what we made and after I replied "pizzas" they turned to me and asked "What are pizzas?" My immediate thought was that it was almost unbelievable for a pair of Americans to not know what pizzas were. I looked at Doug with amazement and he was looking at me in the same way.

'I would like to add that during this brief time I had begun to think that they did look just a little bit strange. They were both rather small, the female had an odd shape to her shoulders—they were lopsided—and the male kept looking around the shop with a sort of amazement as if he had never been in a pizza parlour before. I did, though, begin to think that perhaps they genuinely did not know anything about pizzas.

'They then asked me to make up two pizzas. After I had put on the tomato sauce and cheese (which, by the way, they studied very closely) I asked them what toppings they would like. The female pointed to one of the containers and then asked what was in it. The container had green peppers in it and it was now that I started to think that they were either winding me up or had just landed from another planet. To not know what pizzas were was hard to swallow, but not being able to recognise a simple green pepper was beyond belief. Doug and I were looking at each other in disbelief and thinking that this was a big wind-up at our expense. The female asked if green peppers tasted nice, to which I replied "yes". They both wanted green peppers on their pizzas, which were then put in the oven to cook. During the few minutes their pizzas were in the oven I had to serve other customers who had come into the shop, but I did not notice anything unusual about them standing waiting, except that they stood perfectly still and did not say a word to each other.

'At last their pizzas were ready, they paid me the £8 and I wished them goodnight—it was about 10.15 p.m. What was unusual when they left was that after paying £8 for two pizzas, they both took one bite out of their pizza and threw the rest in the bucket outside the shop. I had read stories on the subject of alien life-forms masquerading as human beings before and that generally they are not very good at doing so. I would certainly say that these two individuals came across acting as humans but also not doing a very good job of it. It was certainly very, very bizarre behaviour and although they did not make me feel threatened, they have left a very lasting impression on me.' Definitely a 'Strange But True' encounter!

Brian's experience does seem to contradict accounts given by some witnesses that aliens are capable of masquarading as human beings. In fact, according to some reports you would not be able to tell an extraterrestrial from 'John Smith', so well do they imitate our behaviour—and common sense might indicate that non-humans among us would not look to draw attention to themselves. On the other hand, this case is reminiscent of accounts given by other witnesses when describing encounters with individuals who they suspect of being of alien origin because of their odd behaviour—as if they were trying to be human yet hadn't quite got their act right, in the same way as spies are caught because they haven't grasped the nuances of a different language. But if abduction experiences tell us anything, it's that aliens come in all shapes and sizes, so we should learn not to expect a 'standard' behaviour pattern.

REPEATER ABDUCTEE

I became involved in the next case through a mysterious phone call late one night. The caller told me of his own experiences, but also related strange happenings that involved a friend of his, David. He asked me if I was interested in finding out more, which I readily confirmed. He closed the conversation by affirming that if David was prepared to meet me he would get back in touch.

A week later the phone rang again. It was Andrew, my contact with the mysterious Dave. Dave had agreed to discuss his UFO encounters and so a meeting was arranged for the following Monday. That gloomy November evening found me parked at a run-down shopping centre on Edinburgh's west side.

As I waited, the radio switched on, I realised with a shock that I had forgotten to ask my contact for a description. I had no idea what he looked like! Mentally I kicked myself for such a basic error. Dave knew I owned a grey Volvo, but I'd been forced to park in a dimly lit space beside a row of similarly dark coloured vehicles. If he didn't come to take a closer look he might easily miss me.

Cursing the cold, I switched off the engine, and following the pot-holes made my way to the bus stop, our pre-arranged meeting place. A couple of men stood chatting to each other. A woman perched on the seat shivered in the cold. Since Dave had said nothing about a woman, I suspected that the two men were the obvious candidates. As I considered an opening line, the awkwardness of my position dawned on me. How do you introduce yourself to a stranger when you intend to have a conversation about UFOs? Would they view me as some weirdo and exact suitable revenge? I glanced at their faces and sized up their 'friendliness quotient'. I mulled over my opening lines like a playwright with his dialogue. Fortunately, the gods saved the day. A number 32 bus came round the roundabout and pulled to a halt by my side. My anonymous chums shuffled forward and climbed aboard. Unless they suffered from an uncontrollable bus fetish, they clearly weren't my customers.

Then I heard voices. Real ones. I turned round and caught sight of three men in their late twenties chatting quietly to one another. They hadn't been there when I crossed the road, but must have arrived while I was rehearsing my lines. As I strove to catch their conversation, I noticed that the woman who had been at the stop shortly before had disappeared, though I hadn't seen her move or catch the '32'. I was beginning to feel as if I'd stepped into someone else's bad dream.

The spell, if that's what it was, was broken when I heard the words 'UFOs' and 'aliens' mentioned. Unless this was a bizarre coincidence this conspiratorial-sounding trio must be my intended contacts.

I went over and introduced myself: 'Hi, I'm Ron Halliday. Are you Dave?' I'd guessed correctly and shook hands with all three, although I noticed that the large chap with blonde hair seemed a little less enthusiastic than the others. I put it down, at this stage, to a reserved nature, something I shared and understood.

We all crammed into my car and drove to Dave's flat, which turned out to be only a few hundred yards away. As I parked my car in a badly lit square I was starting to feel a little bit uneasy. My efforts at conversation were met with a stilted response. The fair man seemed positively hostile. Was this all part of some set-up, with me as the victim? Was I being led up the garden path? The locks festooning the flat door, worthy of Fort Knox, did nothing to allay my suspicions. Something odd was going on here. By now I was convinced of it.

Sitting comfortably round the fireside, listening to Dave and his companions as their stories began to unfold, I started to relax. I was still a little tense, but was less sure of the cause.

David had by now told of his own experience of seeing strange lights over Arthur's Seat in Edinburgh. But he was less concerned with his own encounters and much more interested in having his friend Gary tell me his story.

Gary's problems began on 9 October at around 3 a.m. as he cycled on the track bordering the Union Canal. This ancient waterway had at one time connected Edinburgh and Glasgow. It had long ago fallen into general disuse, but in recent years had been cleaned up and was a favourite stretch for small pleasure boats. For a good part of its length it is possible to walk or cycle alongside it and many people use it as a convenient route into the centre of Edinburgh. Gary, that morning, had turned on to it as a useful short cut to a friend's house.

Gary, pedalling quietly along, noticed a movement in the trees on the opposite side of the water. At first glance he thought it must be a street light which was probably being hidden by rhythmic swaying of branches caught by the breeze. Although he was trying hard to convince himself that the phenomenon was simply a natural effect, he found that he could not take his eyes away from it, staring at the spot in fascination.

Then his patience was rewarded. Over the tops of the trees arose a 'flying saucer', an apt description in this case, as it closely resembled the shape traditionally associated with UFOs. At the front, however, it carried what Gary could only describe as 'a spiky thing'. Beams of laser light which looked solid in the dark? We can only speculate. The object itself appeared as large as a two-storey house, plainly visible to anyone passing, undoubtedly solid and a kind of creamy beige colour.

Gary was, understandably, astounded and while he felt in no way threatened, he was cautious enough to mount his bike and head off in the opposite direction, pedalling furiously. As he glanced back he noticed that the object seemed to be following him, moving silently, close to the ground. Gary couldn't be sure how long the chase lasted, but when he turned off the canal-way at the first opening and looked back, the UFO was nowhere to be seen. Its sudden disappearance, however, did not end Gary's trauma. In fact, it was only the beginning.

A series of disturbing incidents began to plague Gary's life. He received strange phone calls in which a human-sounding voice would warn him to keep quiet about his encounter. Before Gary had a chance to reply the phone would go dead. On one occasion the radio in his living room started broadcasting, even though it hadn't been plugged into the socket.

More disturbing still, strange creatures started appearing to him. Skinny aliens with large black eyes: the ubiquitous greys. Whenever they turned up, Gary would immediately feel paralysed and be unable to move. During one encounter the greys placed a device behind his ear and pressed what appeared to be a control button. A sharp pain coursed through his head. Instinctively, Gary knocked the device to the floor. The grey's response was far from friendly, snarling furiously and showing a row of unpleasantly sharp teeth. Gary was not physically harmed, but the message was clear enough: whatever Gary wanted, his visitors were determined to have their own way. Over the following months the 'aliens' (how else could they be described?) turned up at Gary's home at all hours. He could tell they had arrived by an unpleasant smell, 'like rotten vegetables', which permeated every corner of the room. Even when he moved to a friend's house for temporary refuge, he couldn't escape their attention. One visited him there.

By now Gary was beginning to wonder if his imagination had detached itself from his conscious control. In short, was he still sane? To test himself, the next time a grey appeared he reached out his hand to touch its arm. If it was solid he would know that this was no figment of his imagination. As he stretched his arm forward, his visitor immediately seemed to sense his intention and, showing an incredible strength which belied its puny frame, firmly, but gently pushed Gary's hand away. Gary was shocked to discover the entity was real. The alien, however, showed no resentment at Gary's clumsy gesture, and instead warned him telepathically to keep clear of Arthur's Seat, a hill which, as I have pointed out on many occasions elsewhere, may hold the key to many of Edinburgh's mysteries[3]. The grey then disappeared. By the time I spoke to Gary, the visits had come to an end, although the memory of them still caused him visible concern. Gary's experience may not be unique in the history of ufology, but it is certainly unique in Scotland.

It could be suggested that Gary's experiences have a psychic dimension, but against this is his description of actual physical contact with the alien. As far as Gary is concerned, this was no 'spirit' being.

3. Arthur's Seat, the hill which dominates the skyline of Scotland's capital city, has for centuries been shrouded in mystery—even the origin of its name is uncertain, although there is a possible link to the legend of Camelot. In past times it was said to have been the haunt of fairies and other strange entities. In recent years it has become something of a UFO hot-spot, a site where UFOs of many kinds have been spotted. Is it a coincidence that Scotland's new parliament will be situated in its shadow?

HYBRID ENTITIES

The A70 incident, to take one example, fits into the established tradition in human/alien contact—the unsuspecting witness who, minding his own business, suddenly finds himself apparently confronted by extraterrestrial intelligence.

But can we go one stage further? Is it possible to argue that alien beings are amongst us and may even have married into our species, producing hybrid offspring? The idea may challenge the beliefs even of those who have immersed themselves in the lore of ufology, but, again, I would draw attention to the experiences of people who have confronted this possibility. They are often straightforward, sensible people with no axe to grind and nothing to gain. Their only 'reward' may be to suffer the indignity of laughter and derision, with the unfortunate result that individuals who have experienced strange incidents feel a reluctance to come forward. However, society may have a lot to learn from what they have been through. I have permission to tell one particular story, but, to safeguard the people involved, I have changed names and places so that identification is not possible. The substance of their experiences, however, is as it is told.

June had her first UFO experience when she was ten, at her home in Craigmillar, Edinburgh. She can't be sure of the exact date, but believes it was during 1963. June was asleep in bed but woke with a start. Outside her window she caught sight of a very bright white object moving slowly. It seemed to be getting closer and closer, growing in size. Interested rather than frightened, June called to her father to come and see. He, however, thought there was nothing out of the ordinary in his daughter's sighting and told her it was only 'a big bright star'. Typically, no sooner had he closed the bedroom door behind him than the object, which was now eye-shaped, started moving towards the window again. Eventually, and June can't remember which, the mystery light either disappeared, or she went to sleep!

June can't recall any strange incidents in her teens, but after she was married she experienced a most strange recall. She visited the Island of Barra, situated in the Outer Hebrides, while on holiday. It was her first trip to the place, but during her stay she became convinced that she had lived there previously. She seemed to know the place so well and recalled incidents that had occurred there in the past. June's husband became disconcerted by his wife's familiarity with the island. He knew they were both strangers to Barra and could not understand her conviction that it was well known to her. So strong did June's feeling become of her previous existence on the island that her husband became quite concerned and then even frightened by the implications of June's knowledge. June's reaction was quite the opposite. She felt elated because, as she says, she had 'come home'.

June's life was blighted by tragedy in 1984 when her husband was killed in a car crash, leaving her to bring up two daughters on her own. The night after the accident, her daughter Laurie came running to June, begging her to come and see a 'big star'. The large white object in the night sky seemed to be blinking directly at them. There was no doubt that they felt it was a sign from heaven. The children said 'goodnight' to the star and then it vanished.

The series of strange incidents which intruded on June's life continued the year after she was widowed, during a family holiday to Hull with her brother. Their route took them across an area of moorland, June is not sure exactly where, and because it was a clear night they stopped to watch the stars. It was then that the inexplicable happened. One of the stars started to move and get closer. This so unnerved her brother, who had always been afraid of the dark, that he insisted on getting back into the car and leaving the spot immediately, in spite of June reassuring him 'they won't harm you'. Then, out of the blue, a police car appeared. Neither June nor her brother had caught sight of any headlights or heard the sound of an approaching vehicle. A policeman stepped out and came over to June asking what they were doing. She replied that they had stopped for a minute and were on their way to Hull. He asked them to follow him off the moor and they drove along behind till both cars came to a crossroads. The policeman indicated they should turn right, which they did, and he turned left. When they looked back it was as if the police car had vanished into thin air.

1985 was to be a year of strange events for June. She returned to Barra for a second visit and sensed again that she was 'coming home'. One day during this visit she went down to the beach and saw the figure of a man, standing alone. She immediately felt that this was her dead husband, Ron. June walked towards the figure and as she did so everything around her went quiet, even the breaking waves. She was now within a few feet of the man and only at this point did she realise that it was not Ron. Had June mistaken a complete stranger for a man she had lived with for years? This might be an obvious conclusion except that she heard this mysterious figure say:

'I'm very sorry that I'm not who you think I am, but everything will be okay'.

June was so upset by these words that she fell to her knees and felt herself being lifted back to her feet by an invisible force. She glanced round to check on the children, and when she looked back the strange figure had disappeared. The incident was so remarkable that it was used in a sermon broadcast on BBC Radio Scotland.

For several years afterwards, things were relatively quiet. Then, in 1991, events began to gather pace. In October of that year, June's older daughter was playing at her friend's house. It was situated only a few hundred yards away, but meant walking through an area of wooded parkland, so June decided to walk over and pick her up. By this time, it was evening, but an evening with a different air about it. The lights in June's house were flickering and generally misbehaving. The video recorder would switch itself on and off. The electrical fault, if that's what it was, started with the lights in the living room, travelled to the video, then moved on to the microwave in the kitchen. It was all a mystery to June, and anyway there was Linda to pick up.

On her way back, part of the way through the wooded area, June became aware of a bright blue light. It shone so strongly it hurt her eyes, and every so often as the wind gusted the area beyond the light became visible. And there it was. A solid object hovering (or standing) amongst the trees. And although a strong wind blew, there was no noise whatsoever. June was frightened. She was shouting at it to go away, saying in her head that she had to get home. Then in the blink of an eye the UFO had gone. June was more than relieved. She was convinced that the object had wanted to take both her and her daughter. But if that was true, what had frightened it off?

Later that year June met Ruth. It was a significant event, as she felt that she had known Ruth all her life. It was this relationship with Ruth that would open June's eyes to the possible nature of extraterrestrial contact. Ruth, June learned, had had a miscarriage, but conceived again nineteen days after the tragic incident. Both women felt that these two events were related, but in a way most people would find difficult to accept. For Ruth and June are convinced that Ruth's husband Leonard is either in part or wholly alien. Their child, Christopher, is therefore a hybrid belonging both to the earth and a planet beyond our galaxy.

Let me assure the reader that this account has not deliberately stepped into the realms of science-fiction. These are the facts as related to me by those involved. Is intermarriage between 'aliens' and humankind such an illogical idea? Might it be possible that there are 'aliens' or other beings who are not really so different from us? Entities who can walk and talk amongst us so convincingly that we would not recognise their true origin? Yet, if you looked and watched closely, you might note some differences not discernible to the casual observer.

Leonard, I am told, seems at times translucent. He talks very little. He moves slowly. He has no close friends. He works in a top secret military base.

If Leonard has this odd air, then why on earth (if you'll excuse the expression) did Ruth marry him? It seems, at least according to June, that Leonard singled Ruth out, almost as if he was hunting her down. A strange story starts to hang together. An entity not from this planet seeking a mate, not at all for sinister reasons. Had we been put on planet X, would we not do exactly the same?

Following her marriage, Ruth moved to a west coast city. Soon afterwards she experienced odd goings on in their new home. Lights started to flicker, dim and go out. Electrical appliances would switch themselves on and off.

One day Christopher, then 18 months old, went missing. Somehow he had clambered out of his cot and across Ruth without waking her. Just as Ruth woke up and discovered he was gone, Christopher walked back into the room. His eyes were red, almost as if something had been done to them. After this incident Christopher was extremely agitated and Ruth asked June to come through and visit her. Both women had already noticed that June had a calming effect on Christopher. Was it something to do with the fact that both she and the child were fascinated by the sight of the stars?

During a stay at Ruth's house an incident occurred which convinced June that she really was involved in a case of alien contact. She woke up one night and found herself sitting, freezing cold, on the edge of the bed. She recalled seeing a bright light shining at the rear of Ruth's house with the whole kitchen lit up. She had gone down to the kitchen and caught sight of a white figure standing at the breakfast bar. It glowed forcefully and the impression conveyed to June was one of sheer beauty. The figure was of human form and in height reached June's chest. June is five feet nine inches tall, so the being she saw must have been about five feet. Slowly she (June was convinced the entity was female) reached up and put her hand on June's shoulder.

'Everything is going to be all right as you are a guardian', she told June. At this point, June found herself back in her bedroom.

Was this incident the beginning or part of an abduction sequence? In some ways it does fit the pattern. To June, however, her contact with alien intelligences, and Christopher's, is an incontrovertible fact. Several times both she and Christopher have woken in bed with muddy feet, evidence that they have been led away by alien entities. And if, as Ruth believes, Christopher may have been implanted in her, isn't it likely that this alien race might wish to have contact with one of their progeny? June also points out that ancient civilisations too were obsessed with the stars. Is that a clue to our origins? June is convinced of one fact: aliens 'walk the earth just like we do'. Every night before she goes to bed June goes into the garden and looks to the skies as she knows 'they are out there'.

In general, as could be gathered from June's account, she has a very positive attitude towards her experiences. However, she did suffer one unnerving encounter. This took place in March 1998. As June told it, she had been 'taken up' but 'they' made a botch up. 'They brought me back too quickly'. She was very upset by this incident as she had learned to trust her contacts and took it for granted that they would look after her. This apparent contradiction worried her because not only did she suffer psychologically but physically as well. June told me: 'I woke up before I got back to my bed. My ears were buzzing. My throat was sore. I had a rash up both legs and blotches on my chest. I felt really queasy. I was frightened witless'.

The alien entities, June explained, did try to calm her down.

'There were a few around me', she recalls. 'One was patting the duvet. They were trying to reassure me, but I was too petrified to move. I didn't want them doing it to me again'.

Disturbing too were the memories that came back to June. Recollections which she felt held some deep meaning, but which the aliens had not clearly spelt out to her. She told me: 'I was in a room with chairs and a high table, I remember being shown it. I felt I didn't want to be there. It was like a council of some description. I was scared to be there'. June also remembers: 'There were these "beings", exceptionally old and they were annoyed. A particularly old one was doing the talking. He kept indicating that he had been let down. Someone had gone back on their word and he was not happy with it'.

While she was there, June saw another woman. She was about 5 feet 8 inches, blond hair, medium build, late 30s with gold rimmed glasses and appeared very frightened.

Meanwhile, June was taken to a box-like object which the entities opened. She saw lying on its side what she can only label as 'something'. An incredibly old entity with its legs slightly bent and its arms up against its chest. June told me: 'It wasn't dead but hanging by a thread'. A voice said to her: 'We now have to teach them a lesson'. June had no idea to whom or what this referred, but was sure that 'something is going to threaten a lot of people'.

I had never seen June concerned about her alien contact before, and was relieved when a few days after I spoke to her she rang me up to say that the matter had now been fully explained to her. Whatever it was that had gone wrong had clearly been resolved.

TWO-WAY COMMUNICATION

If alien beings can contact us, shouldn't it be possible for us to contact them? Of course, there are many individuals who will come forward with claims to have met and talked with extra-terrestrials. There are few, however, who can show you such a being. Perhaps there is only one such person. Certainly I know of only one in Scotland. His name is Alex and he wishes no publicity, arguing sensibly that no-one will believe it even if they see what he can do. And if I were to add that what Alex does is to show you the *spirits* of past aliens (as well as humans) then you will realise just how incredible this story is. It really is beyond belief. Unless you have seen these faces. Sitting in Alex's living room, in full light, people have reported several different types of non-human entities. Spirits of our ancestors also appear. It seems the earth is being given a message. Humans and aliens are all part of one vast universal family, but we cannot count forever on the toleration of those from outside this planet. From what is reported, it appears that these beings have no ill-will towards us and that in the dimension beyond we will all come together as one. The universe is both vast and small. Earth has its place, but Mankind is by no means alone.

THE ELUSIVE 'HOT-SPOT'

THE BORDERS, EAST LOTHIAN, UFO WAVES

HOT-SPOTS, WAVES AND WINDOWS · EARLY DUMFRIESSHIRE INCIDENTS · SOLWAY SPACEMAN
· GIANT CRAFT OVER DUMFRIES · FOCUS ON MOFFAT · FIREBALLS IN THE SKY · LIGHTS OVER
LOCHSIDE · 'A LOT GOING ON . . .' · GEORGE ADAMSKI IN EDINBURGH · DUNBAR ORANGE
BALL · THE EARTHLIGHT THEORY · MYSTICAL ASPECT · CASE STUDY: THE BONNYBRIDGE
PHENOMENON

Game-show host Michael Barrymore has a catchphrase to
introduce the television quiz show *Strike It Lucky*. He calls out,
'What is a hot-spot not?' The audience's response is rendered
unintelligible by the resulting blast of voices so I've never yet
heard the answer. I don't know if Michael is interested in
UFOs but his meaningless catchphrase certainly highlights
the difficulties of defining the 'hot-spot' phenomenon. UFO
'hot-spot' is a phrase loved by journalists and over the years
areas from Southern Scotland to Aberdeen have been awarded
the title. In recent years Bonnybridge, Fife, West Lothian and
Blairgowrie have made the grade as sites of special interest to
ufologists, but in the past other locations have for a while

attracted large numbers of UFO sightings. These have now disappeared back into obscurity, but at the time they too grabbed the headlines. It's a strange phenomenon within the whole UFO mystery. Why do 'hot-spots' move around? Why is it that for a few years one area is awash with spectacular UFO sightings and then becomes quiet again. Is it due simply to fluctuating media interest or does the phenomenon itself interact with the environment, possibly at an inter-dimensional level.

HOT-SPOTS, WAVES AND WINDOWS

On a personal note I should say that I have had first-hand experience of watching hot-spots develop. In particular, I was involved in the Blairgowrie area, West Lothian and in aspects of Bonnybridge. Other ufologists who carried out their own investigations into incidents in these 'hot-spots' no doubt have their own interpretation of what is going on as sighting after sighting piles up within a small radius. I can only offer my own interpretation, drawing on what I observed as these phenomena developed. One factor which strikes me as curious is that throughout the 1980s Scotland had no designated 'hot-spot', in spite of the fact that a 'UFO wave' appeared in 1987. The '70s had a 'Scottish Triangle', the 1990s a 'Falkirk Triangle', but the period in between seems to have been largely quiet.

We should also separate the term 'UFO wave' from 'UFO hot-spot'. A 'wave' is usually taken to refer to a spate of sightings from a wide area over a specific period. The years 1992-93, for example, saw a huge rise in reported incidents from across the whole of Scotland and not just at one location.

Within that wave of reports certain areas seem to have attracted many more UFO sightings than others and become 'hot-spots'. A 'UFO window' is similar to a 'hot-spot' although it does bring with it mystical associations that maybe it does not deserve, as it suggests that UFOs are a phenomenon that can be seen at will in a given location, rather than a seemingly random occurrence. It should be noted that studies by Canadian scientists Michael Persinger and Gyslaine Lafreniere do support the idea that UFO sightings cluster in specific areas. So a 'hot-spot' may not be just the product of media speculation.

EARLY DUMFRIESSHIRE INCIDENTS

The extent of UFO sightings in the Dumfriesshire area was unknown till UFO investigator Robert Rogerson decided to compile a record of UFO incidents in the area. Over a period of a few months Robert unearthed an amazing number of UFO incidents, on which this account is based. From his research it seems clear that for a period Dumfriesshire was a centre of UFO activity and a key part of the 'Central Scotland UFO triangle', as the press described it.

Dumfriesshire is probably better known today the world over because of the tragic downing in 1988 of Pan-Am flight 103, allegedly by Libyan terrorists. This was a deliberate act of sabotage, the exact circumstances of which may never be known, but in the 1970s several small aircraft crashed in mysterious circumstances in the area leading to speculation that UFOs were involved.

In July 1976 several people died when a private aircraft, a

Piper Aztec, ploughed into a hillside ten miles north-east of the town of Moffat. The previous September another light plane came down near the village of Dalmellington resulting in the death of its four passengers. Even stranger was the mysterious disappearance of pilot Jane Whylam while flying near Hawick. Neither the plane nor her body could be found.

This was during the period from 1975 to 1980, during which reports of UFO activity reached a peak in the Dumfriesshire area, although there had been the odd sighting before then. There is an RAF radar station at West Freugh near the town of Luce on the Solway coast, and in the 1950s a UFO incident leaked into the public domain. It emerged that the station had tracked an unidentified object 'for some considerable time'. Predictably, the station's commander, Wing Commander Whitmark, was unable to comment on the report, apparently under orders from the Air Ministry (as it then was), but he did assert that there was 'no question of the radar playing tricks. It was checked on screens twenty miles apart. I am not allowed to say at what speed or in which direction it was travelling'. However, a member of the public came forward to claim that he had seen the object as he was driving through Cumbria to Dumfries. The witness was a 44-year-old lorry driver, James Emmerson, who came from Collin in Dumfriesshire. He reported that he had first noticed a reflection on his windscreen which he took to be the lights of another vehicle. He pulled over and switched off his own lights to get a better look. It was at this point that he noticed a mysterious object hovering above him which, he said, was 'shaped like a half moon and glowed bright yellow. The outer edges were golden russet colour and it moved silently'. He added, 'I watched it for a few seconds and then it suddenly turned on its edge and darted at a fantastic speed out of sight. It was impossible to estimate its size or height, but it seemed only about three feet wide and could not have been very high in the sky'.

Although, perhaps, the area's first publicised sighting, it wasn't the first UFO incident. As early as 1948 a Dumfries ironmonger, James Jardine, spotted a 'large spherical object' hovering over New Abbey in Kirkcudbrightshire, and then in 1955 Mairie Brazier observed a cigar-shaped object travelling over the Galloway Hills.

There appears to be a gap until the next sightings although in neither of these reports do I have a definite date for the incident. One probably dates from the late 1950s or early 60s. A number of witnesses had spotted strange bright objects over the Solway Firth. Walter King from Silvermount, Annan, an electricity board salesman, stated 'It was just after three o'clock on Friday afternoon when I saw the object. It had a very bright outer right and something like a rod through the middle'. At midnight on the same date a vivid blue flash was seen by witnesses all over the area, including a farm-worker James Lamont of Gardruin Farm, Eastriggs. He told interviewers: 'I have never seen anything like it before. It lasted only a few seconds. There was no aeroplane about at the time'.

SOLWAY SPACEMAN

The Solway effectively forms part of the boundary between Scotland and England so one would expect reports of activity over the Firth to feature in both Scottish and English cases. One intriguing incident, which involved a photograph, occurred on the English side of the Solway. Fireman Jim Templeton (44) had taken his wife and daughter on a picnic to the Solway Marshes. It was a sunny day and Jim decided to take a family photo. At the instant that he took the picture he was sure that there was nothing in his viewfinder except five-year-old Frances and, in the background, Chapel Cross atomic power station, six miles distant on the far side of the Solway Firth.

When Jim had the film developed, however, he was in for a surprise. A strange figure appeared prominently in the photograph of his daughter. Jim explained: 'The man seems to be wearing a white padded suit with headgear and standing with his hands on his hips'. It dumbfounded Jim who decided to go to the police and see if they could make any sense of it. He handed the negative over to police photography experts in Carlisle for examination. Tom Oldican, Chief of Cumberland CID eventually reported: 'It is a mystery. We thought it was probably a double exposure, but it isn't. The picture shows someone "in white" but Mr Templeton is adamant that there was no-one else about. It is very puzzling'. Jim, however, wasn't sure if the police had taken his claims that seriously and he eventually concluded: 'The police seem to think that my wife or Frances crept in front of the camera. But I know they did not'.

GIANT CRAFT OVER DUMFRIES

These were sporadic sightings, but in the late 1970s a flood of incidents were reported and the area came to the forefront as a UFO 'hot-spot'. On 31 December 1978 hundreds of people around the town of Dumfries watched a mysterious-looking object hovering in the sky. Given the number of witnesses to the incident it is understandable that descriptions of the UFO varied. Some definitely described it as a 'spaceship' although others likened it to a 'huge aeroplane'. Individuals contacted the police to report the sighting and they in turn were in touch with Air Traffic Control at Prestwick Airport. Air Traffic were aware of the UFO and claimed that 'we have been tracking an object in the sky and have received various reports. It has been identified as a giant meteorite'.

This explanation didn't satisfy some of the witnesses. George King, a timber merchant from Locharbriggs, retorted: 'This was no meteorite. I was driving from Dumfries to Locharbriggs with my family at about 7 p.m. when we saw this object in the sky. It was like a huge plane or airship and was travelling much too slowly for a meteorite. We had plenty of time to observe it and could make out rows of windows like you see in a jumbo jet. There was no noise from it and we all feel it was a strange and weird experience'.

Other witnesses corroborated Mr King's version of events. Colin McIntosh from High Beach near Heathhall reported: 'We were at the front of our house when we saw it and it was such a clear night that we had a perfect view and plenty of time to watch it crossing the sky. We could see a row of portholes which were all brightly lit. There was no noise from it. We have seen meteorites before and this was nothing like them. I have never believed in flying saucers or anything like that before, but now I am not too sure. Instead of coming down as we thought at first it appeared to vanish very quickly in the direction of Tinwald'.

At the same time as Colin was observing the object an off-duty policeman, David McLintock, also caught sight of it then thought it so curious that he stopped his car and phoned his wife so she too could get a glimpse. He confirmed that it was very high up and with a vapour trail 'looked like a meteorite'. To Mr McLintock, however, the significant difference was that 'it was travelling more slowly than any meteorite I have ever seen before'.

Interestingly, there were a large number of UFO sightings from across Scotland at around this time. Typically, the Ministry of Defence dismissed them as space debris from old satellites. But since when does space debris have portholes!

FOCUS ON MOFFAT

The above incident occurred right at the year's end. By November of the following year the area seemed to be attracting UFOs by the dozen and much of this activity centred around one witness, Joyce Byers. Mrs Byers hit the headlines after she announced that for almost a year she had been keeping a diary of UFO sightings. She claimed that she had logged over 100 separate incidents and that the town of Moffat was a focus for UFO activity. In assembling this information, Joyce had the help of a neighbour, eighty-year-old Mary Watson, who was convinced that the UFO threat was real and presented a danger to local inhabitants. Objects recorded by Joyce Byers included flashing white and blue balls, swirling saucers and one shaped like an egg timer. Both Joyce and Mary also claimed to have seen an enormous spaceship which they named 'Big Bertha' and saw come down and land on one of the Moffat Hills. Mrs Byers linked the appearance of 'Big Bertha', which she believed to be the 'mother ship', with the various missing planes detailed earlier. Her view was that in some way the UFOs resented the intrusion of these other flying craft.

According to the diary, a particularly intriguing incident took place on the night of 13 April 1978. 'Big Bertha' would announce her arrival with a massive rumbling noise, like water cascading over a waterfall. That night Joyce heard the craft earlier in the evening but had to wait till around 9 p.m. before she caught a glimpse of it. She guessed that as on previous occasions 'Big Bertha' was dropping mysterious small objects which it would then pick up some hours later. This time, however, there was an unexpected interruption. A plane appeared which, according to Mrs Byers, flew around apparently taking photographs of the UFO. The spaceship's response was quick and direct. It flew straight at the 'plane in an obvious effort to drive it away. Mrs Byers didn't indicate whether there had been any crash although it seems unlikely that an impact could have occurred without it becoming generally known. It does, however, appear on the surface to be an aggressive act by the UFO.

Incidents like this led Mary Watson to declare: 'These objects are afraid of nothing. I have seen them circling slowly, almost cheekily, low in the sky and watched through binoculars the most fantastic sights. I have never seen beings or anything of that nature but I am adamant and would argue with any so-called expert about what I have witnessed, fantastic though it may seem'. Mary added, 'I am sometimes jeered at by local folks who don't believe me, but then it is not surprising when you consider the lack of comment and explanation from the powers that be. Our government chooses to ignore UFOs, but

I feel that in the near future America will make an official pronouncement about them'. In that, unfortunately, Mary was wide of the mark. Although there certainly has been more openness recently on the subject of UFOs both by government departments and the military, generally the attitude persists that UFOs of alien origin are a mere figment of the imagination. Over the years since Mary's statement there have been many occasions on which UFO investigators have claimed that important official announcements regarding ET contact are on the verge of being made, but so far nothing has materialised.

I would add as an afterthought here that Joyce's reference to a rumbling sound as 'Big Bertha' appeared has strange echoes of the arrival in past years of fairies. Individuals who had contact with these entities and were taken away by them would report a strange rumbling noise as hillsides opened to receive the fairy band, and other strange rumbling sounds would be heard as they passed through what seemed to be an underground kingdom.

There have been so many claims by UFO groups that we are on the verge of receiving important official announcements that it becomes increasingly difficult to place much reliance on them. At one point I was informed that a group of NASA astronauts and scientists were planning to hold a press conference at which they would tell the world that contact with ET was a reality. UFOs did exist and there was nothing to be afraid of. Certain individuals made a good living for a while promoting these ideas, but it seems unlikely now that such a press announcement will ever be made. Well organised groups such as CSETI[1] continually press the US government for the release of information and challenge them to face up to the public's right to know, but in spite of continual lobbying by ufologists the lips of western governments remain tightly sealed.

FIREBALLS IN THE SKY

Back in 1979 Mary Watson was sure that her sightings over the Moffat Hills were evidence to the world that the UFO phenomenon was a reality. But should the reports of an 80-year-old in rural Scotland be expected to convince world leaders? The answer is surely not, because on the surface at least governments seek to explain all UFO incidents in conventional terms. Mary, however, despite (or perhaps because of) her eighty years, was far more open-minded. She had personally witnessed the UFOs and had a story to tell. One such incident Mary recalled took place in November of 1979. She reported: 'It was about 7.40 in the morning that I watched one with my field glasses. It started as a red glow in the sky above the horizon. It was also visible with the naked eye and I followed it until it disappeared behind the hill'. From her experiences Mary believed that the UFO exerted some kind of force, claiming that the electric current in her home was affected when one of the craft passed low over her home—her room lights and television set both switched themselves off. It was this definite physical effect of UFO activity that particularly alarmed her and made her feel that the government

1. CSETI (The Center for the Study of Extraterrestrial Intelligence) is an organisation based in the USA who believe that alien intelligence not only exists but has been in contact with us for many years. They argue that the US government is engaged in a huge cover-up, and have made many attempts to force the authorities to release information about their involvement with alien entities.

should be taking action on the matter. As she said: 'They [the aliens] may be a power, but the government should remember that they are responsible for our safety. We know that planes have been sent up to look at these objects, but no official statements are ever made about the results'.

Mrs Watson played a significant role in drawing attention to the area's UFO activity, but as has been noted she was not the only witness to sightings, which were reported by a wide variety of observers. In the same month as Mary's sighting described above, Betty Palmer from Lockerbie, a cleaner at Lockerbie Academy, reported her own UFO incident. She said that the object was 'like a red ball of fire at the front and had a yellow arrow-shaped tail. It wasn't going very fast and appeared to be falling towards the ground. It may have come down in the hills towards Langholm'.

In fact there were a variety of objects sighted during this period. Stella Kirk (72) caught sight of a red flare in the sky. She reported 'It suddenly seemed to grow bigger and it came down very low. It looked like four plates stuck together. It was red and there were flames coming from it. I could feel the heat coming from it and it had a sort of beautiful brightness about it. . . . Then it just vanished'. Two months earlier, in February 1980, two police constables also caught sight of a strange object. This incident took place over the village of Kirkconnel as the policemen were out on patrol. The UFO looked like two bright car headlights and after they switched their car engine off the constables could hear a distinct whining noise like a tumble dryer. The noise seemed to stop then started again as the UFO changed direction. A beam of light then shone down but looked as if it was surrounded by a very strong haze. It then switched off and the UFO disappeared. Contact with Air Traffic at Prestwick confirmed that there were no aircraft in the area. At the same time Agnes Carruthers described the 'rocket-like' UFO she spotted from her bedroom window. She claimed 'it was a round disc shape at the front which was a dull wine colour, and it had a tail of white light'. It hardly needs to be added that the authorities yet again put these sightings down to a 'piece of space debris or a meteor'.

It cannot be denied that meteors and space debris could account for some sightings. But to use this explanation as a blanket answer for all such incidents borders on the ludicrous. Joyce Byers and Mary Watson described solid looking objects which bear no relation to the amorphous ball of light skidding across the sky that would be seen by witnesses of a meteorite or other falling debris (see Fig 13).

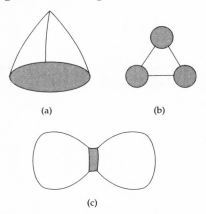

(a)   (b)

(c)

Fig 13. Bizarre objects witnessed over the Moffat Hills

    (a)   Brilliant white cone shape
    (b)   Orange triangular shape
    (c)   'Egg-timer'—bright silver with dark central band

Although these objects appear quite different it is possible that they may be the same structure viewed at different angles. An altered viewpoint can quite radically affect one's perception of the make-up of an object. But what these diagrams do prove beyond doubt is that Joyce and Mary were observing a structured craft.

LIGHTS OVER LOCHSIDE

Unfortunately, Joyce and Mary's UFO sightings attracted considerable ridicule, so much so that Joyce eventually withdrew from publicising her encounters. The incidents continued, however, although the volume of reported incidents seems to have declined. In August 1980 several witnesses reported a sighting over the town of Lochside. An oblong-shaped cluster of lights was seen hovering to the north-west of the town. Interestingly, the witnesses included a number of police officers. Sergeant Bill McDavid (39) certainly saw the mysterious object and said 'I have never believed in UFOs . . . but it certainly was baffling at the time'. It must have been, as despite the early hour—one o'clock on a Saturday morning—both the police and an aircraft from Prestwick were sent out to investigate the report. Police Sergeant McDavid (accompanied by police constable James Smith) reported: 'I couldn't see the exact outline, but it looked oblong-shaped and like an airship and there were five or six white lights in a row. I drove to a higher vantage point on the A 75 for a better view but lost sight of it'. The plane sent by Prestwick to investigate spotted nothing out of the ordinary. However, Post Office engineers came forward to claim that they might have been responsible for the reports. They, it appeared, had been working overnight on a transmitting station at a site called Riddingshill which was several hundred feet above the site where the witnesses to the UFO were located. The lights in the station had been switched on, but possibly obscured from time to time by passing rain clouds. Had this been the UFO seen by the witnesses? It is possible although difficult to explain why people, including police officers, would be confused by lights from a building which they must have known existed. Curiously, a press conference was convened to 'explain' the sighting. An act bound to fuel the suspicions of the conspiracy theorists.

I have to repeat that all of this information would have been overlooked if it had not been for a phone call I received one evening in 1997. The caller introduced himself and explained that for various reasons he had some time on his hands, and was there any part he could play in UFO investigation. He told me that he came from the Dumfriesshire area and that there did not seem to be a lot of UFO activity in the area. I told the caller that I wasn't aware of any incidents in the area at the present time, but had heard it said that there had been something back in the 1970s. If he was interested he could check with the local papers. By good luck that caller turned out to be Robert Rogerson who has a real interest in the UFO phenomenon. By diligent research Robert has not only turned up a host of fascinating cases, but has also brought to our attention a recent UFO encounter in the area.

On Sunday 23 November 1997, Effie Crow and Betty Williams from Kirtlebridge were travelling in a car from Dumfries to Annan when at around 4 p.m. they noticed a bright ball-shaped object in the sky glowing with a tangerine colour. The UFO vanished after a few seconds, but then an arrow-shaped object, coloured silver this time, emerged from the same part of the sky where the orange ball had been hovering and headed across the Solway Firth. Mrs Crow, who had previously worked for the Ministry of Defence, claimed: 'We were both stunned by what we saw. I don't know what the tangerine ball was but it seemed to disappear into thin air. The silvery object came from the Langholm direction and slowly descended westwards until it disappeared behind the rooftops of Annan. I think it must have come down in the Solway. I'm fairly certain it was not a conventional aircraft although it looked solid and could have been some kind of craft'. Interestingly, HM Coastguard control centre in Liverpool was contacted and the response will, I believe, amaze UFO researchers. Their spokesman commented: 'We did receive reports of unusual lights in the sky over Dumfries and Galloway . . . but that was eventually put down to the lightning. *There seems to be a lot going on in the sky over the Southern Scotland coast as we get more reports of unusual sightings there than anywhere else'.* (My italics.) I wonder how many of us have been aware of this fact which official bodies clearly have known about. There has been an area of 'hot' activity of which most UFO researchers have been entirely ignorant (including this one!). Mrs Crow, it should be explained, does not accept the 'lightning' explanation. She said: 'I do not think we have the technology to develop something like this. The only explanation I could come up with is that there is something top secret being tested by the MoD at RAF Spadeadam'. A spokesman for the MoD, however, claimed that although Spadeadam had at one time been a rocket testing base it now dealt in ground-level weapons and did not launch surface-to-air missiles.

Effie's co-witness Betty, who had been driving the car at the time, explained that 'It was a fairly bright afternoon with good visibility. The orange object was dazzling and very distinctive, but soon vanished. The silver-shaped one was also clear and was visible for fully two minutes. It was hard to estimate its size but it travelled for a while at the height of a low-flying jet'.

When the witnesses' report was made public, others came forward in support of the sighting. Mark Toner, president of the Dumfries Astronomy Club, made the reasonable suggestion that the 'late afternoon sighting sounds to me that it could be a comparatively rare occurrence know as "sun dog" that is a mirage effect caused by refraction of the sun's rays. This requires a complex set of circumstances and can look similar to a tangerine ball'. Mr Toner had not witnessed the phenomenon himself so while it might be a reasonable explanation, it does not mean that it is the actual solution. Mr Gow, a former member of the Royal Observer Corps, should be allowed the last word: 'What we saw was solid and certainly unlike any conventional aircraft'.

It will be interesting to see if Dumfriesshire becomes an actual 'hot-spot' again or whether these are isolated incidents.

GEORGE ADAMSKI IN EDINBURGH

As I mentioned earlier, my own interest in the paranormal concentrated at first on such standard fare as ghosts and hauntings. Consequently, when I began research into the UFO phenomenon I tended to assume that sightings of 'strange objects in the sky' were only a relatively recent phenomenon in Scotland. Although in a way that may have been true, as the frequency of reports in the 1990s was unparalleled, it is not entirely correct. Just how wrong I was, I learned one day in 1992.

At that time I was working closely with Ken Higgins who ran his own group, Scottish Research into UFOs (SRUFO). Ken and I were happy to co-operate, as our work together in Blairgowrie shows. I was in regular touch with Ken and one night he mentioned to me a phone call from a man called John Spark who stayed in Pathhead, an old mining village in East Lothian. I was amazed to learn that Mr Spark had been active in UFO research in the 1950s and that there had even been an active society of UFO enthusiasts at the time. I just had to go and find out more.

In his terraced house situated on the road to Crichton Castle, former residence of the Earl of Bothwell, paramour of Mary, Queen of Scots, John enthused over his period of active involvement in UFO research and amazed me with his account of interest in the subject in the 1950s. He told me of an early incident in the East Lothian area, one that had led him to become involved in active investigation. Several 'tattie-howkers' were returning home in a lorry along the Musselburgh to Edinburgh road when they found themselves being followed by a UFO. Mary Howie first caught sight of the object, which she described as being 'the size of a large dining-room table'. She explained: 'It was domed on the top and bottom and seemed to be a light grey colour. As the object followed us about a quarter of a mile high in the sky one of the women became hysterical. We were all shaking. We hammered on the cab to try to make the driver stop, but he thought we were fooling and drove on. The object seemed to be coming lower all the time, that's what made us so scared. It followed us for between five and ten minutes. I never believed in flying saucers before, but I certainly do now'.

As John Spark explained to me, the fact that the potato pickers had really been frightened was highlighted by their decision to report the incident to the police. He also drew my attention to the evidence of Tony Gore, who talked of 'a ring of flame round the rim. A silvery-green light was coming from a small bubble underneath. It followed us along the road, coming close. Once or twice the thing came so low that we all ducked'.

The incident John described seemed very like those we investigated in the 1990s. And it was cases like these which led John to set up the Scottish UFO Research Society which flourished at the end of the 1950s. Another local enthusiast was the Reverend Joseph Ritchie, who had experienced his own UFO encounter when he witnessed a silver-coloured object which disappeared in the direction of the Lammermuir Hills. Fascinating stuff! But I almost fell off my chair when John told me that he had helped to arrange the visit of world famous UFO contactee, American George Adamski, to Edinburgh. Adamski was, and perhaps may still be, the most famous witness to direct alien contact. From his base in California he claimed not only to have met 'Venusians' but to have been taken on space flights beyond our solar system. His book *Flying Saucers Have Landed* was a best seller. It was the first inkling I had had that this leading personality of ufology had visited Scotland in 1958 and addressed a packed meeting at the Methodist Central Hall, Tollcross.

Sadly, this early UFO group had gradually faded away and all its records appear to have been lost. John did not have them, but he did suggest someone who might, although I was unable to track down this former member.

As the society declined, so did reported UFO activity in East Lothian, and there seems to have been a large gap in incidents right through the 60s, 70s and even 80s.

DUNBAR ORANGE BALL

However, in the 1990s unexplained events have put East Lothian back into the news. Strange orange balls of light have been seen travelling over both land and sea, one of the first such incidents being reported by Mrs Coutts of Dunbar. On Thursday 11 January 1995 she was travelling from Dunbar to Edinburgh. At 11.05 a.m. her car had reached the Beltonford roundabout, where the main A1 trunk road meets the A1087. As she glanced towards the Firth of Forth she caught sight of an orange circular ball travelling in a straight line at about tree-top height. Mrs Coutts, however, also stated that its altitude could be compared to that of a low-flying aeroplane, so that it would probably be correct to assume that the object was a few hundred feet from the ground rather than thirty or forty. She was sure, however, that the UFO was not a plane as she was familiar with their movements. Furthermore, it was a clear day with a bright January sun. Mrs Coutts found it difficult to give a more detailed description of the object she saw, but did say it reminded her of something glowing hot. So convinced was she that she had seen something odd that she was certain that others must also have seen it. She knew it had travelled towards Dunbar golf course and felt that anyone out playing that day would have been bound to have seen it. She suggested I contact the local paper, the *East Lothian Courier*, in case other witnesses had called in.

My resulting appeal brought in several witnesses, and provided a possible explanation. Mrs M McNeill informed me that there were several orange balls attached to cables close to where the 11 January sighting occurred and that this might explain the incident. It is, however, clear that there had been a variety of objects seen around the same period. What was intriguing was that the reports, although differing in a variety of details, brought together similar aspects. Had the same object been seen for several years over the East Lothian area?

Monica Cameron wrote to me describing an 'orange star' and 'three small flashing lights moving in the sky'. At first she assumed it was an aeroplane, but then noticed that one of the lights was moving faster than the other two. As the faster moving light caught up with the slower one, 'the slower light just disappeared'. The light then hovered in the air for a few seconds, before heading back in the direction from which it had come.

Two years previously John Bridges, then a twenty-year-old farmer, had also witnessed a pulsating light. This encounter occurred on 29 October 1992 as he drove between Haddington and Pencaitland. Beside a wood to his left, Mr Bridges caught sight of a brown-coloured object which he described as 'the size of two cars on top of each other'. The UFO was only 400 yards away from him at the time and about 100 feet off the ground. So although it was 11 o'clock at night, the sky was clear and he got a good look at it. He could be sure of what he had seen because at the base of the UFO was a big light which lit up both the object and the surrounding area.

The golden light phenomenon had also appeared on Christmas Day when Mrs Aitken from Musselburgh rang UFO investigator Ken Higgins to inform him that zig-zags of gold were traversing the sky to the east of Musselburgh. Then in November 1995 Thomas McGreig and his wife saw two red lights hovering over the Firth of Forth. However, it remains a mystery as to why orange and gold objects and pulsating lights should be seen so frequently in the area.

The spate of sightings continued right into 1996 when a twenty-year-old female witness who does not wish to be named sent in a report of an encounter near Torness power station. She told SEMR: 'I was travelling along the A1 from Eyemouth on Wednesday 17 January 1996 back home to Edinburgh. It was very cold, a clear and dry night. I had never driven home on this road in the dark before and was concentrating very deeply because at that particular spot the road seemed very narrow and dark. I hadn't noticed any house or street lights for a few miles [although] occasionally I would see headlights behind me in the distance and coming towards me. At approximately 5.50 p.m. (I had left Eyemouth at 5.10 p.m. and got back to Edinburgh at approximately 6.20 p.m.) I could see Torness power station to my right in the distance. It is illuminated at night and very bright. All of a sudden a bright red light flashed in front of me coming from my left and off to my right. It gave me a terrible fright because of the darkness. It was bright red and about the size of a pea [and was] about 200 feet from the road. It seemed too low to be a plane [and] if it was a plane the pilot was on a suicide mission flying so near Torness power station.'

One of the strangest UFO sightings in recent years occurred over agricultural land in East Lothian. Maureen Clark, a 49-year-old housewife from Edinburgh, was travelling through the county with her husband on Saturday 31 October 1992 (Halloween!). As they passed south of Haddington her husband, who was driving their car, noticed a bright light which he judged to be over a nearby hill, just below the cloud line. It was 3.45 p.m. on a cold though dry and windless afternoon. Mrs Clark describes the object as 'a bright light tinged with yellow, not a white light like a spotlight, more mellow'. The light appeared to be circular, 'but flattened on top with a dark mark'.

They managed to keep the light under observation as their route led them closer to the source, The object, meanwhile, remained stationary until their car drew alongside the hill. Then, according to Maureen, it suddenly shot 'very quickly upwards into the clouds'. Up to that point the sky had seemed smothered in grey cloud. But now a break appeared at the exact spot into which the light had disappeared! Through the gap the couple could make out a thick, white, vertical column of a cloud-like substance, resembling a vapour trail. However, it was much denser, wider and straighter edged, starting at cloud level and pointing heavenwards. The mystified pair searched the sky for the cause of the strange phenomenon, but could see no obvious explanation. Certainly, there was no sign of the strange object initially observed, which now seemed to have disappeared. In Scottish UFO sightings we can find no exact parallel to this mysterious incident.

Curiously, however, Malcolm Archibald of Gorebridge may have seen something similar in reverse on 16th October 1992. He reported seeing a column of bright lights 'apparently connected, descending at great speed'. As is frequently the case they, or it, 'vanished very suddenly' in the 'vicinity of the Pentland Hills'.

THE EARTHLIGHT THEORY

Are we dealing here with objects from beyond the stars, or another dimension? Or can we locate the source in the bowels of the earth? Do flying balls of light prove the existence of 'earthlights'[2] rather than extraterrestrials? Consider the following two cases and make up your own mind. These two incidents also show that certain types of UFO phenomena can sometimes be linked to a particular 'hot-spot'—I don't know of any similar cases in Scotland where strange lights were seen close up at ground level.

At two o'clock on the morning of 4 December 1995, Mrs Allan of Cockenzie was driving along North Grange Avenue near the town of Prestonpans. Glancing in her rear view mirror, she caught an unexpected sight. Travelling towards her at a

2. 'Earthlights' are balls of energy which come out of the ground in places where rock is under pressure. For a fuller description, see Chapter 9.

furious rate was a bright ball of glowing green light. She was struck by its huge size, as large as a car, and its direct line of movement, as if locked on to an invisible course. Before she had time to be frightened, it soared over her head at house roof height and shot up into the night sky. In its wake it left a trail of red light. This incident made such an impact on Mrs Allan that she contacted Edinburgh Airport, which (UFO investigators will be interested to learn) asked her to complete a questionnaire on her encounter. Paul Devereux, renowned earth mysteries investigator and for many years editor of *The Ley Hunter*, was convinced that this incident was indeed an example of an earthlight. I have to agree that the evidence for this is strong. In pursuing my enquiries, I contacted the British Geological Survey in Edinburgh. Peter Morrison of the Global Seismology Research Group wrote to me on 14 June 1995: 'We have no explanation for the phenomenon observed by the lady near Prestonpans on 4 December last. Earthlights have been reported as a phenomenon accompanying very large earthquakes and that can be discounted in this case! Earthlights, however, have also been reported where earthquakes are absent, so I am not wholly convinced by this, although the existence of such lights seems a recognised fact'.

With the Allan sighting there was no evidence of intelligent life controlling the object. The same is not true of the object seen by Mr and Mrs Buckley of Musselburgh. In the early hours of a cold and frosty winter morning in 1981 (the month was either November or December) they were walking along a pavement close to their house when they spotted an object which appeared like a brilliant white tennis ball. It was hovering beside a lamppost and at first glance the couple took it for a lamplight. Then, however, it started to move. As it did so, they realised that there were, in fact, two balls close together. As the objects moved closer Mr and Mrs Buckley were struck by the intense whiteness of the two balls, 'a fierce white colour', Mrs Buckley described it. They looked like 'metal, boiling hot'. When first seen the objects were about twenty feet off the ground, but they descended to within an inch or so of the pavement, then moved in front of the Buckleys as they walked along the street. What makes the incident even more intriguing was that the couple felt that the balls seemed 'to have a mind of their own' and 'it was as if the balls were playing a game with us'. Furthermore one ball 'seemed more dominant than the other'. Strange though this encounter may be, it does correspond to incidents reported from other parts of the world and documented in Paul Devereux's book *Earthlights*.

MYSTICAL ASPECT

Bright lights and the Pentland Hills seem to go together. In *Mysteries of the Scottish Landscape* I argued that the Lothian area was a place of special and mysterious significance. The focus for that was the Pentland Hills. I also pointed out that in December (the period of the Winter solstice) the silhouette of the hills can take on the appearance of a great goddess figure. In fact it can be argued that the whole of the Lothian region is riddled with ancient sites of mystic significance. Cairnpapple, near Bathgate, with its neolithic temple, is reckoned to be one of the most important examples of its kind in Europe. Arthur's Seat boasts a plethora of prehistoric settlements. Did the people of ancient times recognise that this area possessed some strange significance? Have UFOs been visiting these parts for perhaps thousands of years? It is a question to which we may never have the answer.

CASE STUDY: THE BONNYBRIDGE PHENOMENON

But will we arrive at an explanation for the 'hot-spot' phenomenon before then? If so then we may have to accept that 'hot-spots' as a phenomenon are independent of UFO reality. That in a way we the public and UFO investigators in particular are helping to create 'UFO windows'. I have examined Bonnybridge in the context of the overall phenomenon in Chapter 5. What I would like to do here is look at it in relation to 'hot-spot' creation. I have a special interest in this—I live only a few miles from Bonnybridge, personally investigated some of the incidents, and also found myself accused by other investigators of writing off Bonnybridge as a 'hot-spot'! I should say that I have never doubted that the area around West Lothian to the edge of the town of Stirling, including places like Falkirk, Grangemouth and Stenhousemuir, has experienced incidents out of all proportion to its population. What I have tried to establish through detailed investigation is why the village of Bonnybridge became intimately linked to the 'hot-spot' and what part other factors played in its rise to media stardom. I believe that if ufologists are honest about their investigations then at the end of the day the subject itself benefits. So here goes!

At the height of its fame, between 1993 and 1995, Bonnybridge in central Scotland captured world-wide interest as an alleged UFO hot-spot. Film crews from Japan, Germany and the United States (amongst others) visited the area. It was also strongly featured in both the initial *Strange But True* television series and the accompanying book (1994). Almost every newspaper featured reports of UFO activity in the area, not only the tabloids (as might have been expected), but the 'heavies' such as the *Guardian* where the matter was treated relatively seriously. Perhaps the pinnacle—or nadir, depending on your point of view—was reached with Nick Pope's statement in his book *Open Skies, Closed Minds* that there had been over 8,000 UFO incidents reported in Bonnybridge. (This, it should be noted, is in fact greater than the population of the town.)

One might argue over the number of reported sightings but anyone interested in UFO investigating has to ask whether it was UFO reports alone that brought the area such attention or were other factors at work?

Although it is the town of Bonnybridge that has come to be recognised as a UFO hot-spot, many of the alleged incidents were reported by individuals over a much wider geographical area and larger population base. Sightings were reported from witnesses in Falkirk, Grangemouth, Larbert, Denny and surrounding villages such as Slamannan. This increases the potential witness pool substantially to around 100,000 and the geographical area involved to around 144 square miles. Even so, 8,000 incidents for 100,000 witnesses is still an extraordinarily high ratio.

Remote or isolated areas are often seen as particularly susceptible to UFO activity. However, it would be incorrect to classify any part of this area as 'remote' or isolated. In Grangemouth, for example, a few miles from Bonnybridge, there is the biggest petrochemical site in Western Europe. In this part of Scotland, people are only 30 minutes by car from the Glasgow conurbation and the same distance from Edinburgh. The M8, M9 and M876 motorways cut through the heart of the area and Bonnybridge is only minutes from all these roads.

It is possible, however, that aspects of the geography of the area did play a part in encouraging UFO reports. Drive two minutes out of Bonnybridge, or Slamannan, or Falkirk, and you arrive on high, relatively isolated ground with a good view across miles of countryside, and at night a relatively low level of light pollution. The Shieldhill area, for example, continues to attract UFO buffs convinced that strange phenomena are still to be seen in the area. It is reckoned to be one of the best skywatching sites in Scotland. So it is possible that the natural aspects of the local landscape did play a part in the increased level of reports. But it can hardly explain the sheer scale of the phenomenon, or the area's continuing reputation as a world UFO hot-spot, since there are certainly other areas of Scotland that would qualify almost as well. The West Lothian area, for example, which had at least as many *documented* sightings as Bonnybridge.

Villages like Slamannan and small towns like Bonnybridge do have higher rates of unemployment. Slamannan, for example, is an old mining village with the mines long since gone. There are more people around with time on their hands. Time to gaze at the night sky? More time to imagine things? Possibly, but highly doubtful unless we can show that the unemployed or others with lots of spare time played a significant role in boosting the number of UFO reports. One major problem is that so little material has been released by those involved in the investigation that witness analysis is inevitably limited in scope. But from what little is available (and that mainly via the press), unemployed people did not form a significant proportion of the witnesses. Bored people with nothing to do but report UFOs is no explanation for Bonnybridge.

One could look at various options covering the psychology of the inhabitants and the sociology of small communities, but one might not come out of it any the wiser. Although describing himself as a psychic investigator, Malcolm Robinson has no explanation as to why Bonnybridge became such a 'hot-spot'. I would suggest that the explanation for the development of Bonnybridge as a UFO 'window', and probably the answer to a lot of UFO excitement, lies in a combination of the personalities involved and the media. It is no coincidence that the UFO reports became intimately linked with the town of Bonnybridge when one of the key players was Billy Buchanan, councillor for the Bonnybridge area. But let us take the media first.

Scotland is awash with competing local and national newspapers. In the Bonnybridge 'triangle' there can be found a variety of local papers. The main local journal was the *Falkirk Herald*, but other papers such as the *Stirling Observer* can also be bought and also less 'local' papers, but carrying local news, such as the *Edinburgh Evening News* (with an office in West Lothian, bordering the 'triangle') and the Glasgow-based *Evening Times*. Naturally, however, the real battle lay between the tabloids. Scotland's chief selling daily is the *Daily Record*. In the run up to events at Bonnybridge the *Record* was under attack from Rupert Murdoch's *Sun*, which had adopted the title *The Scottish Sun*. To give an example of the intensity of the circulation battle, the *Record* has been traditionally seen as a supporter of the Labour Party. As the political battle in Scotland is between Labour and the Scottish National Party, and younger voters are more inclined towards nationalist politics, *The Sun* prior to the 1992 general election came out in favour of Scottish independence. This was viewed as a direct attempt to eat into the *Record's* readership.

On top of this, traditional English-based papers, such as the *Daily Express* and the *Daily Mail* moved to increase their Scottish readership and began running Scottish editions with more Scottish stories. Another example of this trend (although after Bonnybridge was at its height) was the decision of the Aberdeen *Press & Journal* to move out of its traditional northern heartland and set up an office in Stirling (beside the famous 'triangle'). All part of a general readership struggle. This period also saw the establishment in the Central Belt of several new press agencies (one based in Falkirk, another in Stirling) all seeking and attempting to sell stories on UFOs. I would suggest that this atmosphere of intense competition for exciting stories largely explains why Bonnybridge became so prominent in the media. And when journalists in radio and TV saw their newspaper colleagues publishing UFO stories, they quickly joined in. The whole affair began to feed on itself.

However, media interest cannot be seen as the whole story. The catalyst, I would suggest, was the presence of an influential individual who could give credibility to the story. Billy Buchanan, a councillor on Falkirk District Council representing the Bonnybridge area, was well known to sections of the media before the UFO stories broke. He was viewed by journalists as a 'colourful' character and was generally well liked. A powerful and persuasive speaker, Buchanan on his own was enough to provide local papers with good copy, but until 1993 the story remained almost wholly of local interest.

In November 1992, one of Councillor Buchanan's requests for help was broadcast on Central FM, a local radio station. It was heard by UFO investigator Malcolm Robinson, who immediately contacted Buchanan. By December 1992, witnesses were beginning to come forward, several of whom were prepared to talk publicly. With an elected councillor who lived in the very village in which sightings were taking place and who believed the witnesses' claims, and an official investigator from BUFORA, from outside the area, who could be seen (by the press) as impartial and could further justify their decision to publish UFO stories, events really began to take off.

In January 1993, Buchanan announced to the press that he was holding a meeting to discuss UFO reports in the village. The story was well covered by Scotland's best-selling Sunday, the *Sunday Post* (reputed readership 1 million in a population of 5 million). The story included a photograph of Buchanan holding a notice announcing the meeting. The story ran: 'A town plagued by UFOs has called in the experts as concern grows among residents', and included the statement: 'some will even be hypnotised in a bid to find any subconscious memories of being taken on board alien spacecraft.'

This account must have heightened expectations, and although the hypnotist did not turn up, experienced investigator Malcolm Robinson gave a talk to an audience of over 200. He discussed the world-wide aspects, including some of the sensational South American cases.

Nonetheless, the presence at the centre of the phenomenon

of an elected councillor meant that whatever way the story developed, it retained, as one respected radio journalist put it to me, 'a strong element of credibility'. It was Buchanan's involvement which encouraged serious papers like *The Scotsman* (with an office in Falkirk) to run stories such as that of the arrival of a Japanese film crew in Bonnybridge to cover the UFO reports.

It is worth noting that, as the media coverage intensified, so did the number of UFO reports. Four hundred in January 1993, according to Cllr Buchanan, 600 by the beginning of October 1994, 2,000 by the end of October 1995, and finally 8,000 according to Nick Pope (August 1996). When I interviewed Malcolm Robinson in August 1996 for *Phenomenal News*, the magazine of SEMR, he informed me that the number of reports from the famous triangle comes to between 250 and 300. Malcolm blames the TV programme *Strange But True* for hyping the reports to 2000 although, to be fair, large numbers of alleged incidents were being claimed by Billy Buchanan before then.

The Bonnybridge saga descended into farce with the affair of Zal-us, an alleged alien who, it was claimed, had been in contact with Cllr Buchanan and was going to appear at a meeting in Falkirk Town Hall. The story was largely press nonsense, but, it could be said that 'those who live by the sword . . .' It might be argued that the press who had worked hard to build up the story in the end helped to kill it off. However, the key element in the decline was undoubtedly the withdrawal of Cllr Buchanan and Malcolm Robinson from the UFO investigations. It is noticeable that after this the number of UFO stories dealing with Bonnybridge fell dramatically.

When BBC Scotland organised a live radio broadcast from Bonnybridge Community Centre in December 1996, they clearly expected dozens of local people to turn up and report their sightings. In fact, of the half a dozen people who did report a UFO sighting, only two involved incidents in the Bonnybridge area. Evidence which points to the conclusion that although Central Scotland has many reported UFO sightings, the fame achieved by Bonnybridge may have been due more to human efforts than extraterrestrial activity.

In the case of the Bonnybridge 'hot-spot', then, circumstances other than the sheer volume of reports played a significant part. But in spite of these additional factors it is clear that many more people were coming forward to report UFO sightings than in most other areas. It may be that at the core of the 'hot-spot' phenomenon lies a 'warm-spot'—a greater than normal volume of UFO reports taking place within a restricted area. Once this 'warm-spot' is established, a whole range of other aspects come into play which lead to national prominence, so that the 'warm-spot' becomes a 'hot-spot'.

THE NUMBERS GAME

STATISTICAL ANALYSIS OF DATA

SOURCES OF DATA · U.K. VS SCOTTISH REPORTING · NUMBER OF WITNESSES · SEX OF WITNESSES · GEOGRAPHICAL LOCATION · REPORTS BY YEAR/DECADE · DISTRIBUTION BY MONTH · TIME OF DAY · COMPARISON WITH OVERALL U.K. FIGURES

Statistics are a notorious minefield for the uninitiated. Mark Twain's famous saying about the art of Politics consisting of 'lies, damned lies and statistics' points to the fact that the presentation of numbers can indeed be a game twisted in support of any axe an individual has to grind. I have no axe to grind, but it is right to be wary of any collection of figures and the conclusions that may be drawn from them. On the other hand it would be wrong to avoid this aspect of ufology as it may give us some insight into the nature of the UFO phenomenon. Are there any obvious patterns, for example? If so what light does this shed on UFO reports? If there are no patterns then are witness sightings simply a chaotic mass of individual incidents which have no collective significance?

SOURCES OF DATA

It may be instructive to consider how the information on which this chapter is based was drawn together. It arose, initially, out of discussions I had with Ken Higgins of SRUFO. Ken, articulate and dedicated, was the first Scottish investigator that I was aware of who had started to build a database of Scottish UFO sightings. In the spirit of co-operation which in the early 1990s brought Scottish ufologists together, Ken and I pooled our UFO reports and, on his computer, compiled a list of several hundred incidents, although the information on each incident varied in detail depending on the source. Unfortunately, Ken was unable to continue the exercise because of extensive work commitments, but he did pass to me a comprehensive list of UFO incidents. This formed a nucleus for my own database which rapidly expanded as the number of reported UFO sightings escalated right through the 1990s. I would admit that if I had a full-time office with secretarial support I have no doubt that the information I have collected over the years would be more systematically stored. However, given all the factors that have to be taken into account—time, energy, finance, other commitments—the information SEMR has gathered is quite comprehensive, although the route along which the information has arrived does affect the level of detail available.

Best of all from my point of view are the sightings forms completed by witnesses themselves which usually (but not always!) provide comprehensive details of what the witness has seen: basic facts such as time, date, location, descriptions, etc.

U.K. vs SCOTTISH REPORTING

Such report forms are a key source of information for Scottish ufologists as far as the 1990s are concerned.

The further you go back, however, the less often this information is available. There have been Scottish UFO groups active at various periods since the 1950s, but no organisation continually in operation as has been the case with the London-based BUFORA. As a result there has been no systematic collection of Scottish UFO incidents from the 1950s to date. BUFORA has been receiving Scottish UFO reports during this period and so more information does exist, but it is locked into BUFORA's filing system. To shed light on UFO incidents earlier than the 1980s it is necessary to go in most cases to other sources—newspapers, UFO magazines, books—to pick up basic information about individual incidents. As you might expect these do vary in the detail recorded. Some reports, the Bob Taylor incident for example, are extensively covered, while others give only the briefest of details. However, they do allow us to build up a more comprehensive picture of the UFO phenomenon in Scotland. I have, of course, over the years received many phone calls and letters from individuals who wish to report a UFO sighting, but who for their own reasons have no wish to complete an official form. I have used these reports only where I have the name, address/phone number of the person involved.

As a compilation of UFO information the SEMR database gives, I believe, a broad picture of UFO activity over Scotland although this picture is clearer, inevitably, for more recent years. The results presented in this chapter are based on a random selection of 395 cases. Why 395? Initially, I selected 400 as the target, but having made that selection eliminated 5 cases because of the scarcity or incomplete nature of the details, and kept the remainder.

NUMBER OF WITNESSES

So what does the analysis show us? If we examine, as a first step, the number of witnesses involved, it would seem that in Scotland the 'typical' incident is witnessed by a single individual: this accounts for 59% of the cases included in the survey.

Cases involving two witnesses comprise 20% of the sample, three witness cases make up 4% and four witness cases account for 2% of the sample. In 6% of cases we know there was more than one witness but are unable to determine the exact number involved. In 9% of reports the number of witnesses is unknown—though presumably, even with new physics, we can assume there was at least one witness! But in the absence of more information it seems sensible to remove this group from the equation. Consequently, we have a situation in which we find that although the largest group consists of single-witness cases, 32% of incidents involve two or more people. It should be noted that these figures are rounded to the nearest 1%.

Of course, to use the term 'single-witness case' is exclusive. Who is to say that, in fact, there was only one witness to a particular incident? In some cases, for example Bob Taylor's (see Chapter 1), we can be fairly sure that only one person saw the UFO. In others, particularly those involving unexplained lights in the sky, several witnesses may not have reported what they saw, for a variety of reasons. It is probably more accurate, then, to talk of single-witness 'reports', though it has to be admitted that such a redefinition takes us a good bit back down the road we just came up.

Bob Taylor's famous encounter is perhaps the best known Scottish single-witness incident, but it (and Pat Macleod's Edinburgh sighting—see Chapter 1) stand up well in comparison with several multi-witness cases where natural phenomena have clearly been misinterpreted. I would, therefore, suggest that having several witnesses does not immediately label a UFO incident as more difficult to explain than a single-witness case. In Scotland, we have substantial incidents involving both groups.

SEX OF WITNESSES

Is UFO reporting in Scotland a sex specific occurrence—that is, is it linked predominantly to men or women? Common sense and the history of UFO incidents in other countries would lead one to believe that there is no such link. The evidence in Scotland would tend to support this, although men were in a majority, reporting in 42% of incidents, compared to a figure of 35% for women. This is close enough statistically to appear like an even split, although it may be that men are slightly more likely to *report* an incident. Note also that the sex of the person making the report is unknown in 7% of cases, while in 16% of cases the witnesses were of both sexes and both (or all) came forward to give their accounts. Overall, the evidence relating witnesses to either sex does not produce startling insights. Both sexes report and are witnesses to UFO incidents, although it appears that men may be more likely to report such an encounter than women. It does not show, however, whether men or women are more likely to have a UFO experience.

GEOGRAPHICAL LOCATION

Turning to geographical location we enter even more uncertain ground. For example, what do we use to define such a concept? We can pick a city, such as Edinburgh or Glasgow, which gives a reasonably recognisable area, but if we say Fife or Perthshire does it make any real sense? And, when you consider it, does relating a UFO to Glasgow or Edinburgh really stand up? What we are talking about in most cases is an airborne phenomenon which may be at any point in the sky, so that a viewer in Edinburgh may be witnessing an object miles away. Essentially, what the database has documented is the spot from where the witness saw the incident and thus we may have a general approximation of the area where the incident occurred. I can't give any solid reason for the geographical divisions in Table 1 except that they refer to areas which have long been recognised as having an individual identity, cultural or otherwise.

The figures in each of the following Tables are all rounded to the nearest 1%.

Table 1: Geographical Locations

Edinburgh and Midlothian	32%
West Lothian	21%
Aberdeen/North of Scotland	8%
Glasgow	9%
East Lothian	5%
Stirling/Clackmannanshire	5%
Ayr/West Coast	4%
Falkirk/Bonnybridge	4%
Fife	3%
Borders	2%
Dumfriesshire	2%
Outer Glasgow Conurbation	2%
Perth/Blairgowrie	2%
Dundee	1%

Clearly the area west and south of Edinburgh and including the city itself stands out. With the addition of West Lothian this area account for 53% of reported incidents. This compares startlingly with the Glasgow area, which accounts for 11% of sightings. No other area compares with the Edinburgh area. Fife, in spite of a recent spate of sightings, accounts for 3%, although arguably that might come within the Edinburgh ambit as a number of sightings were reported over the Firth of Forth or along the coastline, certainly within sight of Edinburgh. Further north, Aberdeen and a general area labelled 'The North' accounts for 8%, although Orkney and Shetland have been included in this designation and, on their own, account for a significant proportion of these cases. Some areas of Scotland come in at a surprisingly low level. The Borders, for example, account for 2% only, although the area covered is quite large and though not heavily populated does include some significant centres of population. It is also notoriously plagued by military aircraft on low-level manoeuvres, so that a significant proportion of military 'UFOs' would be expected. The results, though, do not reflect this. It is anomalous, too, that other extensive areas such as Dumfries and the well populated area round Perth also register low down the scale, both at 2%, in spite of a number of key UFO incidents and periods as UFO 'hot-spots'.

The reason for the consistent predominance of the Edinburgh area is not clear. On a strict population basis, one would expect the Glasgow area, with at least double Edinburgh's population, to account for the largest number, or at least come near to meeting the East Coast's tally. Surely misidentified planes cannot be the answer as both Edinburgh and Glasgow have airports in close proximity to the city centre, with regular military and civil flights crossing over both cities.

A further curious fact is that UFO incidents decrease significantly at Edinburgh's eastern border. East Lothian accounts for only 5% of incidents compared to Edinburgh and Mid Lothian's 32% and West Lothian's 21%. Why? True, the airport is located on Edinburgh's west side, so that fact may account for some part of the difference, but the area is frequently flown over by all types of aircraft and people are well used to plane movements. Indeed it is the fact that objects clearly are not planes which leads witnesses to report their sightings.

Admittedly, it could be argued that the location of SEMR will have a bearing on the number of reports sent in from different parts of Scotland. The focus of a number of UFO groups has been the Edinburgh area, the defunct SRUFO for example. SEMR is based near Stirling. Given the proximity of the Edinburgh area one might expect a greater volume of sightings to come to the attention of active ufologists. On the other hand, SEMR has made consistent attempts to gather information from, for example, the Glasgow area. There are a number of UFO groups active in the West of Scotland, notably the West of Scotland UFO Group, with which SEMR does exchange information. But even publicity about UFOs does not produce anything like the volume of cases which flow from the Edinburgh area. It is also worth noting that if only a proportion of the alleged 8,000 sightings from the Bonnybridge area were included, the dominance of the area between Edinburgh and Stirling would be utterly overwhelming.

We have a real puzzle here. Even though factors indicated above presumably load the figures towards an Edinburgh predominance, this by no means explains the conundrum.

REPORTS BY YEAR/DECADE

UFO sightings were reported in Scotland as early as anywhere in the western world following the Arnold incident. The earliest encounters we have recorded, however, date from 1947 in Edinburgh and 1952 in Glasgow. From 1947 to 1997 there have been regular reports of incidents, although 1979, the year of Bob Taylor's famous encounter, produced a notable peak which continued into 1980. Thereafter reports continued at the pre-1979 level till 1986 when there was a significant rise. That year seems to have heralded the start of a dramatic increase in UFO reports in Scotland as thereafter (1987 apart) the number of reported incidents has remained well above previous levels. The 1990s has undoubtedly been the decade of the UFO as far as Scotland is concerned. It's surprising to note, however, that the biggest group of UFO reports came not during the 1991/2 period when the Bonnybridge 'hot-spot' was at its hottest, but during 1995/6 when there was no particular 'hot-spot' of note. In fact, looking at Table 2, what we seem to be experiencing is successive waves of sightings during the 1990s:

Table 2: 1990s Reports by Year

1990	5%
1991	14%
1992	24%
1993	1%
1994	5%
1995	19%
1996	26%
1997	6%

It's interesting to compare Table 2 with figures sent to me by Nick Pope, then of the MoD. The details he sent me (relating to the whole of the United Kingdom) also indicated a 1988/89 peak, but a slight drop in 1990/91 and a rise through 1991, 1992 and 1993. This doesn't fit with the Scottish figures which start a dramatic rise through 1990 to 1992 and a sharp decline in 1993.

If we look at the proportion of reports by decade we find the following:

Table 3: Reports by Decade

1990s	75%
1980s	13%
1970s	7%
1960s	2%
1950s	2%
1940s	1%

Clearly, of all the figures these must be the least reliable, and they underscore the problem of any UFO investigator working from a limited database. The data collected represents periods when UFO groups were increasingly active in Scotland, from the mid 1980s onwards. The 1991/2 peak in part represents the phenomenal response to the UFO hotline set up by SEMR and SRUFO, which produced a flood of reports relating not only to the year 1992, but for the whole period from 1950 onwards, although the greatest number were for relatively recent cases. On the other hand the 1995/6 peak is harder to explain, as it seems not to be linked to any one area or incident. It may simply have been the result of the considerable interest in the subject generated by the media.

The truth is that we won't have a clearer view of UFO incidents in Scotland over the last 40 years until considerably more cases are brought together on a single database and analysed. This, of course, is also true for all the aspects of UFO data that has been surveyed in these pages, but especially so if we wish to assess annual fluctuations in UFO reports which, I would suggest, is a key problem in this whole mystery.

DISTRIBUTION BY MONTH

Accepting that months are arbitrary divisions of time, none-theless it is interesting to note the fluctuations in the levels of UFO reports from month to month. Variations over the years or between regions should not significantly affect these results. Again, however, we are looking at a broad picture based on overall figures rather than fluctuations in any particular year. The distribution of reports by month produces the following table:

Table 4: Distribution by Month

Month	Percent
January	11%
February	11%
March	3%
April	5%
May	3%
June	7%
July	3%
August	12%
September	6%
October	14%
November	17%
December	8%

The October to November period stands out, although the reasons for this peak are not immediately obvious. Sceptics might point to the Guy Fawkes celebrations of 5 November, with their displays of fireworks brightening the night skies. Superficially, this might seem an attractive solution, but the argument would only hold if the types of UFO reported were different from objects seen at other times of the year, or if November's UFOs had some common feature which would lend itself to this explanation. In fact, November sightings are much the same as incidents witnessed in spring or summer, equally intriguing whatever the season.

Furthermore, there is no evidence that after 5 November there is a steep decline in UFO reports. In fact, what we see is a rise from September (6%) to a peak in November (17%). The level then falls back through December, but rises again into January and February which both come in at identical levels of 11%.

Mystics, of course, might point to the October/November peak and its association with the pre-Christian Celtic calendar. 31 October is Hallowe'en, and the start of the old Celtic year (Samhain) is on 1 November.

The proportion of reports from March to July remains consistently lower than for the other months although June (7%) does rise a little above September. On the whole though, the months of greater hours of light produce fewer reports than the darker months. August is the great exception and at 12% comes third in the league table. I can't think of any reason for this as there is a noticeable dip in September (6%) and July accounts for only 3% of reports. Why should July be so low down, sandwiched between June and August. It may be due to the fact that July is the traditional holiday month in Scotland, schools having broken up at the end of June. Perhaps there are simply fewer people around to report? On the other hand, with time to spare you might think that there would be more attention paid to unusual lights in the sky. The Press at this time of year is particularly desperate for stories. Whatever the reason July, like May, comes way down the league of monthly UFO sightings.

Despite the upward surge in August most sightings occur during the months of early darkness, that is, October to February, which account overall for 61% of the total. Before jumping to conclusions, we should also bear in mind that if long hours of either darkness or light affect the number of reports, why does December account for only 8% and May a lowly 3%? The position may be a little clearer when figures relating sightings to hours of the day are considered (see below). In broad summary, the evidence seems to point to there being more UFO reports in the early and latter part of the year than in the middle months. There is no clear explanation for this. Furthermore, these figures do not relate to an annual or even a ten-yearly cycle. Even so, it is perfectly possible that the monthly incidence of reporting has altered over a period of time and analysis of past decades might produce a different picture. There is not enough data to provide a definite conclusion, but at least I hope I have given some food for thought for those who might wish to investigate further.

TIME OF DAY

UFO sightings generally happen in the evening. A remarkable 42% of incidents take place between 9 p.m. and 1 a.m. It is a safe bet that after that most potential witnesses are fast asleep, although the lowest incidence of reports doesn't occur till between 4 and 5 a.m. (1%). Remarkably the early morning period between 2 a.m. and 4 a.m. accounts for almost 8% of reports! Afterwards, while there are some variations, the rest of the day moves within the range of 1% to 4%. The period between 9 a.m. and 10 a.m. accounts for less than 1% although the lunch hour 12 p.m to 1 p.m. registers an astonishing zero return.

The late evening to early morning bulge might explain why the darker nights predominate in the reports. Less light makes objects harder to identify, produces more lights in the sky and leads to more reports. Interestingly, there is a considerable overlap between objects classified as unidentified lights and those where a solid object is reported. The appearance of humanoids represents only a fraction of incidents, around 4%, while contact with alleged aliens in Scotland happens in only a handful of cases, although it may be that with increased publicity over alleged abductions there will be a corresponding rise in Scottish reports. It will be a good measure of the reality of the UFO phenomenon to document its development over the next few years in Scotland.

COMPARISON WITH OVERALL U.K. FIGURES

How do UFO statistics north of the border compare with elsewhere? No comparison has been carried out in the sense of an agreed range of questions set against a comparable database drawn from, say, England or the United States. Such an exercise would be a fascinating one to follow through. In the book *Fact or Fantasy* Jenny Randles does report an analysis of UFO incidents carried out for the United Kingdom (which presumably included Scottish cases) for the period 1975 to

1979. It is a fascinating account and it is interesting to compare that sample with our Scottish one to see what, if anything, is similar and what is different. Does this comparison shed any light on UFOs? As might be guessed, the highest proportion of cases involved unidentified lights in the sky (about 87%). This is probably a slightly lower proportion than might be the case in our survey, but is in general line with it, that is, the single largest aspect of the UFO phenomenon involves a reporting of mysterious lights.

In terms of the number of UFO witnesses, the survey reported by Jenny Randles gives only the *average* number of witnesses, which comes to 2.19. I'm not sure that this statistic can tell us a lot about the nature of sightings, as it is obviously an amalgamation of witness figures which might vary significantly. Still, it does point to the fact that the number of witnesses to UFO incidents tends to be low, and this is also true in the Scottish survey.

On the sex of the witnesses, there does seem to be a significant difference. 68% of the non-contact UFO cases were male and the figure for UFO contact cases was similarly high. This compares with 42% of male witnesses in Scottish cases. The difference seems difficult to explain, even if we assume that by the 1990s women were more inclined to report a UFO encounter than in the 1970s (which is a questionable assumption). It may be that the data simply does not have the accuracy or the sheer bulk to provide a useful comparison. It does, however, point to the broad conclusion that men are more likely than women to report a UFO incident.

On the issue of the time of day at which one is most likely to see a UFO (which is then reported), the UK survey named

9 p.m. The Scottish survey noted that 42% of reported sightings take place between 9 p.m. and 1 a.m., although no particular peak point in time was identified.

Statistics are a well known quagmire, particularly to the non-specialist, so it would be wrong to come to any definite conclusions at this stage, though the UK and Scottish surveys do point broadly in the same direction. It would be interesting to go further—to compare sightings from different periods from various areas within the UK, and see what trends emerge. If there is one sensible conclusion to be drawn from the data currently available, it is that a lot more research needs to be done before we can paint a clear picture of the nature of UFO sightings in Scotland and the UK.

AN ENDURING ENIGMA

OVERVIEW OF THE PHENOMENON

Given that the UFO phenomenon has been with us for over 50 years you might think that with the passing of time we would have moved nearer to a solution. It's a paradox that the opposite seems to have happened. In place of increased clarity we have growing confusion, with people from every part of the globe making claims about what they have seen or been involved in. It's a fascinating scene unless you are someone who wants the definitive answer now. Alternatively you can be the sceptic who dismisses it all as sheer fantasy. To do this would, I believe, be a pity because the UFO mystery, in my view, opens up a whole spectrum of questions even going as far as the origins of life on earth itself.

A SCEPTIC'S VIEW

No-one has been more critical of the reality of paranormal phenomena than the Canadian-born, now naturalised US citizen, James Randi. I use Mr Randi as a distinguished standard-bearer of those opposed to the reality of the world of the paranormal as he has been involved in high profile exchanges of views with leading 'paranormalists' and in court cases involving, among others, Uri Geller. He has also offered an as-yet-unclaimed $10,000 to anyone who can prove their psychic ability to a committee of scientists. It is not surprising then that in his book *Supernatural from A-Z* Randi dismisses everything from the abominable snowman to zodiac signs as unproven mystical notions and writes that 'no paranormal, psychic or supernatural claim has ever been substantiated by proper testing'. Of Unidentified Flying Objects he claims that 'endless reports . . . have come in, most of them actually weather balloons, science projects, meteors, regular airline flights and other relatively mundane events'.

Mr Randi might be amazed to learn that most investigators who have spent time looking at UFO reports would not disagree with this assessment. It's a well established fact that the vast majority of UFO reports can be put down to straight-forward natural phenomena. No serious researcher is going to pretend otherwise.

Mr Randi also makes the pertinent point that the 'size and distances [of UFOs] . . . cannot be determined without the use of proper instrumentation, a comparison object or another properly recorded, independent report. It is a delusion most people have that they can tell the size and/or distance of an object without these advantages . . . and it is just not true'. Randi's criticism of size/distance estimates are undeniable, but again a competent UFO investigator and most witnesses I have come across readily accept that estimating the distance to an object they saw and its size is not possible with accuracy. Most people are perfectly well capable of realising this themselves. They readily accept that when set against a night sky an object can be of any size, and either many miles away or hovering over an adjacent field.

However, many sightings do take place against a solid background, and in broad daylight when there are plenty of features against which to set an anomalous object. A substantial number of reports involve an object seen within a few hundred feet of the observer when size and distance can be readily determined. Ufologists do not just have to rely on sightings of a solitary bright light seen in the heavens at midnight.

OCCAM'S RAZOR

Mr Randi also makes use of the concept of 'Occam's Razor' which was devised by, or came to be associated with, the sage William of Occam, who lived in the 13th century. In essence his theory was that if there are two possible solutions to a problem, the simpler one must be correct. Mr Randi explains it in this way: 'If there exist two answers to a problem or a question, and if for one answer to be true, well established laws of logic or science must be rewritten, ignored or superseded in order to allow it to be true, and for the other answer to be true no such accommodation need be made, then the simpler—the second—of the answers is much more likely to be correct'.

This argument is fundamental to criticism of paranormal and 'strange' incidents. Is it more likely that a person has seen an extraterrestrial spaceship or simply misidentified an aeroplane? Well, we might say the latter, but Occam's Razor cannot in all circumstances answer such questions as it assumes that we all know everything there is to know about the nature of the universe at the point that we apply Occam's test. In fact, Occam's Razor is a bar to increasing our knowledge as it would deny any development which did not fit in with current thinking.

Take a 1920s inhabitant of New Guinea. For various historical reasons the peoples who inhabited these islands lagged behind in the field of technological developments which transformed countries like the United Kingdom, Japan and the USA. An old man of high intelligence looking out from his forest home at the sky and seeing a plane circling above him would say, according to Occam, that the plane could clearly not exist as it was a physical impossibility and that he had imagined the whole thing. And, according to his state of knowledge, that would be a logical deduction to make. However, a person in Scotland, though he might be of less intelligence than our friend in New Guinea, would know differently simply because of the state of his knowledge of the world. He has the background information which those in new Guinea did not have. The same might equally apply to sightings of UFOs. They make little sense to us, but to others the challenge they seem to pose to our known laws of science or of the universe may just not exist. The problem may not be the existence of UFOs, but our own inability to recognise them.

*   *   *

I would like to ask sceptics like Mr Randi what they make of bizarre incidents such as the following, which defy logic and common sense yet actually happened. It was related to me by a woman I will call Sandra, who I have known for several years. She holds down a responsible job. She has no axe to grind on the matter and has herself struggled to make sense of this strange event. Sandra had her car stolen and reported the matter to the Strathclyde Police. A little while later a man and woman turned up at her office and though not in uniform claimed to be police officers. Sandra felt that there was something odd about the couple, but was assured that they must be who they said they were because they had her name and knew that her car had been stolen. The man had with him a bulging black plastic bag. Without asking permission the couple emptied the contents of the bag onto Sandra's office floor and asked her if any of it belonged to her. Sandra was completely taken aback. It was simply a pile of odds and ends which seemed to have no link whatsoever to the stolen car she had reported. She told them that none of the items were hers and asked them to leave. They picked up every bit of rubbish and left.

I'm sure by now you will not be surprised that Strathclyde Police disclaimed any knowledge of the individuals involved. To the sceptics I would say 'look around you'. Strange incidents happen all the time and show that the Universe is not the fixed entity some would have us believe.

AN INTERNATIONAL PERSPECTIVE

The above points are relevant, I would argue, because UFOs form part of a broader picture and should not be viewed in isolation from other unexplained phenomena. But before we proceed further, let's fit the Scottish UFO experience into the overall picture.

Are Scotland's UFOs any different from those witnessed in the rest of the world? Is there anything distinct about the UFO phenomenon in Scotland? These are the type of questions investigators should be asking if they want to determine the reality or otherwise of the phenomenon. Of course, some would argue that the sheer volume of the reports is convincing proof in itself that 'something strange' is taking place in Scotland's and the world's skies. Others would also argue that the number of abduction cases, particularly in the United States, must lead to the inescapable conclusion that we really are being visited by alien beings from another civilisation. On both counts I would urge a note of caution. Steuart Campbell in his book reviewing the photographic evidence for the Loch Ness 'monster' has shown that the sheer number of snaps of Nessie do not prove its existence. If we take each alleged photograph on its own merits, then the 'evidence' disappears because each individual photograph does not stand up to scrutiny. Are UFO reports in the same league?

My own concerns centre on the substantial difference between the volume of reported abduction cases alleged in the USA compared with the British Isles. I do not have accurate figures (if there are any) but to state that there are at least 100 such reported cases per million of population in the US would certainly not be an overestimate. In Scotland that proportion of abductees would give us 500 cases and in England over 2,000. Yet in Scotland we are talking about a handful of reported incidents—perhaps a couple of dozen. There are not many more than that reported from England.

So are we really suggesting that aliens find Americans more worthwhile to abduct than English or Scots or other Europeans? It is an anomaly, and one that can't easily be explained or wished away. I write this more in puzzlement than with any desire to downplay the experience of abductees or those who have encountered alien entities. The experiences for these individuals are too real, frightening and baffling to dismiss. I believe that such people have seen 'something' that is not imagination or hallucination, but on the other hand does not fit easily into the ET hypothesis. Are these really beings from a distant planet, light years away from Earth? For centuries people have experienced encounters with strange beings. I am reluctant to accept such experiences as simply a 'modern myth'. Eyewitness testimony may be suspect, but vast areas of life are ruled by the reality of what we as human beings see and experience. Why should seemingly bizarre encounters be dismissed simply because they do not fit the rules of a world order that we ourselves have established? Perhaps our picture of the universe should be redrawn in a less fixed and certain manner.

LIMITATIONS OF EYEWITNESS REPORTS

Yet, it does seem to me largely true that the vast majority of UFO reports are explicable as natural phenomena. One evening in October 1996, for example, I received a number of telephone calls from the town of Irvine on Scotland's west coast. The callers told me basically the same story. A big light shaped like a spoked wheel was clearly visible in the sky. The UFO had been hovering in the same spot for two hours and looked big, larger even than the full moon. The urgent tone of these witnesses excited me and I urged them all to video, photograph or draw the object for later analysis. Could this, I wondered, be the evidence ufologists had been looking for?

Irvine was too far away for me to get to that evening, so I immediately rang Air Traffic Control at Prestwick Airport. This transatlantic stopover is only a few miles from where the spoked-wheel UFO was being seen. ATC were well aware of the excitement as they had been swamped by calls from anxious residents worried by the appearance of the strange object. They were in touch with the police who were, even as we spoke, investigating the incident. They suggested I call back after 10 p.m. when air traffic would be quieter and we could discuss the matter further. When I rang back the incident had been solved. A nightclub, the 'Aquarian' (how apt!) had bought a powerful spotlight and the new gadget was projecting an image onto the clouds. Our UFO! The police had asked them to turn it off and the town had gone quiet. Much to the relief of Prestwick Airport! An understandable mistake for the townsfolk, who quickly forgot about it, but an incident of longer term concern for ufologists.

That odd light was an unusual object for the witnesses, but what are we to make of 'less excusable' reports? Venus is regularly misidentified as a mysterious object. Perfectly sincere, rational individuals have videoed it believing they have caught something weird on film. Why? The fact that individuals do report Venus or Sirius or Mars as a UFO undoubtedly fuels the scepticism of those who would dismiss the whole business as nonsense. Clearly, when people see Venus as an alien spaceship, they may well be seeking to create mystery out of nothing.

This doesn't detract from the evidence of those who have had a close encounter or witnessed lights behaving in strange ways. It does, however, remind us all to be cautious. A mysterious light in the sky could be all sorts of things, or nothing. No UFO investigator should be frightened of declaring a UFO to be an IFO (Identified Flying Object). It enhances rather than detracts from UFO research if it can be shown that ufology is about real and not imagined mysteries.

However, at the end of the day, if we go through all the likely explanations for what a strange light might be and discover that none of the obvious explanations fit, for example civil aircraft, planets, etc., what exactly are we left with? The problem is that we are left with nothing in particular, to be exact. All we have is an unidentified object—not an alien spacecraft. Given that the vast majority of UFO sightings consist of 'lights in the sky', are we talking about a phenomenon of any significance whatsoever? Isn't this as David Clarke and Andy Roberts argued in their book *Phantoms of the Sky* simply a 'modern myth'? A fantasy projection by our twentieth-century minds? A twentieth-century folk tale 'developed to combat our fear that we are alone in the Universe'? Today we see 'UFOs', three hundred years ago it would have been witches on broomsticks and 'fairies', or something equally unlikely.

THE QUESTION OF SOLID EVIDENCE

This argument, any reasonable person would have to accept, has some substance to it. Given that no alien spaceship has landed in Glasgow's George Square or Edinburgh's Princes Street or outside the White House, where is our proof? Pointing to thousands of sightings of lights flashing or hovering in the sky doesn't itself undermine the case of sceptics. Frankly, sceptics don't worry me too much, but it is of concern that the evidence to counterbalance their scepticism does seem on the surface weak. It is weak because it does not come across as scientific, and science is extremely important in the twentieth century in establishing the validity of a point of view. Of course, it is not the sole criterion on which we base our judgement, otherwise religion and 'spirituality' would have no place in our society. This is not the case—on the contrary, they are growing. It can thus be argued that, while there is no getting around the materialistic scientific outlook, eyewitness accounts and a person's belief that he has experienced something strange do still count for something.

Some readers may be puzzled at this point. They may ask, 'Do we really need to rely on eyewitness accounts? What of the physical evidence? Traces on the ground? Photographs? Bits and pieces of extraterrestrial craft? Surely there is enough of this type of evidence to back up whatever has been recorded by the naked eye'. Obviously UFO encounters are a worldwide phenomenon. I don't want to state the obvious, but sometimes we overlook the obvious. If we remember that UFOs are global, then we can also realise that over the last fifty years there have been many tens of thousands of

UFO sightings. In Scotland alone there are over a thousand documented cases out of a population of only five million, with many more seen but not recorded. Yet out of all these incidents, how many encounters have left behind definite scientifically provable traces? How many nuts and bolts from interstellar craft do we find littering our highways and byways? As much as any UFO investigator I dream of finding that piece of metal which definitely is not of earthly origin. In 1993 I thought I had got lucky.

One afternoon I received a phone call from Ian Kyle, then of the *Edinburgh Evening News*. A walker on Dechmont Law had discovered a strange metallic tube. It was about a foot high, a few inches in diameter, with a gold coloured base. It looked as if it had been badly burned. The object had been taken to the police station in the nearby town of Livingston where it was being kept under lock and key by George Martindale, the station custodian. The police had no idea what the object was. It was something completely out of the ordinary. They had asked around, but everyone seemed baffled and could offer no solution.

So now the question was: 'Could it have come from a UFO?' The object had been found on Dechmont Law, not too far from where Bob Taylor had experienced his 1979 encounter. There had been sightings in the area over the years, so the possibility did not seem too far-fetched. In the United States, for example, there had been many claims that whole spacecraft had been locked away in secret hangers. Was it so unlikely that in Scotland a piece of the galactic jigsaw would turn up by chance? At the time, put on the spot, I suggested taking it to the nearest university laboratory where it could be properly examined. If it was made of unknown materials then its non-terrestrial origins would quickly emerge.

The story with my comments appeared in the papers the next day, accompanied by a photograph of the object, which looked unremarkable. However, it had been associated with UFOs and, therefore, had been cloaked in an aura of mystery. The mystery soon evaporated. That night I received a call from a local Roman Catholic priest. He had seen the story and recognised the object. It was an incense burner stolen from his church the previous week. He was delighted to get it back and sorry he had spoiled a good story. The sceptics had a field day.

I would make it clear that I am not deriding all alleged physical evidence, only urging continual caution. Supposed parts of spacecraft have tended not to stand up to scrutiny. They may not have been disproved, but they do not provide substantial evidence. I would agree that there are interesting eyewitness accounts of secret machines tested far from the prying eyes of the public. I too have heard reports of mysterious goings-on at Machrihanish. On several occasions I have been in receipt of phone calls from an individual who has claimed to have documented evidence that 'alien craft' were stored and tested at that West Coast base. I even arranged a meeting in Glasgow, to which my mystery caller did not turn up. The evidence that alien technology has been tested and flown over Scotland may well be in existence, but so far it has not been brought into the public domain.

Have we been more successful with other aspects of physical evidence? Several cases have occurred in Scotland where strange objects have been seen either on or near the ground. There are other incidents where odd markings have been discovered on their own or in conjunction with bright or unexplained lights. Have these encounters left evidence that might provide proof of extraterrestrial contact? The Bob Taylor incident once again provides a good example of the kind of problems faced when dealing with evidence of this nature. At the site of Bob's encounter there were both ladder-type impressions in the ground and circular marks. This seemed to corroborate his account in so far as it provided proof that a solid object of some type had been in the vicinity. However, was this object one that would shatter the sceptics' view of ufology? Steuart Campbell's view was that the markings could be explained by engineering or other equipment that had been left in the area not long before. It could not be proved conclusively, but there was no doubt that official groups had been active in the woods during this period. The depressions left on the ground could certainly have been produced by equipment left overnight or longer. As any gardener knows, marks can be visible on grass for a considerable time after they have been made. So there is an open verdict on whether the marks that were investigated could be linked to the craft seen by Mr Taylor.

Unfortunately, other incidents associated with physical evidence have in all probability not been so thoroughly examined. The evidence is not significant. Where soil or wood samples have been analysed by SEMR, the results have been inconclusive with no confirmation that any inexplicable chemical or molecular change has occurred. The results of the 1977 Elgin case (see Chapter 3) are not available, but if they had proved to be significant I dare say that they would be public knowledge by now.

Some people have pointed to the occurrence of crop circles as proof that flying saucers have landed. This evidence is less enthusiastically promoted than it was a decade ago, but it still has some supporters. The crop circle debate has been an extensive one and it is not my intention to enter into it. However, crop circles have appeared in Scotland and so some comment is relevant.

As far as Scotland is concerned, there is not a great deal to link crop circles with UFO sightings. A major problem is that there have been so few circles in Scotland compared with the south of England. A worrying aspect, perhaps, if we accept the reality of crop circle incidents. Of the few circles that have been known about none can be definitely linked to a UFO sighting. It is true that circles have appeared close to areas of UFO activity, for example at Blairgowrie (one time 'UFO capital'), and at Corpach beside Fort William. However, so many areas experience UFO incidents that the proximity of a crop circle is statistically a near certainty, I would suggest. It is interesting that West Lothian with its hundreds of UFO reports has only one known crop circle—at the side of Linlithgow Loch in 1992.

ELECTROMAGNETIC HYPOTHESIS

But do we need physical evidence to prove that witnesses have genuine UFO experiences? It may be that these experiences do not involve solid objects. One suggestion has been that powerful emissions of electromagnetic energy might stimulate an individual's perceptions and so allow that person to see into other dimensions. This would explain why a particular witness might experience a strong and vivid incident that another person might be completely unaware of. Returning to the Bob Taylor sighting, electromagnetic stimulation would account for the fact that whilst the object he saw appeared perfectly solid over most of its parts, sections of it appeared translucent so that Bob could see through it. Bob, in effect, caught sight of an object that was partly in and partly out of our dimension. If we recall also Pat Macleod's encounter on a busy Edinburgh road, or Tom Coventry's sighting in Glasgow, both in broad daylight, both (it would have been thought) easily visible to others, then the electromagnetic explanation does provide an answer. The stimulation affects the individual and thus the UFO sighting is really limited to that one person. Multiple-witness sightings might be explained by the strength of the stimulation which at certain times in certain areas might affect individuals in a wider area. Some have argued that there is no need to add inter-dimensional viewing as an explanation—the electromagnetic stimulation could simply produce a type of sensory hallucination.

It does appear to be the case that laboratory tests can stimulate paranormal type experiences. But simply because an experience can be simulated in a laboratory, does that nullify the experience of the witness in the field? I don't think so, because one problem with the electromagnetic explanation is its ability to focus on an individual rather than a crowd. Can it be argued that electromagnetic energy can focus itself so readily? It does seem unlikely. Although in this theory's favour it is undoubtedly true that certain areas experience many more sightings than others, and this might well be linked to a concentration of electromagnetic activity. It could also be the case that some individuals are more susceptible to its effects.

SCOTLAND AND EARTHLIGHTS

An explanation which has enjoyed considerable vogue has been expounded for many years by respected investigator and author Paul Devereux. He coined the term 'earthlights' as a neat summing up of his theory that UFOs were, in reality, an earthbound phenomenon caused by releases of energy from rocks under pressure. The results of this escaping energy were bright lights shooting across the sky—UFO lights in fact. This explanation has always appealed to me as a reasonable, scientific solution to some UFO sightings. However, when I attempted to relate 'rocks under pressure' in Scotland to UFO sightings I ran up against some problems.

In Chapter 8, I indicated that 1996 was a peak year for UFO incidents in Scotland. It seemed reasonable, therefore, to compare earthquake activity for 1996 with UFO reports to see if time and place of both bore any relation. I used as my source the annual *Bulletin of British Earthquakes*. I should explain that 'earthquakes' is a broad term. Experts use the 12-point Richter Scale, which runs from '1' describing a quake 'Not felt, even under the most favourable circumstances', to '12' which is 'completely devastating. Practically all structures above and below ground are heavily damaged or destroyed'. In 1996 not a single Scottish earthquake made stage '3', a tremor which registers as 'Weak . . . is felt indoors by a few people. People at rest feel a swaying or light trembling'. The nearest to a '3' was a movement on 18 May 1996 at Loch Fyne, which hit '2.9'.

Virtually all of the one hundred recorded tremors for that year registered less than a '1' or between '1' and '2'. On the other hand the number of 'earthquakes' averages one per three days so there is quite a lot of movement in total. Unfortunately, the relationship between earth movement and UFO sightings seems on the face of it non-existent. The quakes in 1996 were mainly in certain areas—Clackmannan and Musselburgh between them account for 54 incidents. Yes, there were UFO reports from these areas, but not to the extent that they could be directly linked to underground rock movement. As was noted in Chapter 8, East Lothian (where Musselburgh is situated) has not registered a high number of UFO reports in recent years. Moreover, there were UFO reports from many other areas where no tremors appear to have occurred even though the slightest of movements—as low as '0.1'—are recorded. I will admit, however, that the Edinburgh area, in close proximity to Musselburgh, has had a great many sightings. It definitely is a UFO hot-spot. So there may be a connection which requires further investigation.

THE REALITY OF EXPERIENCE

If strange lights in the sky do not provide substantial evidence, can we so readily dismiss the close up encounters? Let's leave aside the abduction cases for the moment. What can we say to incidents like those of Pat Macleod (see Chapter 1) where the sighting of the object is perilously close. Perilously close for scientists and sceptics, I mean. Those who pour scorn on UFO sightings adopt two basic attitudes to close encounters such as this: the witness is either deliberately lying or otherwise he or she imagined it—the 'mirage of Venus' scenario put forward by Steuart Campbell. If you adopt this response to the subject, then whatever the incident you will always have an explanation. For example, Steuart Campbell can explain away Pat Macleod's sighting as yet another mirage—the planet Mercury on this occasion! There is an attempt in such cases to put forward any scientific-sounding explanation which may provide a solution even where that solution seems more unlikely than the incident itself. I have no idea what Pat Macleod saw, but I don't believe it was a mirage of Mercury. Nor do I believe that Bob Taylor's encounter was a mirage of Venus, an epileptic fit or ball lightning. If sceptics feel more comfortable when they have 'solved' incidents in this way, then so be it. UFO investigators should happily leave them to it and get on with the real work of exploring the unknown. Whatever rationalists and sceptics might say, or argue, incidents do occur which simply cannot be explained.

Unfortunately, with abduction cases we enter a difficult world (in several senses). Having spoken to those involved in these cases, I know only too well just how severely individuals can be affected by their experiences. The last thing these people need is to be derided or have their sanity questioned. This is particularly true in Scotland where the number of abduction cases will always be relatively small because of the limited population. Yet many of the stories related by Scottish abductees correspond to accounts given by abductees from other parts of the world. Are we dealing here with a global alien phenomenon? Possibly, but on the other hand the use of hypnosis and the many portrayals of alien contact on screen make it difficult to determine where fact ends and fiction begins. Sceptics will have none of it and dismiss the whole phenomenon as fantasy. UFO researcher Malcolm Robinson stated that he had become convinced of the reality of alien contact through his involvement with one particular case, the alleged abduction incident on the A70 (see Chapter 7). However, is a witness's sincere conviction that he or she has been abducted sufficient evidence of the reality of the phenomenon? Should we accept an individual's claims simply because of repeated assertions that they are true? And if hypnosis is the only evidence that we have, are we bound to accept its results as proven facts?

The difficulty in answering these questions is that each person is different, and our acceptance of an account may vary according to our own judgement of the individual concerned. I accept, from my own research, that we have difficult incidents to explain, but it is a leap from that to argue that we are being visited by aliens from another planet. I have no truck with those who simply put it down to a modern myth, but my own feeling is that we are dealing here with an area that might be more complex than the proverbial 'men from Mars'. Surely there are advanced civilisations—those who have found ways to turn light years into mere inches of travel, just as we now orbit the world at a speed unbelievable even a hundred years ago. On the other hand, can we be so sure about the material nature of our world and the heavens around it. What do we really perceive? Is our knowledge, perhaps, limited by our own human senses, while beyond those senses lies another 'world' which we can rarely, but sometimes do, experience? By nature I'm inclined to both possibilities, but whatever answer we eventually find, or whether we continue searching for ever, I am sure that there is far more to life in the universe than we have even started to dream about.

CHANNELLING

There are individuals even in Scotland who claim that there is nothing unusual about abduction incidents as they are regularly 'abducted' and in contact with alien intelligence. According to the *Sun* newspaper Graham Wyllie from Dundee set up a 'telephone helpline to counsel people claiming to have been kidnapped by invaders from space'. Mr Wyllie had, it seems, undergone such an experience, having been 'kidnapped by a friendly alien called Josef'. He expressed the view that there might well be an invasion and takeover of the Earth by alien 'greys', and this would come about when a certain proportion of the Earth's population had met the aliens. Mr Wyllie might be correct. I can't claim to have spoken to any aliens, but I suspect that any extraterrestrial beings who are capable of visiting the Earth and kidnapping individuals would have little trouble in taking over the whole planet. A galactic war involving Earth and ET hardly seems a viable option.

There are so many channellers of alien messages that it has become hard to know exactly which, if any, messenger is relaying accurate information. Certainly, they can't all be right. If there are genuine messages, and true mediums through which this information is being conveyed, then their efforts are being swamped by an unfortunate pile of junk mail. Let us hope that any urgent communication eventually gets through.

ALIEN INTELLIGENCE: TWO HYPOTHESES

In recent years a number of individuals have gained world-wide attention with their views on alien intelligence. These ideas are often well thought out, eloquently expressed—and completely different.

David Icke, in his book . . . *and the truth shall set you free*, expounds his belief that there are many extraterrestrial intelligent life-forms. For many millennia, he claims, the Earth has been trapped in a shroud of what he calls 'negative vibrations' that cut Man off from his higher self and prevent him reaching his full potential, both as an individual and as a race. This, he says, is the result of an intergalactic battle between negative and positive extraterrestrial intelligences where, at present, the negatives are in the ascendant, at least in this quadrant of the Universe. These negatives feed off the negative energy our misery produces. They have controlled the Earth to produce war, famine, plague and death through the machinations of their stooges, a global elite (whose main focus is the United States, but which also includes highly placed politicians, business executives and international agency members throughout the world) which they, themselves, control.

The positives, centred in the Pleiades, are now on the verge of making a breakthrough, and, with the help of increasing positive thinking from an ever-expanding number of people and organisations, they may be on the verge of a breakthrough.

Icke produces a powerful and convincing body of evidence to support this viewpoint.

Zecharia Sitchin's thesis is very different (although the two viewpoints are not, in fact, mutually exclusive). A scholar of ancient languages, Sitchin describes in his book *Genesis Revisited—has modern science caught up with ancient knowledge?* how the story of Earth's origins and the birth of Man as told in 6,000-year-old Sumerian texts is being confirmed by modern scientific research.

The Sumerians described the solar system as having 12 'planets'—the sun, moon and 10 planets. In modern times the ninth planet, Pluto, was only rediscovered in 1930. The tenth planet, called Nibiru by the Sumerians and Marduk by the Babylonians, was pulled into the solar system from outer space by the sun's gravity and entered an elliptical, retrograde orbit round the sun that took 3,600 years to complete. This caused it to crash into the planet Tiamat, then in the orbit of the asteroid belt, splitting Tiamat, knocking half of it into a new orbit where it became Earth, and the remaining shattered fragments became the asteroid belt. Modern data gleaned from space exploration now confirms much of this story and many astronomers have become convinced that there is indeed a tenth planet.

The Sumerians tell how the Annunaki, the technologically advanced people who had evolved on Nibiru, came in their spaceships to Earth about 5 million years ago to mine for gold. They developed slaves called 'adams' to work the mines for them. These 'adams' were made by a process of in vitro fertilisation and surrogate motherhood, using eggs from the apemen (or rather women) who had developed on Earth, and Annunaki sperm. This hybrid was initially infertile, but became fertile after DNA manipulation. Modern DNA research suggests that such manipulation would in theory be possible.

Mr Sitchin completes his book with the fascinating hypothesis that the Annunaki, who seem to have been fairly quiescent for many millennia, are returning to our orbit. The loss of Phobos 2, sent to investigate Mars, and other clues from anomalous factors in Martian photographs, appears to indicate that they may have reactivated their ancient space base on that planet, and don't want us to know about it. . . .

The author's scholarly knowledge of ancient languages and wide ranging information on current research gives his book a powerful credence. He is not tied to the micro-view of academic researchers, but is able to take a macro-view of many disparate strands, ranging from medicine, linguistics, astronomy, biochemistry and archaeology to religion, to produce his shattering, but convincing, thesis.

THE SCIENTIFIC VIEW

Scientists, of course, have been divided about the possibilities of life existing elsewhere in the universe. The American astronomer Francis Drake examined the possibility that advanced civilisations might be found on other planets. Using various calculations, he concluded that there might exist in our own galaxy alone many 'earths' capable of supporting life and potentially developing the technology to achieve interstellar travel. Sir Arnold Wolfendale, former Astronomer Royal and President of the Institute of Physics, told a conference at Stirling University that he did 'believe there were intelligent beings somewhere else in space'. He explained: 'I think there is life out there, but it is less common than people think. . . . The distances are incredible and I think that means that the chances of getting visitors are pretty small'. Sir Arnold also made the point that it was far more likely that alien civilisations would attempt to contact us by radio first rather than attempt to visit us. Of course, it might be argued that aliens would do it their way rather than the way we might predict!

EUROSCEPTICS

Attempts by the European Union, according to *The Scotsman* newspaper, 'to set up an observatory in France to search for UFOs' sparked a storm of protest from British politicians. Sir Teddy Taylor, a Conservative MP with anti-European Union views, declared it 'a madcap venture'. He was concerned that there were 'a lot of MEPs who are rushing around Europe asking people whether they have seen a flying saucer. . . . The whole idea seems to have been cooked up in some kind of ethereal dream world', and he was particularly concerned that they were studying the 'extent of aliens taking control of areas of outer space around the world'. He described this as 'the biggest piece of nonsense I have ever heard in my life!'

In response to Sir Teddy *The Scotsman* published an article I wrote which pointed out that many government and military establishments, including those in France, Russia, the US and Britain, had been interested in UFO sightings for many years. I concluded: 'Many people have now claimed to have seen something in the sky which they cannot explain. Europe has recognised that the UFO phenomenon requires investigating. Is that really an outlandish objective?' Surely the interest shown by the governments of various countries and by their military is evidence that UFOs are not at all 'phantoms of the sky', but genuinely inexplicable phenomena.

When, for example, conversations of the following nature occur, aren't we, the public, entitled to wonder what is going on, and to receive some explanation?

> Glasgow Air Traffic Control (ATC): 'Cleared to land.'
> Pilot: 'Has somebody just taken off?' (Urgent tone in voice.)
> ATC: 'No. Why?'
> Pilot: 'Some lights are oscillating at the end of the runway, going back and forth, oscillating fairly rapidly.'
> ATC: 'OK. We'll check it out. Where exactly is it?'
> Pilot: 'It's half, or one, mile from the end of the runway, oscillating rapidly. One dot either side of the runway centreline.'
> ATC: 'OK, we'll make sure and check it out.'
> Pilot: 'It's very strange indeed.' (Obvious puzzlement in voice.)

This incident took place on 26 February 1996 at 7.18 p.m. In spite of our enquiries, no explanation has been forthcoming.

CONSPIRACY THEORY

There has been in recent years a considerable amount of video footage taken in Scotland, including UFOs caught by Margaret Ross in Stenhousemuir, Barry Macdonald in Falkirk, the Malcolm family in Lanark and several others. Much of this video footage has been of excellent quality, yet no matter how good the video evidence, it will always be suspect in the eyes of sceptics. We still want the one hundred per cent convincing piece. It may, of course, never come. If UFOs are really intelligently guided extraterrestrial craft then, presumably, they will be seen when they want to be and not before. Unless, of course, one crashes. Mysterious balls of light crashing into the ground have been seen on many occasions in Scotland, but without any evidence of a metallic craft being involved. There are plenty of military areas within Scotland where a 'spacecraft' could be stored, but in spite of numerous sightings, associated particularly with Machrihanish, we still await disclosure from anyone who has worked there.

Naturally, in this kaleidoscope of views and claims, the more outrageous the story the more attention it grabs. Claims of world-wide channelling-receiving centres would fill a whole section.

So is there really a government cover-up? The call by an international group of scientists for serious investigation to be carried out into UFO sightings points to the fact that at least some recognise that there is indeed evidence worth looking at. But, in theory at any rate, we're well away from a government sponsored review of the subject. I write 'in theory' because in fact the military in both the UK and the USA have been following UFO reports for decades. Nick Redfern in *Covert Agenda* has revealed how extensively and for how long UFO reports have been recorded by various branches of the govern-ment and armed services. While researching this book I wrote to the Ministry of Defence, as I wanted to gain access to reports from the 1950s and 1960s which related to Scotland. I also asked if Scottish UFO reports were kept separately from those relating to other parts of the British Isles. As it turned out they were not (as they certainly should be), but I was also told that Scottish UFO reports were included in any declassified document available in the Public Records Office in London. Not exactly convenient for Scottish researchers! But it does point to the fact that Scottish UFO incidents were being recorded during a time when this was being officially denied.

On the surface at least the MoD have been substantially more open about their interest in the UFO phenomenon than in the past. They have, for example, made the great step of admitting their interest and that they have a section which deals with UFO reports. However, they still claim that their concern is limited to clarifying whether or not a UFO is a threat to the country's defences. This seems to me a quite reasonable attitude on the MoD's part. The big question is whether their interest runs beyond that. Does our government have knowledge of extraterrestrial life-forms and, if so, have they in fact been in contact with them.

The problem here is that there are so many claims made by various individuals that it's almost impossible to be sure whether we're dealing with a deliberate smoke screen designed to spread confusion, people who just love publicity, or insiders with definite knowledge of ET contact. I have to say again that though I have spoken with several people who have claimed, passionately in some cases, that our government knows a great deal about life 'out there', and that alien technology has definitely been tested in Scotland, I have yet to see any documentary or other proof to back up these claims. I would say that I firmly believe that the government has a lot more information—including film and photo evidence of UFOs, but maybe even those with access to vast resources are as confused as the rest of us by the nature of the phenomenon. Or maybe, like the professional sceptics, they just don't want to believe.

*   *   *

Those who hold to the view that we on Earth really are alone were shaken by claims that life might have existed on Mars—claims made by respected scientists. This controversy arose because of impressions of primitive organisms found in rocks in Antarctica: rocks, it was argued, which had arrived from Mars. Hard on the heels of this revelation came the discovery of a large planet, about the size of Jupiter, orbiting the unimaginatively-titled HR3522 star in the constellation of Cancer, 40 or more light years from Earth.

Neither of these finds proves that extraterrestrials are visiting Earth or even that advanced life-forms exist elsewhere in space, but they are a reminder that we cannot be certain we are alone in the Universe. Chance would surely point to the existence of many planetary civilisations, and if they are out there, wouldn't they share with the inhabitants of Earth a wish to find other life-forms? If the Universe is bound by universal laws, then we must all, surely, be driven by the same inner force—to seek and find anyone, wherever they are, whatever they are, who shares this vast inexhaustible space we call our own.

FURTHER READING

We have still a lot to learn about Scotland's UFOs although more cases are coming to light every day.

In every sense, *UFO Scotland* represents the fruits of primary investigation. Recent years have seen the production of a variety of Scottish UFO magazines. First of these was *Enigmas*, which I started with Malcolm Robinson in 1990. It ceased publication in 1996. *Phenomenal News*, edited by Viv Alexander and published by Scottish Earth Mysteries Research, is now Scotland's foremost UFO magazine. David Colman has produced much interesting material—particularly in relation to the Fife Abduction incident—in *Cover-Up*, and (despite the title) *Haunted Scotland*, edited by Mark Fraser, has regular UFO reports.

Otherwise, Scottish UFO incidents have appeared mainly in the newspapers and various English-based UFO and paranormal magazines. My column 'Scotland's X-Files' in the

Glasgow Saturday Times regularly looks at the Scottish UFO phenomenon.

Allingham, Cedric: *Flying Saucers From Mars*
(Muller, 1954)

Arnold, Kenneth & Palmer, Ray:
The Coming of the Saucers (1952)

Campbell, Steuart: 'Close Encounters at Livingston'
(Case History No 1, BUFORA, 1982)

Campbell, Steuart: *The UFO Mystery Solved*
(Explicit, 1994)

Clarke, David & Roberts, Andy: *Phantom of the Sky*
(Robert Hale, 1990)

Daniken, Erich Von: *Return to the Stars* (Corgi, 1972)

Devereux, Paul: *Earthlights* (Turnstone, 1982)

Evans, Hilary: *UFOs 1947-1987* (Fortean Times, 1987)

Halliday, Ron: *Mysteries of the Scottish Landscape*
(Aura, 1988)

Halliday, Ron: 'Bonnybridge Bites Back'
(*Northern UFO News* No 164, 1994)

Halliday, Ron: 'The Truth About Bonnybridge'
(*New Ufologist*, 1997)

Halliday, Ron (Ed.): *McX: Scotland's X-Files*
(B&W Publishing, 1997)

Halliday, Ron: *UFOs: The Scottish Dimension*
(Scottish Paranormal Press, 1997)

Hough, Peter: *Supernatural Britain* (Piatkus, 1995)

Hynek, J Allen: *The UFO Experience* (Corgi, 1974)

Jenkins, John: *Of No Defence Significance*
(Pen-y-Coe Press, 1997)

Keel, John: *UFOs: Operation Trojan Horse* (Souvenir, 1970)

Leslie, Desmond & Adamski, George:
Flying Saucers Have Landed (Werner Laurie, 1953)

Mantle, Phillip & Nagaitis, Carl: *Without Consent*
(Ringpull, 1994)

Oakensen, Elsie: *One Step Beyond* (Regency Press, 1996)

Pope, Nick: *Open Skies, Closed Minds* (1996)

Randles, Jenny: *Abductions* (Robert Hale, 1988)

Randles, Jenny: *The Paranormal Year, 1993*
(Robert Hale, 1993)

Randles, Jenny: *Star Children* (Robert Hale, 1994)

Randles, Jenny: *Strange But True* (Piatkus, 1994)

Randles, Jenny: *UFO Retrievals* (Blandford, 1995)

Redfern, Nick: *A Covert Agenda* (Simon & Schuster, 1997)

Robinson, Malcolm: 'Central Scotland in Grip of
UFO Wave' (*Enigmas*, Feb/March 1993)

Robinson, Malcolm: 'UFOs: The Study Goes On'
(*Enigmas*, May/June 1993)

Robinson, Malcolm: 'Japanese Film Crew Probe
Bonnybridge Mystery' (*Enigmas*, August/Sept 1993)

Robinson, Malcolm: 'The Fife Incident' (*Sightings*, 1996)

CLASSIFICATION OF PHENOMENA

Two widely-used systems for the classification of unexplained phenomena are detailed below.

The **Hynek System** is named after Dr J. Allen Hynek, a professor of astronomy who took part in a US Air Force investigation into UFOs, code-named *Project Blue Book*, which began in 1952. The project was terminated in 1969, after it was officially discredited. However, many now accept rumours that reports which could not be explained away were mysteriously 'lost'—and that those in authority must therefore not have intended *Blue Book* to succeed.

In 1973, Dr Hynek formed the Center for UFO Studies, the first scientific UFO group. It is from the Hynek System that we get the familiar Close Encounter types.

The Hynek categories are:

Nocturnal Light (NL)—Any anomalous light(s) seen in the night sky whose description rules out the possibilities of aircraft lights, stars, meteors etc.

Daylight Disc (DD)—UFOs seen in the distant sky. May be any shape.

Radar-Visual (RV)—Where UFOs are tracked on radar, and can simultaneously be seen at the corresponding location.

Close Encounters:

Of the First Kind (CEI)—Where a UFO comes close to the witness (within 500 feet).

Of the Second Kind (CEII)—Where the UFO either leaves markings on the ground, causes temporary injury to humans, frightens animals, or interferes with electrical or radio apparatus, etc.

Of the Third Kind (CEIII)—A CEI or CEII in which occupants are visible.

Of the Fourth Kind[1] (CEIV)—Abduction cases.

Of the Fifth Kind[1] (CEV)—Communication occurs between a person and an alien.

The **Vallée System**, created by Dr Jacques Vallée, a French astrophysicist, is based on Hynek's work, although the list of categories has been greatly expanded in order to be applicable to other areas of paranormal research—Vallée's view is that there may be a psychic dimension to the UFO phenomenon.

---

1. Later additions to reflect the growing number of such reports.

The Vallée categories are:

AN (Anomaly) Rating—classifies any anomalous behaviour.

    AN1—Anomalies which have no lasting physical effects, e.g. amorphous lights.

    AN2—Anomalies which do have lasting physical effects, e.g. where objects are moved or materialised, crop circles.

    AN3—Anomalies with associated entities, e.g. ghosts, 'monsters', nature spirits, etc.

    AN4—Witness interaction with AN3 entities, e.g. religious or near-death experiences, out-of-body experiences.

    AN5—Anomalous events resulting in physical effects on the witness, e.g. spontaneous human combustion, unexplained wounding or healing.

MA (Manoeuvre) Rating—describes mobile behaviour of a UFO.

    MA1—A UFO which travels in a discontinuous/non-regular trajectory, e.g. sudden changes in speed or height.

    MA2—MA1 in which the UFO leaves physical traces of its presence.

    MA3—Where entities are observed on board.

    MA4—Manoeuvres accompanied by a sense of reality transformation for the witness, e.g. being taken on board.

    MA5—A manoeuvre which has a physical effect on the witness.

FB (Fly-By) Rating.

    FB1—A simple sighting of a UFO travelling in a straight line across the sky.

    FB2—FB1 leaving physical traces.

    FB3—Where entities are observed on board.

FB4—A fly-by accompanied by a sense of reality transformation for the witness, e.g. being taken on board.

FB5—A fly-by which leads to physical effects on the witness.

CE (Close Encounter) Rating—similar to the Hynek Close Encounter ratings.

CE1—UFO comes within 500 feet of the witness, but with no after-effects or physical traces.

CE2—A CE1 that leaves landing traces or injuries.

CE3—Where entities are observed on board.

CE4—Where the witness is abducted.

CE5—CE4 which leads to permanent psychological/physical effects on the witness.

SVP (Source/Visit/Possible explanation) Rating—measures the credibility of a report. A score from 0 to 4 is awarded for each of three categories—source reliability, site visit, and possible explanation. The scores are written consecutively, e.g. 201. A rating of 222 or higher is considered good.

Source Reliability Rating.

0—Unknown or unreliable source.

1—Report attributed to a known source of unknown reliability.

2—Reliable source, secondhand.

3—Reliable source, firsthand.

4—Firsthand personal interview with witness and proven reliability of source.

Site Visit Rating.

0—No site visit, or answer unknown.

1—Site visit by a casual observer not familiar with the phenomenon.

2—Site visit by someone familiar with the phenomenon.

3—Site visit by a reliable investigator with some experience.

4—Site visit by a skilled analyst.

Possible Explanation Rating.

0—Data consistent with one or more natural causes.

1—Natural explanation requires only slight modification of the data.

2—Natural explanation requires major alteration of one parameter.

3—Natural explanation requires major alteration of several parameters.

4—No natural explanation possible, given the evidence.

FURTHER INFORMATION

Scottish Earth Mysteries Research (SEMR) produces a quarterly magazine, *Phenomenal News*, edited by Viv Alexander. For information about subscriptions, or to submit articles, please write to:

Viv Alexander, 4 Linden Avenue, Stirling, FK7 7PG.

REPORTING AN ENCOUNTER

If you have had a UFO experience, or have video footage or photographic evidence that you would like to report, please write to Ron Halliday at:

SEMR, 35 Fountain Road, Bridge of Allan, FK9 4AU.

INDEX

C

D

I

J

H

K

N

O

P

Q

R